Tech Giants, Artificial Intelligence, and the Future of Journalism

This book examines the impact of the "Big Five" technology companies – Apple, Google, Amazon, Facebook, and Microsoft – on journalism and the media industries. It looks at the current role of algorithms and artificial intelligence in curating how we consume media and their increasing influence on the production of the news.

Exploring the changes that the technology industry and automation have made in the past decade to the production, distribution, and consumption of news globally, the book considers what happens to journalism once it is produced and enters the media ecosystems of the Internet tech giants – and the impact of social media and AI on such things as fake news in the post-truth age.

The audience for this book are students and researchers working in the field of digital media, and journalism studies or media studies more generally. It will also be useful to those who are looking for extended case studies of the role taken by tech giants such as Facebook and Google in the fake news scandal, or the role of Jeff Bezos in transforming *The Washington Post*.

Jason Whittaker is the Head of the School of English and Journalism at the University of Lincoln. He worked for 15 years as a tech journalist and has written extensively on magazine journalism and digital media, most recently as the co-editor of the collection *Online Journalism in Africa* (2013) and as the author of *Magazine Production* (2016).

Routledge Research in Journalism

19 News of Baltimore
Race, Rage and the City
Edited by Linda Steiner and Silvio Waisbord

20 The Trump Presidency, Journalism, and Democracy
Edited by Robert E. Gutsche, Jr.

21 Russia's Liberal Media
Handcuffed but Free
Vera Slavtcheva-Petkova

22 Critical Perspectives on Journalistic Beliefs and Actions
Global Experiences
Edited by Eric Freedman, Robyn S. Goodman, and Elanie Steyn

23 Economic News
Informing the Inattentive Audience
Arjen van Dalen, Helle Svensson, Anotinus Kalogeropoulos, Erik Albæk, Claes H. de Vreese

24 Reporting Humanitarian Disasters in a Social Media Age
Glenda Cooper

25 The Rise of Nonprofit Investigative Journalism in the United States
Bill Birnbauer

26 Tech Giants, Artificial Intelligence, and the Future of Journalism
Jason Whittaker

For more information about this series, please visit: https://www.routledge.com

Tech Giants, Artificial Intelligence, and the Future of Journalism

Jason Whittaker

Routledge
Taylor & Francis Group

LONDON AND NEW YORK

First published 2019 by Routledge

2 Park Square, Milton Park, Abingdon, Oxfordshire OX14 4RN
52 Vanderbilt Avenue, New York, NY 10017

Routledge is an imprint of the Taylor & Francis Group, an informa business

First issued in paperback 2020

Library of Congress Cataloging-in-Publication Data
CIP data has been applied for.

ISBN: 978-1-138-49997-3 (hbk)
ISBN: 978-0-367-66109-0 (pbk)

Typeset in Sabon
by codeMantra

To Sam for her patience and support

Contents

Acknowledgements   ix

Introduction: Automatic for the People   1

1 The New Ecology   11

2 Distribute and Be Damned   39

3 Zombie Media: Alt-Journalism, Fake News, and
   Robot Editors   71

4 Turing's Test: Automated Journalism and the
   Rise of the Post-Human Writer   99

5 Citizens: The Voice of the People in the
   Age of Machines   126

   Conclusion: The Future of Journalism   163

   Bibliography   173
   Index   183

Acknowledgements

This book has developed over a series of discussions with a number of colleagues, students, and friends who have had the patience to sit through presentations and debates on various aspects covered in this book over the years. I would particularly like to thank Deborah Wilson-David, John Cafferkey, Ola Ogunyemi, Hayes Mabweazara, John Cafferkey, Gary Stevens, Rob Brown, and Julia Kennedy, as well as Eleanor Simmons and Felisa Salvago-Keyes at Routledge who helped to develop this book from initial idea through to final publication.

Introduction

Automatic for the People

In August 2018, financial reporters around the globe became extremely excited at news that the tech company Apple had passed the $1 trillion mark in terms of its market capitalisation, the value of all its shares at that time. The BBC announced that it was "the first public company worth $1 trillion", remarking that its shares had risen by more than 50,000 per cent since it had first been listed in 1980. Likewise, *The Washington Post*, *Bloomberg*, *Fortune*, and many others remarked its status as the most highly valued company, at that time the most exclusive club in the world with one member, although on 4 September, Amazon briefly joined before dropping down to a mere $995 billion.[1] The more carefully written of these stories tended to mention that this trillion-dollar record referred to a "publicly-owned" or "US" company, as Apple would at best be the *second* trillion-dollar company in history. As *Forbes* writer Lucinda Shen pointed out the previous November, the state-owned oil and gas producer, PetroChina, had briefly topped the magical mark on the Shanghai stock exchange in 2007.[2] PetroChina also saw the biggest-ever stock market losses, with some $800 billion – or approximately the size of Italy's stock market in 2017 – being wiped off its shareholder value. Incredible drops in oil prices, combined with plans to move towards alternative sources of power in China and a clampdown on excessive swings in Chinese stocks in the aftermath of the 2007 global financial crisis demonstrated the fragile nature of such high-risk speculation.

It is no accident that a book on tech giants, artificial intelligence and journalism begins not with innovation and ideas but with the effect of share prices. In the business world, the value of the major technology companies is extremely significant news and, in many quarters, reporting about technology is synonymous with financial journalism. In March 2017, *Fortune* ran a piece that is typical of the speculative opinion pieces familiar to anyone interested in such stories, betting on whether it would be Alphabet (the parent company of Google), Amazon, Apple, Facebook, Microsoft, or Tesla that would hit the trillion-dollar mark first.[3] With the exception of Tesla (whose name is only featured here because its charismatic but sometimes erratic founder, Elon Musk, suggested it), these five companies will be returned to again and again throughout this title. Their value is a reflection of their power in a number of areas – including the ways in which we consume and perceive the media in the twenty-first century. For anyone sceptical about how important these companies are to contemporary society, it is worth reflecting on an article written by Ryan Derousseau at the time that Apple hit the magic target, and which noted five historical companies that would have been worth more. Leaving aside PetroChina, companies such as the Dutch East India Co., the British South Sea Co., and Standard Oil all had immense impacts upon the societies of their day – often enriching the countries in which they were based or bankrupting them as with the South Sea bubble.[4] Apple has shown nothing remotely akin to the volatility the South Sea Co., nor even that of PetroChina and its trillion-dollar mark is unlikely to be its highest point. Since the second quarter of 2013 (when it briefly traded the top spot with Exxon Mobil), Apple has been the most highly valued company in the world according to its market capitalisation, rising from a value of nearly $416 billion at the beginning of 2013 to $921 billion by the end of 2017 according to the Fortune 500. Indeed, the value of the top ten companies worldwide at the end of 2017 was equally revealing as shown in Table I.1.

Although Walmart dominated the Fortune 500 in terms of revenue (alongside petrochemical companies, energy conglomerates, and even car manufacturers), it was tech firms that held the top spots in terms of their overall market value. In the first decade of the twenty-first century, the highest valued companies were energy giants such as Exxon Mobil, PetroChina, Gazprom, Royal Dutch Shell, and BP. The relative decline of oil prices in the second decade means that, Exxon aside, such companies have almost never made the top ten in recent years and that since 2011, a very noticeable change has occurred: the Fortune 500 in terms of market capitalisation has largely been dominated by Apple, alongside Microsoft

Table I.1 Top ten valued companies in 2017

Company	Market cap (2017, Fortune 500, billions)
Apple	921
Amazon	765
Alphabet	750
Microsoft	746
Facebook	531
Berkshire Hathaway	492
JPMorgan Chase & Co.	388
Exxon Mobil	349
Johnson & Johnson	332
Bank of America Corp	315

Source: Fortune 500.

(the one consistent technology company to appear in this company since the 1990s), and regularly the top positions are held by Apple, Alphabet, Microsoft, and Amazon as these organisations jostle for the top spot of most highly valued company. A comparison of 100 years of the market made by Visual Capitalist using data provided by Forbes rather than the Fortune 500 offers a similar comparison to the top companies in 2017 but also allows a much wider contextualisation. Thus in 1917, the John D. Rockerfeller's Standard Oil and J. P. Morgan's US Steel dominated the US stock exchanges, stalwarts of the industrial era although at this time Standard had already been broken up through antitrust action. Fifty years later, in 1967, Standard Oil (soon to be renamed Exxon) remained important but this was now the emerging domain of hardware and tele-communications companies such as IBM and AT&T, as well as other manufacturers such as Eastman Kodak and Polaroid.[5] It is slightly too early to define the second decade of the twenty-first century as the decade of digital platforms: the volatility of market values is clear over a period of years, but it is remarkable just how stable Apple has been at the top of the pile. In the future, emerging markets such as those around health and medicine, or indeed a resurgence of energy in alternative forms to gas and oil, could see a revolution in the capitalisation of companies, but to all intents and purposes, the 2010s have been the decade of the Big Five.

This brief excursion into the financial status of contemporary tech-nological companies is one means of emphasising the significance of big tech. Nor should it be forgotten (Apple and Microsoft aside) just how recent this transformation has been: until 2015, Amazon, Facebook, and even the mighty Google never made to the top ten list of companies, while until 2003, Intel and even IBM remained significant players. The impact of Apple, Google, Amazon, Facebook, and Microsoft reaches into a great variety of areas of everyday life, but for the purposes of this book, their significance can easily be weighed by comparing their market value to those for more traditional media companies (Table I.2).

Table I.2 Value of top tech companies versus top media companies

Tech company	2018 Q3 value (billions)	Media company	2018 Q3 value (billions)
Apple	1,091	AT&T[b]	248
Amazon	976	Walt Disney	173
Microsoft	877	Comcast	161
Alphabet	839	Twenty-First Century Fox	85
Facebook[a]	473	Thomson Reuters	32

Source: Fortune 500.

[a]Number six on the overall list behind Berkshire Hathaway.
[b]Owner of Time Warner Inc. since June 2018.

The message is clear: with the exception of Disney, flush with the success of the Star Wars franchise among other elements, AT&T and Comcast (which both have extensive telecommunications components as part of their business) the larger, more traditional media companies lag behind the main tech companies by a factor of at least ten. The companies on the right of the aforementioned chart are responsible for producing the vast majority of media consumed by audiences around the world and yet, increasingly, it is the companies on the left that enable the majority of that audience to consume media in the first place. When Ben Bagdikian outlined the companies that controlled the media in the USA in 2004, his five conglomerates were: Time Warner, Walt Disney, News Corporation, Viacom, and Bertelsmann.[6] Just over a decade later, it is the Big Five who are the subject of this book that, increasingly, control access to the new ecologies of media distribution in the twenty-first century.

"Big tech" is a phrase that will recur frequently in this book, and is often associated with the "Big Five" (Alphabet/Google, Amazon, Apple, Facebook, and Microsoft) although it is not entirely synonymous with them. The phrase itself evolved slowly, beginning with Eric Schmidt's reference in 2011 to the "gang of four" – Amazon, Apple, Facebook, and Google – which at that point were worth half a trillion dollars combined and which, in his opinion, were shaping consumer technology.[7] At this time, the Big Four were considered the most exciting and dynamic companies in the world and were imbued with a certain glamour: Apple had reinvented itself as the manufacturer of what would become the world's most popular hardware device, the iPhone, Amazon stunned the stock market with its continued growth and acquisitions, Facebook was on the verge of launching the most expensive initial public offering (IPO) in history, and Google had shot into the top five of the best companies to work for in the world, offering beanbags, pool tables, and polka dot walls.[8] Unlike traditional multinationals, these were companies that were cool and fun, and the omission of Microsoft from Schmidt's "gang of four" was deliberate: throughout the late 1990s, Microsoft had come to represent the aggressive, power-hungry aspects of big business that companies such as Google defined themselves *against,* taking up the motto "Don't be evil" as a reminder of what not to turn into.

Within a decade, however, the Big Four had become the Big Five and the return of Microsoft to the ranks of big tech demonstrated that there was less to distinguish these major, multinational corporations that had existed in the previous decade. It was Theodore Roosevelt who first began to label "big business" as an enemy of the people in 1906, when he began to attack corporations and anti-labour decisions in the courts, and throughout the twentieth century, the addition of "Big X" indicated a general disillusion with an industry, whether Big Phama, Big Tobacco, or Big Oil. Such descriptions indicated popular perceptions that a particular industry was out of touch with its consumers, more interested in its shareholders as in Jacky Law's 2006 book *Big Pharma*, which portrayed the pharmaceutical industry as self-serving against the interests of its customers – and this was a sector that was excoriated for earning $200 billion among its ten largest players.[9] By 2016, the Big Five had become Big Tech, and, as with those other industries that were distrusted by voters, taxpayers, and consumers, the epithet was not intended as a positive one. As Olivia Solon could write at the end of 2017, this was the period in which "the world turned on Silicon Valley", blaming it for poor working practices, extreme tax avoidance, and undermining democracy.[10] Whereas Amazon had been filled with titles such as *Are You Smart Enough to Work at Google?* and *The Google Resume: How to Prepare for a Career and Land a Job at Apple, Microsoft, Google, or Any Top Tech Company*, now top selling titles are as likely to include *World Without Mind: The Existential Threat of Big Tech* or *Antisocial Media: How Facebook Disconnects Us and Undermines Democracy*.

This book shares much of the critical view of more recent titles regarding tech giants – although the use of big tech is also intended to demonstrate that my own scepticism is more concerned with exploring how technology alters our patterns of behaviour, in particular with regard to how we consume journalism. The shift from media producers (Big Media, if you like: certainly different media sectors such as music or publishing have their Big Fives or Sixes who monopolise content creation) to distributors has incredibly important consequences for the future of journalism, but this is not simply an intention by those major tech companies to grind all media into the ground. As thoughtful writers such as Franklin Foer and Scott Galloway frequently indicate, the current monopolisation of communication by the Big Five often stems from utopian impulses as much as greed, although the consequences of those impulses are frequently unintended. One such outcome has been a dramatic loss of confidence in mainstream media which has demonstrates just how unstable the public sphere – that loose conglomeration of public opinion and influence – has become, notably in large-scale upsets for established opinion as in votes for Brexit or to elect Donald Trump as the president. As I shall argue in more detail throughout this book, the ultimate causes of these problems within the public sphere often have their roots within legacy media itself, not least its own rush towards monopolisation in the late twentieth century, but the speed and efficiency with which big tech has harnessed automation (the preferred term throughout this book for what is commonly called artificial intelligence) have greatly influenced changes in the public's behaviour.

The role of technology in the public sphere has been a contentious one since the 1990s, when the World Wide Web first attracted attention. Initially, such discussions were largely positive: in 1995, for example, Sclove sought to explore how technology could be used to liberate social activities as well as how it could increasingly restrict public freedoms, while Kellner argued that the Internet, by encouraging participation, had "the potential to invigorate democracy".[11] In more recent years, the view has tended to be much more ambivalent, as much due to the monopolisation of digital technologies and spaces by big tech. Balnaves and Willson welcomed the decreasing homogenisation of the Internet-using community, but that the increasingly "black box" relations that users had with digital technology meant that they could not understand it and that this could result in a relative disempowerment for users in terms of sociopolitical engagement, while Lee Salter began to question whether the Internet could even be considered as a public sphere at all.[12] Such criticism was relatively gentle at that moment when the Big Five were only starting to emerge as a techno-oligarchy, and more recently their effects on the potential use of the Internet as a public sphere in the sense discussed by Habermas have come increasingly under scrutiny. Thus, Fenton more recently has described its effects as those of a "fake democracy", while Pfetsch draws attention to an increasingly disconnected audience.[13] Similarly, Nguyen observes that while online resources provide a source of information undreamed of by previous generations, the practice of communication online via filter bubbles tends towards further fragmentation and "the intensification and radicalisation of viewpoints" as we are more likely to converse with those who think like us and hear fewer and fewer oppositional points of view.[14] Some commentators, such as the contributors to *Managing Democracy in the Digital Age*, explore practical considerations and challenges for encouraging participation, but are also fully aware of the dangers not simply of censorious, authoritarian regimes but with a sense of growing disenfranchisement among voters in liberal democracies.[15]

Some of the ways in which technology affects our patterns of behaviour are considered in Chapter 1, which explores in more detail notions of media and technological determinism, the idea that new technologies shape human culture and society. In its widest form, it is clear that the development of our societies has always been influenced by the technological innovations we introduce, but a failure of much so-called "hard" media determinism has been an assumption that technology is somehow "outside" society, and that its introduction will implement changes in a reductionist fashion. This is a common assumption among those engaged in tech companies: for example, Mark Zuckerberg and other founders of Facebook appear to have blithely assumed that social media was a tool that would bring people together through simpler communication, applying a simplistic model of cause and effect that in recent years has proved woefully inadequate to describe the actual consequences of Facebook across a wide range of incidents. The impact of technology is dynamic and frequently turbulent: just as the invention of printing led to a whole series of consequences from the Reformation to

the rise of mass participation in democratic elections that its origina-
tors simply could not envisage, recent innovations in digital technologies
cannot be fully mapped out via any straightforward models of cause and
effect. One particular example has become evident to me while writing
this book. At the turn of the century, a wide range of commentators
believed that the widespread adoption of digital devices such as cameras, laptop computers, and mobile phones, along with newly emerging
platforms to effortlessly distribute information, would give rise to a new
generation of "citizen" journalists, breaking down the barriers between
professionals and amateurs that had grown up in the nineteenth and
twentieth centuries as the means of production had become ever more
expensive. Dan Gillmor famously described this transition to a grassroots journalism as the shift "from journalism as lecture to journalism
as a conversation"[16] and I, like many, welcomed the opportunity that
new innovations presented to a variety of people who wished to get involved in reporting their own circumstances and communities. What
none of us realised was another effect of this breakdown of barriers
to publication, that the simplicity of communicating with millions via
Twitter and Facebook would be even more effective in the service of
automated bots and trolls seeking not to report facts but to disseminate
fake news as widely as possible. As such, Chapter 1 posits a much more
complex approach to the issue of a media ecology which must never
forget the law of unintended consequences, particularly as developments
in artificial intelligence (or, more accurately, automation) will certainly
ripple outwards far beyond their original purposes.

Chapter 2 explores a major shift that has taken place within the media
ecosystem within which journalism operates, whereby financial rewards
have moved from the producer to the distributor. How we get the news
has traditionally been a somewhat dry subject, and media producers
have always relied on complex (and usually expensive) systems of distribution. There are plenty of historical examples where such systems have
existed in a symbiotic relationship with media organisations, whether
it is train and transport networks for print or broadcast infrastructure
for television and radio. In the twenty-first century, however, the digital duopoly of Google and Facebook realised that the dissemination of
news online was ripe for disruption via its model of financing journalism through advertising. Using automation on a massive level, these two
companies were able to drive down the costs of advertising and thus
monopolise digital spend to a level never seen by the older media monopolies, in part because legacy corporations were still trying to maximise
the investments they had made in print and broadcast even as more and
more readers were shifting to purely digital platforms. The disruption
caused by big tech is another example of unintended consequences, in
that while frequently seeking to avoid being labelled as media companies (because of the additional regulations this will bring), sites such as

YouTube and Facebook are now responsible for more media consumption than any other group.

The following two chapters are related insofar as they explore some more of the consequences, intended or otherwise, of automation, first in the role of gatekeeping and disseminating information, and then in the form of robot or algorithmic journalism produced by software. With regard to automated gatekeeping, Chapter 3 begins first by looking at how simplicity of distribution online has affected journalism produced by people, especially insofar as the lowering of the barriers to distribution which were originally welcomed as a renaissance of citizen journalism has also resulted in a surge in highly partisan "alt"-journalism or even outright lies and propaganda as fake news. Because of the vast quantities of information that are shifted across their servers and networks, big tech companies such as Facebook rely on software to manage that flow of data and, as recent events such as the 2016 presidential election and European Referendum vote demonstrated, that automated process of gatekeeping has been very open to being gamed. This is not a case of technology somehow being "outside" (and thus responsive to) social and human decision-making: what came to light after these highly contentious votes was the level to which large organisations were highly culpable as they sought to monetise their systems. Chapter 4 concentrates on the role which automation is taking in the production of news. For practising journalists, this perhaps represents the greatest threat to their profession personally, and certainly media organisations facing financial pressures caused by the shift in such things as advertising are looking to cut costs. However, the evidence as it currently stands draws attention to the limitations as well as the successes of artificial intelligence: where it is good – as in writing millions of articles to deadlines that no group of professionals could ever match – algorithmic journalism is very good. Yet, such journalism is highly dependent on structured information that is not always presented in this format in the chaotic and messy environments in which journalists must frequently work. As in many other areas of technological innovation, algorithmic journalism will probably drive out humans in very restricted topics but, for the foreseeable future, it simply cannot reproduce the vast range of cognitive tasks that we take for granted.

Finally, in Chapter 5, we return to the impact of technology on journalism and the public sphere via three extended case studies which explore the relations between journalists and the citizens they purport to serve. In the first instance, the recent high-profile example of Infowars, this is an exploration of the dark, unintended consequences of the new distribution systems for data, by which social media first allows fake news to spread without interruption but then, in the space of a few days, closes down such sites because of the monopolistic power of tech giants. Against this – and with much longer-lasting consequences – the chapter continues to examine the changes wrought by Jeff Bezos, a twenty-first-century Citizen Kane, at *The Washington Post* and how, under his tenure, a flagship print newspaper became one of the ultimate digital media companies just at that moment when Donald Trump changed the news cycle completely. The fact that one of the most successful news sites in the world is controlled by the world's richest man will also have a far-reaching effect on the reporting of the world's most powerful democracy. Finally, the chapter ends with a turn away from the heavily American-centric focus of this book (inevitable when the biggest technology companies are based in the USA) to examine some of the ways in which various aspects of the media ecology considered in this book come into play in smaller scale reporting in Africa. Big tech may be viewed, rightly in my opinion, with ever-greater suspicion, but the desire to use technology to communicate with others is fundamental to the development and future of journalism.

Notes

1 Chris Johnston, "Apple is the First Public Company Worth $1 Trillion", *BBC News*, 2 August 2018, www.bbc.co.uk/news/business-45050213; Thomas Heath, "Apple is the First $1 Trillion Company in History", *The Washington Post*, 2 August 2018, www.washingtonpost.com/business/economy/apple-is-the-first-1-trillion-company-in-history/2018/08/02/ea3e7a02-9599-11e8-a679-b09212fb69c2_story.html; Mark Gurman, Mira Rojanasakul, and Cedric Sam, "How Apple Overcame Fits and Flops to Grow Into a Trillion-Dollar Company", *Bloomberg*, 2 August 2018, www.bloomberg.com/graphics/2018-apple-at-one-trillion-market-cap/; Kevin Kelleher, "As the Stock Market Closes, Apple Is Officially the First Trillion-Dollar U.S. Company", 2 August 2018, http://fortune.com/2018/08/02/apple-trillion-dollar-stock-price/.
2 Lucinda Shen, "Apple Is Worth Over $900 Billion. But It Won't Be the World's First Trillion-Dollar Company", *Fortune*, 8 November 2017, http://fortune.com/2017/11/08/apple-stock-amazon-trillion-aapl-iphone-x/.
3 Lucinda Shen, "Amazon and the Race to Be the First $1 Trillion Company", *Fortune*, 31 March 2017, http://fortune.com/2017/03/31/amazon-stock-trillion-dollar-company-apple-tesla-google/.
4 Ryan Derousseau, "Apple Isn't the First to Hit $1 Trillion In Value. Here Are 5 Companies That Did It Earlier", *Money*, 2 August 2018, http://time.com/money/5282501/apple-trillion-biggest-companies-in-history/.
5 Jeff Desjardins, "Most Valuable U.S. Companies Over 100 Years", *Visual Capitalist*, 14 November 2017, www.visualcapitalist.com/most-valuable-companies-100-years/.
6 Ben Bagdikian, *The New Media Monopoly*, Boston, MA: Beacon Press, 2004, p. 3.
7 Rafe Needleman, "Eric Schmidt: 'Gang of four' Rules Tech", *CNET*, 31 May 2011, www.cnet.com/news/eric-schmidt-gang-of-four-rules-tech/.
8 Bryan Glick, "Beanbags 2.0 – The New Google Office", *Computer-Weekly.com*, 26 July 2012, www.computerweekly.com/blog/Downtime/Beanbags-20-the-new-Google-office.
9 Jacky Law, *Big Pharma: How the World's Biggest Drug Companies Market Illness*, London: Constable, 2006.
10 Olivia Solon, "Tech's Terrible Year: How the World Turned on Silicon Valley in 2017", *The Guardian*, 23 December 2017, www.theguardian.com/technology/2017/dec/22/tech-year-in-review-2017.

11 Richard E. Sclove, *Democracy and Technology*, New York: Guilford Press, 1995; Douglas Kellner, "Intellectuals, the New Public Spheres, and Techno-Politics", in Chris Toulouse and Timothy W. Luke (eds.), *The Politics of Cyberspace: A New Political Science Reader*, New York: Routledge, 1998, p. 174.

12 Mark Balnaves, and Michele A. Willson, *A New Theory of Information & the Internet: Public Sphere Meets Protocol*, Frankfurt: Peter Lang, 2011, pp. 3–4; Lee Salter, *Conflicting Forms of Use: The Potential of and Limits to the Use of the Internet as a Public Sphere*, Riga: VDM Verlag, 2010, p. 10.

13 Natalie Fenton, "Fake Democracy: The Limits of Public Sphere Theory", in Slavko Splichal (ed.), *The Liquefaction of Publicness: Communication, Democracy and the Public Sphere in the Internet Age*, New York: Routledge, 2018, pp. 28–34; Barbara Pfetsch, "Dissonant and Disconnected Public Spheres as Challenge for Political Communication Research", in Slavko Splichal (ed.), *The Liquefaction of Publicness: Communication, Democracy and the Public Sphere in the Internet Age*, New York: Routledge, 2018, pp. 59–65.

14 Dennis Nguyen, *Europe, the Crisis, and the Internet: A Web Sphere Analysis*, London: Palgrave, 2017, p. 271.

15 Julia Schwanholz, Todd Graham, and Peter-Tobias Stoll, *Managing Democracy in the Digital Age: Internet Regulation, Social Media Use, and Online Civic Engagement*, New York: Springer, 2017.

16 Dan Gillmor, *We the Media: Grassroots Journalism By the People, For the People*. North Sebastopol, CA: O'Reilly Media, 2004, p. vi.

1   The New Ecology

In 1983, the American media company Knight Ridder, in conjunction with AT&T, launched an online news service called Viewtron. Initially a "videotex" service (similar to Ceefax, launched by the BBC in 1974), Viewtron initially required a specialised terminal but very quickly moved to being available on home computers. Launched in Florida first, Knight Ridder began its news service offering *The Miami Herald* online (the company itself was based at that time on the top floor of the Miami Herald building), requiring subscribers to pay $600 for a terminal and, according to company director Morton Goldstrom, offering "all the information I can imagine when I want it, the 21st century genie"[1] Knight Ridder's original plans were to sign up 5,000 customers to the system: in addition to purchasing the terminal, subscribers would pay $12 per month to Viewtron and then $1 per hour to Southern Bell for access to the system. All the information that Morton Goldstrom could imagine came at a significant price, but once Viewtron had jettisoned its specialist terminals, the service managed to extend to some 15 states before being closed in 1986: the service was extremely slow and people ceased to use the system once the novelty wore off. As subscribers departed the service, Knight Ridder lost approximately $50 million and James Batton, then president of the company, observed: "Videotex is not likely to be a threat to newspapers in the foreseeable future."[2]

Viewtron was an experiment a decade ahead of its time, and demonstrates just how important it is that technology is viewed within a wider context of financial and social operations. A recurrent theme among Knight Ridder executives was that subscribers were not incorporating videotex news into their daily habits: as well as the connecting technology being slow and frustrating, users still relied on television, radio, and print for their daily consumption of the news. The entire ecosystem that would support an online publication did not exist. By the late 1980s, Internet service providers such as Compuserve, America Online (later AOL), and Prodigy were beginning to offer news services as part of their package, but it was not until the wider adoption of Tim Berners Lee's world wide web in the mid-1990s that news services really began to take off. The first pioneers included CNN, *The Chicago Tribune*, and Time Inc's *Pathfinder* website. Before this, there existed a specialist series of "fax papers", which had a limited period to gain a foothold in the market before the web removed their reason for existence. Aimed at specialist (usually business) audiences, fax papers took advantage of the proliferation of fax machines in the late 1980s to send news highlights to subscribers for prices ranging from $400 per year (the cost of Tribfax, a product of the *Chicago Tribune*) to $2,500 for the one-page fax paper sent out daily by the *Hartford Courant*.[3] This hybrid of print and digital cultures was doomed to failure as soon as general-purpose computers with Internet connections replaced the fax machines, as well as American news sites web pages for international services such as the *Electronic Telegraph* (1994) and BBC (1997) in the UK began to appear, although the Anglo-American dominance of the web meant that sites in other countries only emerged more slowly: indeed, France's own national videotex service – Minitel – was incredibly successful after its introduction in 1982, with 26 per cent of French homes having access to a Minitel terminal in 1993 (bringing in revenues of $1.3 billion) compared to 13 per cent with a PC and 11 per cent with cable access.[4]

By the early 2000s, online news services were becoming ubiquitous across many parts of the globe, although the grip of news websites was felt most keenly in the English-speaking world. In 1999, John Pavlik was predicting that news junkies had "never had it so good" with news available at the touch of a button,[5] but as the new millennium began plenty of legacy media companies, such as ABC, were still very tentative when it came to rolling out truly multimedia programming[6]: at that stage, connections were still not fast enough and there were still too few users online to justify a wholesale shift online. By 2007, when Apple unveiled the first iPhone, faster Internet and mobile connections and eventually cheaper devices allowed the number of connected users to explode: while online news at the end of the twentieth century had been a novelty, by the beginning of the second decade it had become the norm, with consequences that completely transformed the relationships between news sites and readers. In its annual *Digital News Report* for 2018, for example, Reuters reported that social media – the prime driver of news consumption growth for much of the previous decade – had finally begun to decline in the face of mistrust surrounding fake news; yet in many countries, it remained the primary source of information for many users.[7] Television and radio remain a significant part of the mix for our consumption of news, but the rapid decline of print in the past ten to fifteen years means that for many of us, our mobile devices are the primary means by which we discover what is taking place around us.

Digital Ecosystems, Media Ecologies, and Technological Determinism

"Digital ecosystem" has become something of a buzzword in recent years. The business research organisation, Gartner, for example, offers its services to support organisations that wish to use "digital business ecosystems & the platform economy" to gain the "leverage organizations need to monetize, manage, and measure information as an asset for competitive advantage".[8] Beyond such trite phrases, in the field of information management the notion of digital ecosystems provides important tools for setting up the architecture required to sustain technological innovations in cloud computing and the Internet of things, as discussed by Skilton and Brady among others.[9] Between 2007 and 2013, the concept of a digital business ecosystem formed an important part of the work of the IEEE Digital EcoSystems and Technologies Conference (IEEE DEST), covering a wide array of issues including sustainable infrastructure for businesses, healthcare, and the digital humanities.[10] Nigel Shadbolt, alongside other researchers, has argued that artificial intelligence is contributing to a rise of social machines, in which the persistent environment of mobile and wearable technology, as well as sensors, is increasingly orchestrating human interactions and leading to the emergence of what he calls "social computational power".[11] Shadbolt offers Wikipedia as an example of such social computational power at work, whereby the activity of thousands of volunteers across the globe is co-ordinated not by human agents in traditional terms (editors with a sole prerogative over gatekeeping), but rather the interaction of those people via the software platform itself. Likewise, within the field of digital humanities, theorists such as Sheila Anderson and Tobias Blanke have demonstrated some of the ways in which big data and high-performance computing can transform scholarship in the field by transferring some of the characteristics of e-Science to arts and humanities research. Drawing on the ideas of Thomas Hughes regarding complex systems – in which interacting, interconnected large technology systems can grow from relatively simple components – such an approach may be even more important as an increasing amount of content is commodified behind paywalls: more than ever, scholars in the field must explore and open up the connections between such large technology systems as business seeks to compartmentalise them.[12]

This tension between large technology systems that enable the kind of social computational power discussed by Shadbolt and proprietary, more restrictive ones are very much at play in the confrontations between the Big Five. Although more recently some of these players have begun to recognise the opportunities present in embracing open digital ecosystems – typically because of a failure to monopolise important sectors, as in the case of Microsoft which sought to make its Office software available on as many platforms as possible when its Windows Mobile operating system collapsed – the more prevalent tendency of the past ten years has been to lock users into proprietary systems. The most successful company in this regard is Apple which, in terms of mobile considered from the vantage of profitability, is far ahead of the competition. Yet even the much-vaunted openness of Google's Android platform still seeks to establish other Google services such as search and maps as primary for users, while Amazon is ruthless in its attempts to hook all users onto itself as the main gateway into a vast range of commercial and entertainment opportunities.

When discussing digital ecosystems, the technology and business press tends not to consider the phrase in terms of complex, large-scale technology systems which, theoretically at least, are open-ended and capable of evolving far beyond the plans of those who establish them. Instead, there is a tendency on the part of journalists to accept the definitions offered by the big tech companies themselves and treat platforms as a series of increasingly closed, proprietary systems. Thus, for example, Michelle Evans at *Forbes* can argue that integration between things such as iOS, the iPhone X, Apple Watch, and Apple Pay is transforming digital commerce (all the time keeping consumers within the Apple ecosystem), while John Thornhill observes that iOS can provide an important hub between a huge variety of "digital capitalism" services such as Uber and AirBnB;[13] and yet, as Antonia Villas-Boas observes in the kind of article that has almost become a trope in recent years, "leaving the Apple ecosystem can be a tough thing to do"[14] – intentionally so. If Web 2.0 was intended, among other things, to break down the walled garden between producers and consumers, the Big Five have devoted a great deal of time and effort wherever possible to rebuilding those walls, tempting users to return to a carefully regulated Eden where everything "just works".

As such, this chapter tends to distinguish between digital ecosystems and media ecologies. This is not that the digital ecosystem is not a useful concept – it is – but that its increasingly prevailing use with regard to big tech tends to allow Google, Apple, Amazon, and others to define it in the more restrictive sense rather than as a true ecosystem; by the latter, this book means a system that considers the operations of such companies within a much wider context of interactions between a plurality of structures, economics, regulatory frameworks, organisations, and people. In many ways, the tension is between an assumption that, with enough data, any system can be perfectly determined versus the notion that any ecological system is always inherently complex. The development of complexity theory from the 1990s onwards deals with nonlinear systems capable of exhibiting emergent, self-organised and adaptive behaviour.[15] Such theory is especially suited to the concepts of digital ecosystems outlined by Shadbolt and others, particularly with great advances in computing power. Yet, the desire of big tech to move towards monopolisation of information flows seeks to limit emergent behaviours among consumers so as better to guide them towards a particular platform – aided, as Franklin Foer observes, by governmental tendencies to view antitrust legislation through the eyes of Thurman Arnold's distrust of inefficiency rather than Louis Brandeis's attempts to combat monopolies as antithetical to public values.[16] Because of a tendency to use the phrase "digital ecosystem" in a restrictive sense, media ecology is better suited for my purposes to describing large technology systems that are open to emergent and complex behaviour.

Media ecology as a concept is older than complexity theory: its roots lie, as with so much media theory, in the work of Marshall McLuhan and Walter Benjamin, but in the 1970s, Christine Nystrom and Neil Postman used the term to draw together observations by Kenneth Boulding, Thomas Kuhn, and Pierre Teilhard de Chardin that, during the twentieth century, a fundamental shift had taken place in mankind's world view. As such, media ecology began to be formulated at in the early seventies as a metadiscipline engaged in the study of media and complex communication systems as environments.[17] Lance Strate has recently outlined how the work of figures such as McLuhan and Postman, as well as other scholars such as Walter Ong, has created a rich context for artists, creatives, managers, executives, and even politicians in which the media operates within a field rather than a discipline and a well-defined subject, being fundamentally interdisciplinary.[18] An essential tenet of media ecology, as Dennis Cali, drawing on Postman, observes is that "the introduction of any new agent into an environment changes that environment".[19] Although not discussed by Cali, this approach is particularly fruitful when viewed from the perspective of actor-network theory (ANT) as outlined by theorists such as Michel Callon, Bruno Latour, and John Law, especially insofar as it demonstrates the capacity of nonhuman actors to effect change in a network.[20] While ANT theorists have been criticised for attributing intentionality to nonhuman actors (for example, by Langdon Winner[21]), the demonstrable effects on a whole range of complex systems by nonhuman agents – whether the impact of Milankovitch cycles on climate change or a botnet distributed denial of service (DDoS) – are particularly important to considering the role of technological agents within contemporary media ecologies. Indeed, the recognition that nonhuman agents can function as mediators allows us to bracket off one of the thorny philosophical issues surrounding artificial intelligence, that is whether it needs to be conscious (and thus intentional) to be considered truly intelligent. Termites may lack those attributes we would recognise as demonstrating consciousness, but that has not stopped one group of researchers classifying them as "soil engineers", capable of effecting major changes in tropical and subtropical ecosystems.[22]

As the approach to media ecologies espoused here draws upon ANT, an important addition is the notion of object-oriented ontology, or flat ontology (the latter being the preferred term here). Drawing upon a range of philosophers working in the first decades of the twenty-first century, including Graham Harman, Levi Bryant, Ian Bogost, and Timothy Morton, as well as Manuel DeLanda (who coined the term "flat ontology"), this approach rejects the privileging of human subjects over nonhuman objects, as well as the notion of "undermining" or "overmining" objects. The latter is usually encountered when thinkers argue that objects are manifestations of some deeper, underlying substance or force: this is not necessarily metaphysical in the usual sense, although historically this is where it has been most commonly encountered, as in Plato's notion that physical objects were manifestations of the ideal world, but can also apply to modern physical notions that the perceptual objects of the world – stars, planets, dogs, coffee cups – are better understood via the underlying relations between atoms and forces. This is what is referred to as undermining, whereas overmining deals with nineteenth-century idealism or twentieth-century theories of social constructivism, which holds either that there is nothing beyond what is perceived by the mind or that objects cannot be perceived outside language or the power structures of discourse.[23] The roots of flat ontological thinking lie in the phenomenology of Heidegger and Husserl, and, alongside ANT, the approach is especially important in establishing the reality of nonhuman objects that have agency within a system. A typical criticism of such flat ontologies is that they display a tendency towards nihilism, degrading meaning by reducing human values to "a fluke in an uncaring and fundamentally entropic universe".[24] Such a criticism does not necessarily invalidate the notion of flat ontologies: instead, the assumption that is made in this book is that human values are not essentialist and self-evident, but must always be critiqued and worked through in a system.

While media ecological theories, as espoused here, draw together media theorists and sociological/phenomenological philosophies, they will not completely neglect approaches to ecology more generally which provide the underlying model for the metaphor. As Pablo Marquet *et al* argue, there is something of a mistrust of theory in ecological thinking because theories such as those dealing with island bio-geographies or optimal foraging tend to focus on one or two hypotheses and models and thus fail in the overarching aim of theoretical work, which is to extrapolate from empirical data to advances via deductions from those data.[25] The authors argue that there are some efficient theories that are genuinely useful for environmental extrapolation, such as the optimal foraging theory and the MTE (whereby interplay among processes is affected by individual metabolic rates) – as well as a great many inefficient ones. They also note that deductive models based on inductive approaches will become more important, not less, in understanding biodiversity in an age of big data, and that correlations are not sufficient in themselves. Correlation alone was the approach suggested by Chris Anderson, based on the assumption that big data are rendering scientific method obsolete: in such an approach – what Anderson refers to as the "Petabyte age" – the ability to search, read, and analyse data does not require a visualisation of the data "as a whole" (which is, in any case, impossible). Given a large enough corpus, we can find correlations without "knowing" what the underlying model is – something that, prior to the massive power of contemporary computing, would have been considered just noise.[26] Marquet *et al* acknowledge the inefficiencies of many theoretical approaches to ecology, but still hold that efficient models are important for helping us make predictions dealing with our current global environmental crises. The metabolic theory of ecology (MTE) and the neutral theory of biodiversity (NTB), which deals with the stochastic – or random probability – distribution of data, have demonstrated themselves capable of making accurate predictions. Large populations allow themselves to be studied deterministically, ignoring chance factors such as accidental births or deaths – as with the famous predator–prey population cycles outlined in the Lotka–Volterra model of the 1920s, which showed fluctuations in populations according to the density of prey and predators, respectively.[27] Such deterministic models are much more difficult with small populations, and are more likely to be affected by socially constructed patterns as Shaffer demonstrated in 1978 when examining the effects of the United States National Forest Management Act of 1976, which mandated the maintenance of viable populations of native and desirable non-native species and his own studies of the grizzly bear population in Yellowstone: for small populations, a chance fluctuation can result in extinction and so stochastic models began to emerge to predict the probabilities of such extinctions within a given time frame.[28] What should be becoming clear from these observations is that an appropriate theory of media ecology that can help to explain factors affecting journalism is much more intertwined than the desiccated "digital ecosystem" hype that is bandied around iOS, Amazon's market place, or Android (important as all these elements are to a deeper understanding of media ecologies).

Certain elements of the approach to media ecology considered here mitigate against common notions of media or technological determinism. The strongest forms of technological determinism, for example the assumptions by Thorstein Veblen that capitalism represents a struggle between technology and "ceremonial" culture (the so-called Veblenian dichotomy whereby institutions adjust technologies to make them more instrumental – and thus wasteful[29]) or Jacques Ellul's notion that technologies operate along a form of natural selection,[30] tend to be viewed as simplistic among media theorists today. Among those more heavily invested in the digital economy of the twenty-first century, unsurprisingly, the opposite is true. For them, the notion that technology is the key driver of transformations of human society and culture are self-evident truths, whereby as technologies stabilise so they determine users' behaviours. To give merely one example, though an important one, in an ambitious post in February 2017, Mark Zuckerberg argued that by building a global network, by providing the infrastructure that allowed people to communicate more immediately, Facebook is "bringing us closer together and building a global community".[31] Tools for faster – effectively instantaneous – communication will encourage us to behave as though we are part of a worldwide community. This approach, in the form of hard determinism, tends towards what Claude Fischer calls a "billiard ball" impact analysis of such relations: as a technology is introduced and adopted, so user behaviour ricochets away in a clearly defined response.[32] Fischer is right to draw attention to critics of such hard determinism, who point out that the assumption that technology is somehow "outside" society and thus able to have a clean and obvious impact upon that society is a flawed one. Nor is this something necessarily new. Merrit Roe Smith argues that the belief in technological determinism dates back to the industrial revolution at least, an assumption whose European roots grew more deeply in America so that by the early twentieth century, advertisers and industrialists "quickly mastered the idea of the technological fix"[33] The folly of Zuckerberg's particular technological fix in the light of the presidential election of 2016 will be the subject of a later chapter, but it is also worth commenting on that he suffers from this misconception of technology as separate to society, to history, as something outside which operates on culture and human behaviour, the billiard ball which can ricochet us into the right pocket if only we can control the levers of that technology. As Nicholas Carr correctly observes, Zuckerberg can only entertain the notion of a planetary community because he fundamentally misunderstands what community means, that communities nearly always comprise groups of individuals who have found a way to get along *despite* sometimes fundamental differences of opinion and belief, or which, as in the case of religious communities, may be oppositional to the communities in which they find themselves.[34] In order for his technological fix around community to have the remotest chance of working, Zuckerberg must reduce it – as indeed many theorists of online communities have since the 1990s – to being synonymous with communication. If community equals communication, then enhancing communication will ricochet into a superior community and Zuckerberg's ideal is perhaps best referred to as the field of dreams model: build it and he will come.[35]

Such comments are not intended necessarily to fixate upon Zuckerberg alone: it is a common mindset among the masters of the new digital universe, and Martin Bauer observes that the digital economy relies on a "hall of heroes" whereby the "fables" of billionaire philanthropists such as Bill Gates, Larry Page, and Sergey Brin justify an inevitability of future outcomes.[36] While Bauer is sceptical of this technologically deterministic approach to culture and history, others, such as Tim Jordan, tend to assume that such determinism is inevitable even if it should also be resisted, creating a counter-mythology of heroes in the form of hackers, "the warriors of this everyday technological determinism", who hack to "resist being technologically determined themselves".[37] Behind such assertions is another fundamental myth, that of progress, which, as Michael L. Smith argues, leads to a belief that technological changes are inevitable and unstoppable.[38] Such a simplistic, teleological viewpoint is counter to the media ecology approach throughout this book: this kind of narrative retrofits the evidence to match the final outcome – the rise of Google is inevitable, unstoppable, even though, as Foer observes, it was as much Microsoft's fear of the Department of Justice investigation in the late 1990s that prevented it from wiping the young company from the map (as it had done with Netscape in the mid-1990s) as any "inevitable" technological progress.[39] Similarly, Galloway points out the numerous opportunities that more established media companies had to change the course of history, as when Excite and Blockbuster failed to acquire Google and Netflix in the early 2000s.[40] It is easy to demonstrate in countless ways how the myth of inevitable, technologically determined progress is false – we are all wise after the event. Brian Winston even went so far as to suggest "a 'law' of the suppression of radical potential", whereby new communications media are prevented from attaining their full potential in the short term due to the constraining influences of existing institutions, whether family, home, workplace, church, or political leaders.[41] When treated as an external force operating upon society, an almost divine inspiration that moves mere mortals to behave in new ways, technology becomes a religion suited to the secular, consumerist age. And yet while rejecting this simplistic, reductionist, and frequently self-serving view ("You cannot oppose Apple/Google/Amazon/Facebook: this is the end of times, and only the elect will be judged worthy."), obviously a book on big tech and journalism must believe at some level that technology has an effect on society.

Fernando de la Cruz Paragas and Trisha Lin have offered a much more nuanced examination of technological determinism that corresponds to the media ecology approach adopted here.[42] Rejecting the reductionist stance of earlier critics, and using Burrell and Morgan's four paradigms of social theory as a starting point, they demonstrate usefully the obvious point that technological determinism is a continuum with society rather than a dichotomy. Burrell and Morgan in the late seventies constructed a matrix for discussing the main debates of sociology – whether reality is given or constructed by the mind, whether experience is required to understand something, whether humans have free will or are entirely shaped by environment, and whether scientific method or direct experience is the best way to understanding. These topics could be approached via an interest in regulating to preserve stability or in the search for radical change, as well as either subjectively (individualistically) or objectively (structurally), leading to their four paradigms: functionalist (objective-regulation), interpretative (subjective-regulation), radical humanist (subjective-radical change), and radical structuralist.[43] From this matrix, the functionalist paradigm has often been the default for sociological study, assuming a rationalist approach to organisations and human behaviour, while the interpretative paradigm seeks to explain processes from the individual's perspective the better to understand the world. Radical humanist paradigms are usually opposed to organisations and seek change because individuals are separated from their "true selves", while radical structuralist paradigms, such as Marxism or the current penchant for disruptive technologies, see conflicts as inherent within society and necessary to generate change and progress.

It is tempting to see the radical structuralist and radical humanist paradigms as the *modus operandi* of Silicon Valley in terms of its investment structures and advertising agencies, respectively. Disruptive investors are constantly looking for means to shake up existing practices (and to make a great deal of money in the process) while advertising to consumers and users of these new technologies that old ways of doing things are preventing them from finding their true selves: "think different" and "do the right thing."[44] Paragas and Lin observe that the traditional distinction between "hard" and "soft" determinism – that is between ascribing technology to the necessary and sufficient qualities to effect social change versus being a key factor that may facilitate change – has more recently been reconceived as technological determinism versus social constructivism, whereby according to the latter technology is viewed as a more neutral instrument whose effects are shaped by users and social conditions.[45] By using Burrell and Morgan, Paragas and Lin argue that a refined and more nuanced version of technological determinism can be applied to explore a multiplicity of relations between technology and society, rather than insisting upon a binary opposition whereby we must come down on one side or the other in all cases. Thus, objectivist positions tend to focus on how new technologies can *cause* certain behaviours (for example, whether video games cause certain types of aggressive behaviour or whether online tuition enhances learning), while subjective responses may demonstrate how technology is affected by other social relations (such as men dominating skilled trades during the industrial revolution to the exclusion of women). Technological innovations may indeed result in disruptive and powerful social changes, but at other times, they seem to be constrained by how privileged actors control the design process.[46] While Paragas and Lin provide an immensely flexible and thus more useful model of technological determinism that will feed into many of the discussions of relations between technologies, users, and organisations throughout this book, it is tempting to coin a phrase to better describe those relations: technological stochastism. Rather than attempting to define causal relations within different paradigms, a media ecology based on stochastic procedures would outline the probabilities of particular patterns of behaviour emerging within certain conditions.

Technology companies – the great disruptors of Silicon Valley and elsewhere – have greatly transformed the media landscape of the early twenty-first century. Of that, there can be no doubt: and yet the effects of their innovations are by no means the result of a simple "billiard ball" view of technological and media determinism. As we shall see in subsequent chapters, companies such as Google and Facebook have often struggled to deal with the unintended effects of forces which they have set in motion. What is clear, however, is that the increasing automation of cognitive activities through algorithms powered by increasingly sophisticated computers – what is usually referred to as artificial intelligence – will bring about even more profound changes.

The Ghost in the Machine

In his book *Life 3.0: Being Human in the Age of Artificial Intelligence*, Max Tegmark offers a hypothetical scenario in which an "Omega Team" of researchers produces an artificial intelligence, "Prometheus", that rapidly approaches what some of those working in the field of AI refer to as a "singularity" – that moment when such an intelligence surpasses human capabilities:

> Within a year of the first launch, they had added remarkably good news channels to their lineup all over the globe. As opposed to their other channels, these were deliberately designed to lose money, and were pitched as a public service. In fact, their news channels generated no income whatsoever: they carried no ads and were viewable free of charge by anyone with an internet connection. The rest of the media empire was such a cash-generating machine that they could spend far more resources on their news service than any other journalistic effort had done in world history – and it showed. Through aggressive recruitment with highly competitive salaries of journalists and investigative reporters, they brought remarkable talent and findings to the screen. Through a global web service that paid anybody who revealed something newsworthy, from local corruption to a heartwarming event, they were usually the first to break a story. At least that's what people believed: in fact, they were often first because stories attributed to citizen journalists had been discovered by Prometheus via real-time monitoring of the internet.[47]

Ignoring the many assumptions that take place within Tegmark's scenario (for example, that the Omega Team is not Chinese and thus does
not automatically comprise those favourable to a liberal-capitalist democracy), it is worth concentrating on this passage with regard to the
extensive fantasy it provides surrounding artificial intelligence and journalism. The utopian vision of humanity's future that Tegmark provides
in *Life 3.0* has an important role to play in terms of recognising a special
role for the media: to gain traction, Prometheus needs to operate a media
company, not merely producing high-quality rendered entertainment at
a lower cost than human competitors, but also as a news source. Of interest in this scenario are two particular points which will be explored in
much more detail in subsequent chapters: first of all, the news company
operates as a public service and, in contrast to the rest of its entertainment remit, operates at a loss; secondly, Prometheus is much better at
finding stories because of its "real-time monitoring of the internet". The
third notion that Prometheus can afford to pay more competitive salaries
for news without bringing in any income is, I believe, where Tegmark
enters the world of pure fantasy.

Regarding funding more generally for a news channel, Tegmark –
who is Swedish-American – appears to hanker after the public–private
duopoly that is common in many European countries rather than the
more cutthroat commercial environment of North America. As we shall
see in the next chapter, the advertising-led model that has driven media
growth in the past century or more seems very much broken the tech
giants of the twenty-first century, and Tegmark's idealistic solution is
to build an altruistic public service function into Prometheus and the
motivations of the Omega Team.[48] Software-generated journalism will
be returned to in Chapter 4: because Tegmark is dealing with the notion of a singularity, a climactic moment when AI moves beyond human
comprehension, the ability of Prometheus to find stories that no person
can match as outlined previously is better treated as fiction. As we shall
see, no algorithm yet is capable of generating anything close to human
writers, and the question remains as to whether – without a mythical
singularity – such an activity is actually programmable. Despite my crit-
icisms, however, which are many, I do appreciate that Tegmark considers
journalism a significant activity for AI and also that, as a Professor of
Physics, he has a more idealistic view of the profession than many of
those working in the media.

Tegmark's reference to "life 3.0" is meant to distinguish that in which
hardware, through technological mastery, is able to reconfigure itself,
from life 1.0 (development through evolution) and life 2.0 (development
through software or programming – that is, teaching and learning).
While I am gently mocking the scenario that leads to Prometheus (if
not Tegmark's idealism regarding the media), his book is an interesting definition of some of the myths and concerns surrounding artificial

intelligence, as well as identifying that the real struggle at the moment is not between technological evangelists and luddites, but rather between digital utopians and techno-sceptics as to how feasible artificial general intelligence – AGI, or the ability of machines to think in some semblance of consciousness – is in this century. While the common fear among the public is of some kind of Frankenstein monster that will become evil or conscious, Tegmark observes that among AI researchers, the real worry is about AI becoming competent with goals that diverge from our own. Current AI is very narrow – good at achieving specific goals such as playing games – in contrast to the much broader capabilities of human intelligence. Something that is evident when reading Tegmark – and indeed a number of AI researchers – is the underlying dualism upon which their work is based: memory, computation, and learning (all contributors to intelligence) are "substrate-independent" and can exist on any kind of matter so long as it has multiple stable states, such as the magnetic orientation of a hard disk, the pits and smooth surfaces in a CD, valleys in an egg-box, etc. That information, which is substrate-independent, also allows researchers to experiment with computational alternatives to neurons, such as the NAND gates that control outputs in a circuit or neural networks that can rearrange themselves to improve learning.

The Prometheus scenario, as well as being one of the most recent contributions to AI studies and a good general introduction, is also valuable for demonstrating some of the ways in which artificial intelligence can potentially interact with media sources. In the past decade at least, AI has become an increasingly important part of the mix of digital ecosystems, driving Facebook's Algorithm or Amazon's Alexa, and AI theory in more recent years has, in the words of Petrović, begun to move towards a theory of intelligent action in all agents, not simply humans, that can approximate human levels of interaction.[49] It has its roots in the assumption, following work undertaken by Turing and McCulloch and Pitts in the 1940s and 1950s, that cognition is computational and that neurons can be viewed as computing devices.[50] This approach, sometimes called cognitivism (and formulated in the 1970s in particular in the work of Fodor, Newell, and Simon)[51] is often exemplified by the Turing Machine, a model of universal computation that can take any input, process it, and provide a comprehensible output: as such, the assumption of cognitivism is that the human brain can be treated as a computer and thus modelled and extrapolated.

The original premise of a considerable amount of research into artificial intelligence was that it would be able to build a machine capable of thought, consciousness, and even something approximating human emotions. Herbert Simon laid the roots of this approach – what the philosopher John Searle would later call "strong AI" – when he claimed in 1955 that he, Allen Newell, and J. C. Shaw had created a program that could prove mathematical theorems, and that they had "solved the venerable mind/body problem, explaining how a system composed of matter can have the properties of mind."[52] Strong AI has since evolved into the notion that is more commonly referred to in this book, artificial general intelligence or AGI. When referring to AGI, this means that machines will be able to perform the same intellectual tasks as humans: it is more often than not the stuff of science fiction or futurism, and there is a veritable specific genre of scientific researchers who produce what are, frankly, fantastical applications of AI along the lines of Tegmark's *Life 3.0*, whether resulting in dystopian situations such as the "AI takeover" envisaged by Stephen Hawking or Elon Musk, or a fruitful singularity that promises huge benefits for humanity – the line adopted by Ray Kurzweil in *The Singularity is Near*.[53] This book will not concern itself much with AGI, but instead with what is more frequently referred to as "weak" or "applied" AI. The 1950s to 1970s are sometimes referred to as a "golden age" of AI, but the dream of a universal, general intelligence that can compete with humans seems to be receding even as the tasks of specific automation become incredibly successful. In early 2018, researchers at Carnegie Mellon announced that they were ceasing work on human-like AGI to concentrate instead on refining and engineering particular elements of automation, following calls by figures such as pioneering AI researcher, Geoff Minton, to "throw [current research] away and start again".[54]

This is not for even a moment to deny that automation and applied AI can achieve remarkable things. While not necessarily bringing about either the kind of visionary utopia imagined by Tegmark or Kurzweil, nor leading into a bleak future for humanity ruled by Terminator-style robots, automation can be both incredibly beneficial and destructive for people. Concerns about the role of highly automated machines in warfare are already widespread enough for more than 2,400 scientists to have signed a pledge opposing autonomous lethal weapons at futureoflife.org/lethal-autonomous-weapons-pledge. Less dramatically, automation is set to take over, or is already taking over, a wide range of cognitive tasks that were previously considered the preserve of humans – including many writing tasks. The linguist and philosopher Noam Chomsky assumed that humans are born with a biological predisposition towards language based on the "poverty of the stimulus", that is, there are not enough empirical data in our environments to allow us to learn language solely through experience. We cannot, for example, learn grammar simply through hearing sentences, which led Chomsky to assume – in the language of AI researchers – that human intelligence was not entirely substrate-independent.[55] Functionalist approaches to AI, that the mind and body are separable and that the former can be modelled by software, do not as yet appear to be able to make the leap towards true AGI.

It was in his 1950 paper on "Computing Machinery and Intelligence" that Turing introduced his famous test (called by him "the imitation game" and only later named after him) for determining whether or not it was possible for an interrogator to mistake a machine for a person, offering a setup which originally involved one person asking questions and two other participants, one human, another a machine, providing typed answers to questions.[56] Turing himself considered a number of objections to the consideration of whether we could mistake a machine for a human, some of which (such as religious objections) he dealt with fairly cursorily, while others – notably the argument from the informality of behaviour, later codified by Hubert Dreyfus as the assertion that human reason and behaviour cannot be fully captured in rules[57] – were not so quickly glossed over. While there were some half-hearted attempts to use the test in the 1960s, most famously via Joseph Weizenbaum's ELIZA programme which appeared to fool some humans, it was not fully implemented until 1991 when Hugh Loebner offered a $100,000 pledge to the first entrant to pass the test. Before this, John Searle had offered one of the trenchant critiques of the Turing Test as a means of measuring true intelligence: in his famous "Chinese Room" analogy, presented in his 1980 paper "Minds, Brains, and Programs", Searle offered the analogy of a human operator in a sealed room, which he later summarised more concisely in 1999:

> Imagine a native English speaker who knows no Chinese locked in a room full of boxes of Chinese symbols (a data base) together with a book of instructions for manipulating the symbols (the program). Imagine that people outside the room send in other Chinese symbols which, unknown to the person in the room, are questions in Chinese (the input). And imagine that by following the instructions in the program the man in the room is able to pass out Chinese symbols which are correct answers to the questions (the output). The program enables the person in the room to pass the Turing Test for understanding Chinese but he does not understand a word of Chinese.[58]

There have been responses to Searle's analogy – whether along the lines that just because the man does not understand Chinese does not mean that comprehension has not taken place, to conceding that this is an argument against strong AI but that the process can still be useful for dealing with natural language processing and applied AI. In any case, with regard to Turing's own conception of machine intelligence, the earlier mathematician would have probably not been phased the slightest by Searle's objections: his opening statement is that he will consider the question "Can machines think?" and, within a paragraph, he has dismissed that question as fatuous, replacing it with issues of whether machines will ever be able to mimic humans enough to fool us. Claims were made for the test being passed in 2014 by software called "Eugene", developed in Saint Petersburg and able to emulate a 13-year-old boy: before contemplating that we are on the verge of a singularity, it should also be pointed out that this was an adapted version of Turing's rules that allowed for a success rate of the machine fooling human judges more than 30 per cent of the time (Eugene managed 33 per cent).[59]

Turing's observation regarding mimicry offers a route out of the impasse of AI and AGI, which is, after W. Grey Walter's "mimicry of life" via simple robots in the late 1940s, to consider intelligence as simply that which exhibits interesting behaviour.[60] Based in Bristol, Walter was able to construct mechanical tortoises that were phototropic (able to follow light) and had a bump mechanism to allow them to change direction. His first robots, Elmie and Elsie, were thus able to simulate autonomous motion without human intervention, leading to a branch of robotics development that did not need to concern itself with consciousness and the difficult tasks of cognitivism. As Russell and Norvig point out in their guide to modern thinking about AI, the standard approach to artificial intelligence that is considered and evaluated by the Turing Test (if not actually by Turing himself), "thinking humanly", is only one of four approaches, including acting humanly, thinking rationally, and acting rationally. In practical terms, it is probably the latter, also known as the "rational agent", which tends to concentrate on intelligent behaviour in hardware and software, that offers the most immediate benefits for future development.[61]

The fact that this book is largely concerned with automation and applied AI rather than strong or general artificial intelligence is by no means to assert that AGI is impossible: complexity theory and notions of biological emergence frequently demonstrate that complex systems can arise from situations where there is not enough information, as in termite colonies or traffic patterns. Applied AI has often resulted in more useful models and theories, for example, the modular approach based on Fodor's observations in the 1980s that the human mind is largely composed of task-specific modules,[62] the cognitive processes that allow us to concentrate on winning (or losing) a game of chess. Fodor's approach has been criticised, but it does have practical applications in the field of AI research and robotics. Simulated micro worlds are easier to understand (and program) than the entire universe of cognition, and this is particularly evident in areas such as game playing where computers are becoming better than humans. Rather than simple brute force – an attempt to compute every possible move recursively – such controlled environment simulations work better via heuristics to build up the limited range of moves that are possible in a given situation. As with playing chess, we shall see in a later chapter that this approach to AI is also especially pertinent to certain forms of journalism.

Artificial intelligence is a term that is regularly applied throughout this book, although what is really being discussed is the automation of cognitive tasks. This certainly is possible with regard to *some* writing but, at our present level of technological mastery, there is much within the sphere of journalism that, as Dreyfus would observe, falls into the intuitive, semi-, or unconscious "knowing-how" we achieve certain aims rather than the conscious "knowing-that" steps of problem-solving that can be emulated by an algorithm, the former a contextual "background" that is close to Heidegger's notion of *Dasein*.[63] To repeat, this book is entirely agnostic about the possibility of AGI and the notion of a singularity – sceptical in the sense that I simply do not *know* whether it is possible rather than I do not *believe* – and instead restricts itself to AI in the more limited sense of cognitive automation. Even in that restricted sense, AI is already transforming the media ecology by means of which journalism is produced in the twenty-first century: there is no Prometheus creating omniscient news stories far superior to anything capable of being written by humans. Instead, what we have is a small number of big tech companies that are using such automation to radically transform our economic and sociopolitical environment, one of the most important of which at the time of writing is the richest company in the world: Apple. How it has attempted – sometimes succeeding, sometimes failing – to change the journalism environment is now our extended case study for understanding the relationship between big tech and a media ecology.

The Age of Apple

The history of Apple is very much one of two acts. Founded by Steve Jobs and Steve Wozniak in 1976, its first phase was as the company which, alongside Microsoft, probably did more than any other to transform public perceptions of the personal computer. Fascinating as that story is in its own right, it is of little significance to the development of a media ecology in the twenty-first century. Indeed, after Jobs was forced out of Apple in 1985, the company began a decade-long slide into irrelevance until Jobs, the prodigal founder, returned in 1997, kickstarting Act II of the Apple play and bringing with him a new management style and a new computer, the iMac. As Luke Dormehl observes, the genius of the iMac was really its name – other than a simple ability to plug in simply to the Internet and a bright and breezy design, there was "nothing innately superior about the iMac over any other computer".[64] Nonetheless, the iMac marked a return to profitability at Apple, allowing it to post a $309 million profit in 1998 as opposed to losses of $1.05 billion in 1997, and the coming decades would see the company abandon many more legacy issues than simply removing floppy disk drives. The fact that Apple Computer, Inc. would become, simply, Apple Inc. in 2007 spoke volumes about the future direction of the organisation: the company that had been founded in the garage of Steve Jobs's childhood home in Los Altos to build the original Apple I computer would in essence become a producer of luxury consumer devices, and its first major success in this field was with the iPod.

In 1981, Apple had paid $80,000 to Apple Corps Ltd, the multimedia corporation founded by the Beatles, and promised to stay out of the music industry (so much so that throughout the 1980s, engineers and managers at Apple were suspicious of even developing audio systems on the Mac or software to burn CDs[65]). With the return of Jobs, however, the dynamic between the music industry and the hardware company was to shift completely. While MP3 players had started to become widely available in the late 1990s, none would perform as well as the iPod. When Apple made the decision to enter the market in 2000, digital music players were worth $80 million in the US alone, rising to $100 million in 2001.[66] The original iPod met only with limited success – and, with hindsight, was clearly a piece of hardware with a limited future as smartphones became more widely available – but with the launch of iTunes as an accompanying piece of software for managing and, more importantly, downloading music, Apple was finally able to shift the music industry landscape in its favour. With regard to digital music, Apple was not really the innovator at all although, for a decade, it would be the main benefactor of the changing ecology in which music was distributed and consumed: the dubious accolade of true innovator belonged to Napster.

Founded by Shawn Fanning in 1999, Napster comprised a peer-to-peer file-sharing service that enabled users more easily to share MP3 files between each other. Although not the first file-sharing service (Usenet had allowed such activity since the 1970s), Napster revolutionised the ease with which music could be transferred between participants. Commentators such as John Alderman were right to believe that the music industry was about to undergo a radical transformation; they were, however, wrong to believe that Napster would benefit.[67] Faced with insurmountable legal challenges from the Recording Industry Association of America (RIAA) to prevent the transfer of copyrighted material, the Napster network was shut down in 2001 and, despite various attempts to relaunch as a legitimate file-sharing service, it was declared bankrupt in 2002. Yet while the head of the hydra was cut off, many more would spring up in its place – file-sharing services such as Gnutella, Kazaa, Limewire, and Freenet appeared and frequently disappeared in the space of months, demonstrating a growing hunger for digital music that the major record labels refused to accommodate. During the post-war period, the music industry had – a few years aside – solidified into an apparently stable monopoly comprising the "Big Five": EMI, Sony Music (formerly CBS), BMG, Universal Music Group (formerly

Polygram and MCA Music), and WEA. This group was responsible for 80 per cent of music sales in the world and, as Stephen Witt observes, the conglomerates had long been out of touch with their fans.[68] Rather than embrace digital downloads, they preferred to maintain what had been a very profitable ecosystem based on CD manufacturing and retailing. In 1999, the music industry recorded a high point of $36.9 billion in revenues worldwide – a figure that dropped to $6.3 billion by 2009.[69] Napster was the disruptive innovator, but Apple was the beneficiary. Apple itself was surprised at how successful the iPod was a year after its release, and that the volume of pirated music was even more valuable to consumers once it was made portable. As such, the company increasingly sought to press home a new business model for distributing music: it would sell individual tracks for 99 cents each on iTunes and keep 30 per cent of the revenue. In 2002, companies such as Universal were not interested – by 2005, they recognised that sales of CDs were falling off a cliff.[70]

With the iPod and iTunes, Apple realised its first major transformation of a media industry and this is often held up as a prophetic example of technological determinism, how a visionary leader inspired behavioural change across a generation, frequently being the argument of hagiographies such as Walter Isaacson's authorised biography of Jobs.[71] More thoughtful accounts, such as those by Stephen Witt, draw attention to how such a teleological account is retrofitted to the facts, and that not only was the success of the iPod unexpected by Apple but just how much the company was adapting to consumer behaviour rather than leading it. iTunes and the iPod were indeed part of a new media ecology, but this was the one that very much operated outside of the strict remit of its emerging (and limited) ecosystem as millions of users put the device to frankly illicit purposes in its first years. Nonetheless, by 2013 iTunes accounted for 63 per cent of digital downloads.[72] The level of transformation of one media industry, however, would be completely dwarfed by Apple's next innovation: the iPhone.

When it was first announced in January 2007, perhaps no one had any real conception of just how important the iPhone would be: Jobs himself referred to it as a "widescreen iPod with touch controls" and a "revolutionary mobile phone", but sceptics abounded. Kate Bevan in *The Guardian* observed that £269 was "quite a lot for an 8GB music player", especially one that didn't allow you to use custom ringtones (oh, how priorities have changed in a decade)[73] while CNet gave it a measly 3.5 stars out of 5 and remarked likewise that the memory was "stingy for an iPod".[74] Nonetheless, more prescient commentators such as Guy Kewney were hailing it as a success while its availability in stores by the end of June 2007 led to what would become a regular phenomenon: that of eager fans camping outside Apple stores to get their hands on the new device.[75] Mobile devices had been an important part of personal communications for years, and the Nokia 1100 still remains the bestselling device ever (with over 250 million phones sold, although the iPhones 6 and 6s came close with 220 million). Nonetheless, it was Apple rather than Nokia that truly revolutionised mobile platforms for the twenty-first century, so much so that by 2016, the iPhone accounted for 91 per cent of mobile profits based on a 17.2 per cent market share: more people owned Android devices, but for the majority of manufacturers – including HTC, Sony, and LG, although not Samsung – that meant operating on razor thin margins or at a loss. As Brian Merchant explains in great detail, the iPhone itself was the product of huge levels of collaboration and innovation outside of Apple itself, one that was capable of a "civilisation-scale transformation", although ultimately one that may simply mark a phase in the transition towards more pervasive and intimate technologies.[76] The iPod had prepared the way, but it was the iPhone that led to an explosion in the mobile market – though its effects on news consumption, at least to begin with, were perhaps less important.

Instead, it was with the launch of the iPad in 2010 that Apple effectively introduced another format to market which, once again, transformed the consumption of media. Apple did not invent the tablet format: as Apple Computer in 1987, the company had launched its tablet division under the direction of John Sculley rather than Steve Jobs, an initiative that resulted in the launch of the truly innovative – if little loved – Newton MessagePad in 1993. The 1990s saw a number of ultimately ill-fated devices appear, some relatively successful, such as the PalmPilot, others little more than concepts like the Knight-Ridder tablet video, shown in 1994 as a future device to consume media produced by the company. The most substantial development was the launch of Microsoft's Tablet PC operating system on devices made by original equipment manufacturers such as Hewlett-Packard, pen-driven devices that, however, were too bulky and plagued by display and power issues that made them unsuccessful in the market place. Such were the precursors to Apple's iPad that when, in 2011, it sued Samsung for bringing a similar device to the market, the Korean company argued that the original prototype for tablet computers was the device shown in Stanley Kubrick's 1968 movie, *2001: A Space Odyssey*.[77]

Regardless of the patentable origins of tablet computers, with the iPad, Apple managed to bring together a number of factors that made the device an incredible success. While underpowered in comparison with later tablets, being particularly constrained by only having 256Mb of RAM, nonetheless it offered up to ten-hour battery life and its screen, while a low resolution compared to subsequent devices, was bright, clear, and responsive. Most of all, pricing for the iPad began $499, much less than Microsoft's early devices. In its press release to accompany the launch, Apple described the iPad as "A magical and revolutionary device at an unbeatable price".[78] The iPad also benefitted from being targeted as a consumer electronics product, one designed to consume video, text, and graphics, and, from its very earliest stages, it was also intended to be a *reading* device. Alongside the launch of the iPad itself, Apple introduced a new app, iBooks, as well as a service to complement iTunes, the iBookstore, with titles from major and independent publishers. Electronic readers had been touted since the late 1990s, but it was only with the launch of Amazon's Kindle in 2007 that they finally began to gain market share: by the time Apple entered the market in 2010, Amazon claimed that it had 70–80 per cent of the e-book market,[79] a situation that many publishers considered disastrous as Amazon, in a push to sell Kindles, started limiting all e-book prices to $9.99 or less – even paying publishers more in many cases in order to ensure that its loss-leading e-reader would dominate the market.[80] Into this increasingly toxic market place – where Amazon effectively declared war on some of the Big Six book publishers – Apple entered with a seductive proposition: Apple would use its agency model to allow publishers to set the price of their e-books, taking a 30 per cent cut as it did via its app store and iTunes sales. While publishers were eager to sign up, this, in turn, created further problems as the 1890 Sherman Act forbids organisations from combining to exert control over a market: as the main publishers were in regular contact with each other and Apple regarding the deals that they signed with Apple, in 2012 a suit was filed against Apple and five of the main publishers (excluding Random House). The publishers subsequently settled with Amazon and only Apple went to court and was found guilty, in 2013, of conspiracy to set the retail prices of e-books and, after appeals, was ordered to pay $450 million. As of February 2017, Amazon was responsible for 83.3 per cent of e-book sales in the USA, compared to 9 per cent for Apple, a market share that was more-or-less replicated across English-reading markets.[81] Clearly, there was one competitor that dominated the market and, for all its success as a hardware manufacturer, this was not Apple. And yet, Apple had lost its court case for the simple reason that the Sherman Act considers antitrust actions against consumers, rather than monopolies *per se* directed against other competitors. As Foer and Galloway have observed, the particular nature of antitrust legislation in the United States has greatly benefitted Amazon, which has consistently presented itself as an ally of consumers.[82]

The two examples considered thus far – music and book publishing – show how Apple has intervened in different media ecologies with very different consequences, dominating one completely for the best part of a decade, while being very much a secondary competitor in the other. The two media industries share several key factors, not least that the process of monopolisation had long been taking place before any of the main digital companies entered the fray: mergers and acquisitions from the 1970s onwards had resulted in a Big Five and Big Six in music and book publishing, respectively, that were already affecting consumer patterns. This is not to deny the transformative effects of Apple and Amazon, which have been profound, but it does draw attention to the more complex, probabilistic rather than deterministic relations between production networks and consumers. Apple saw an opportunity to enter a media market – music – and change it considerably, as did Amazon in another – books. Where neither has succeeded as they intended is with the distribution of news and journalism, which draws attention to some of the complexities of this particular media ecology.

In *World Without Mind*, Franklin Foer cites a quotation from Ben Bagdikian regarding the operation of newspapers monopolies from 2001: "By the early twenty-first century, literally 99.9 percent of contemporary daily papers are a monopoly in their own city."[83] Foer then goes on observe just how many of these have since perished since Bagdikian statement, with print circulation down from nearly 60 million in 1994 to 35 million by 2017. In just over 20 years, the print industry for newspapers has been hollowed out while that for magazines, while delayed by a half-decade, has also begun to dwindle rapidly. Many of the factors contributing to this decline – not all of which are due to technological disruption – will be considered in the next chapter, but at this stage, we shall consider one ill-advised intervention on the part of Apple that demonstrates the limitations of simplistic notions of technological determination.

When the iPad was launched in 2010, Apple heralded it as a device that would be especially helpful to publishers. Steve Jobs referred to the first iPad as the "iPod for books"[84], and Celeste Martin and Jonathan Aitken have observed how the device, as one of the second generation of e-readers, allowed for a rethinking of how reading could take place on an electronic device, offering a "permeable" space that shared the interconnectedness of computers but also preserved some of the contemplative modes of traditional reading.[85] A larger screen – even prior to the retina display introduced with the fourth iteration of the device – meant that it was more suited for reading than the iPhone, and with the launch of iOS 5 in 2012, Apple also tried to leverage these additional qualities for newspapers and magazines with the release of Newsstand. In tandem with iTunes, this was intended to woo publishers to the iPad, with Apple and Jobs intending to do for the news and magazine publishing industry what it had done for music (though not necessarily for books). In its announcement for Newsstand, Apple remarked that the app – a "new way to purchase and organize your newspaper and magazine subscriptions" – was intended as a simple, skeumorphic interface that would display covers of titles as though on a physical newsstand and update subscriptions automatically.[86]

Even before the arrival of the app, newspaper and magazine publishers had been looking excitedly towards the new device as the one that would be suitable for their digital content, with *The Economist* referring to it as the "tablet of hope".[87]

Problems soon began to emerge, however. Much of the commentary initially was due to Apple's slicing off 30 per cent of subscriptions as it did with all digital sales, but in many respects, this simply duplicated distribution models for physical copies and was less important to those involved in the publishing industry. More significantly, by failing to understand the media ecology of magazine and newspaper publishing and by seeking to replace it with the much simplified ecosystem of iOS, Apple reduced the scope for publishers to take advantage of the opportunities provided by the iPad. First of all, by imposing strict terms, Apple stopped publishers from striking other deals with existing subscribers, a common tactic to promote sales whereby publishers willingly took a loss in the first year so as to be able to recoup those losses via renewals. As well as preventing publishers from approaching readers directly, thus severing the ties between them for future direct marketing and the collection of information, Newsstand began to look less and less appealing to the newspaper and magazine industries. The launch of the iPad itself had led to a spike in subscriptions, a growth of 268 per cent for Condé Nast, for example, by the end of 2011,[88] but that boost was already declining when Newsstand appeared and in 2015, disappointed by declining interest among users, Apple removed the app from version 9 of iOS. As Glenn Fleishman observed, "after some fanfare, and major publications adopting the Newsstand format... Apple more or less left it to rot."[89]

The failure of Newsstand did not mark the complete end of Apple's engagement with journalism via iOS. News replaced Newsstand in iOS 9, and effectively worked as an aggregator for different news feeds, similar to applications such as Flipboard, which created mobile magazines from multiple sources. With News, however, Apple no longer held out promises to monetise in any innovative shape or form. Being the richest company in the world was not enough for Apple to revolutionise journalism: while the iPad was vastly more successful than the Viewtron terminal, the demise of Newsstand indicated some of the ways in which a thriving media ecology is very different to a digital ecosystem in the ways in which the main big tech companies attempt to define it. As we shall see in a later chapter, while it is possible for an organisation such as Amazon to, effectively, subsidise a part of the journalism industry, none of the Big Five tech companies – individually or together – is able to completely support the production of global media. More than that, their history over the past decade, as we shall see in the next chapter, has been more closely aligned to the disruption of the funding of media through advertising rather than the creation of news.

Notes

1 "Two-Way Data Setup Operating: Viewtron in Florida is First", *The New York Times*, 31 October 1983, p. 6.
2 Cited in Pablo J. Boczkowski, *Digitising the News: Innovation in Online Newspapers*, London and Cambridge, MA: MIT Press, 2005, p. 28.
3 Boczkowski, p. 32.
4 Holly Hubbard Preston, "Minitel Reigns in Paris with Key French Connection", *Computer Reseller News*, 594(1994), pp. 49–51.
5 John V. Pavlik, "New Media and News: Implications for the Future of Journalism", *New Media & Society*, 1.1(1999), pp. 54–60.
6 Richard Tedesco, "ABC News Tests Net", *Broadcasting & Cable*, 130.1(2000), p. 67.
7 Nic Newman, "Overview and Key Findings of the 2018 Report", *Digital News Report, 2018*, Reuters, www.digitalnewsreport.org/survey/2018/overview-key-findings-2018/.
8 Gartner, "Digital Business Ecosystems & the Platform Economy", 2018, www.gartner.com/technology/topics/business-ecosystems.jsp.
9 Mark Skilton, *Building Digital Ecosystem Architectures: A Guide to Enterprise Architecting Digital Technologies in the Digital Enterprise*, London: Palgrave Macmillan, 2015; Matt Brady, *Digital Ecosystem Leadership*, New York: Gabwalker, 2017. See also: Yong Jin Park, Jae Eun Chung, and Dong Hee Shin, "The Structuration of Digital Ecosystem, Privacy, and Big Data Intelligence", *American Behavioral Scientist*, 62.10(2018), pp. 1319–1338.
10 See, for example, the proceedings of the 7th IEEE International Conference on Digital Ecosystems and Technologies (DEST), http://ieeexplore.ieee.org/xpl/mostRecentIssue.jsp?punumber=6596009.
11 Nigel Shadbolt, Max Van Kleek, and Reuben Binns, "The Rise of Social Machines: The Development of a Human/Digital Ecosystem", *IEEE Consumer Electronics Magazine*, 5.2(2016), pp. 106–112, p. 106.
12 Sheila Anderson, and Tobias Blanke, "Taking the Long View: From e-Science Humanities to Humanities Digital Ecosystems", *Historical Social Research / Historische Sozialforschung*, 37.3(2012), pp. 147–164.
13 Michelle Evans, "iPhone X and Apple Watch: How Apple's Vision Will Further Innovate Digital Commerce", *Forbes*, 12 September 2017, www.forbes.com/sites/michelleevans1/2017/09/12/iphone-x-and-apple-watch-how-apples-vision-will-further-innovate-digital-commerce/#1e404bcd598c; John Thornhill, "Now Apple Needs to Reinvent the Digital Economy", *Financial Times*, 17 September 2017, www.ft.com/content/643f845a-9bb2-11e7-9a86-4d5a475ba4c5.
14 Villas-Boase Antonia, "How to Break Free from the Apple Ecosystem", *Business Insider*, 15 January 2017, http://uk.businessinsider.com/how-to-break-free-from-the-apple-ecosystem-2017-1?r=US&IR=T.
15 Melanie Mitchell, *Complexity: A Guided Tour*, New York: Oxford University Press, 2009; Steven Strogatz, *Sync: The Emerging Science of Spontaneous Order*, London: Penguin, 2004.
16 Franklin Foer, *World without Mind*, London: Penguin, 2017, pp. 187–192.
17 Neil Postman, "The Reformed English Curriculum", in Alvin C. Eurich (ed.), *High School 1980: The Shape of the Future in American Secondary Education*, New York: Pitman, 1970, pp. 160–168; Christine Nystrom, *Towards a Science of Media Ecology: The Formulation of Integrated Conceptual Paradigms for the Study of Human Communication Systems*, Doctoral Dissertation, New York University (1973).

18 Lance Strate, *Media Ecology: An Approach to Understanding the Human Condition*, Frankfurt am Main: Peter Lang, 2017.

19 Dennis D. Cali, *Mapping Media Ecology: Introduction to the Field*, Frankfurt am Main: Peter Lang, 2017, p. 10.

20 Bruno Latour, *Reassembling the Social: An Introduction to Actor-Network-Theory*. Oxford: Oxford University Press, 2005.

21 Langdon Winner, "Upon Opening the Black Box and Finding It Empty: Social Constructivism and the Philosophy of Technology", *Science, Technology, & Human Values*, 18(1993), pp. 362–378.

22 Pascal Jouquet, Saran Traoré, Chutina Choosai, Christain Hartmann, and David Bignelle, "Influence of Termites on Ecosystem Functioning. Ecosystem Services Provided by Termites", *European Journal of Soil Biology*, 47.4(2011), pp. 215–222.

23 Graham Harman, *The Quadruple Object*, New York: Zero Books, 2011, pp. 6, 10–12.

24 Matthew David Segall, "Cosmos, Anthropos, and Theos in Harman, Teilhard, and Whitehead", *Footnotes to Plato*, 12 July 2011, https://footnotes2plato.com/2011/07/12/cosmos-anthropos-and-theos-in-harman-teilhard-and-whitehead/.

25 Pablo A. Marquet, Andrew P. Allen, James H. Brown, et al., "On Theory in Ecology", *BioScience*, 64.8(2014), pp. 701–710.

26 Chris Anderson, "The End of Theory: The Data Deluge Makes the Scientific Method Obsolete", *Wired*, 16.07(2008), www.wired.com/2008/06/pb-theory/.

27 Frank Hoppensteadt, "Predator-prey model", *Scholarpedia*, 2006, www.scholarpedia.org/article/Predator-prey_model.

28 Cited in Simon A. Levin, and Stephen R. Carpenter, *The Princeton Guide to Ecology*, Princeton, NJ: Princeton University Press, 2012, p. 522.

29 Thorstein Veblen, *The Theory of the Business Enterprise*, New Brunswick, NJ: Transaction Books, 2013[1904], pp. 13–14.

30 Jacques Ellul, *The Technological Society*, New York and London: Random House, 1967.

31 Mark Zuckerberg, "Building Global Community", 16 February, 2017, www.facebook.com/notes/mark-zuckerberg/building-global-community/10103508221158471.

32 Claude Fischer, *America Calling: A Social History of the Telephone to 1940*, Berkeley: University of California Press, 1994, p. 8.

33 Marrit Roe Smith, "Technological Determinism in American Culture", in Merrit Roe Smith and Leo Marx (eds.), *Does Technology Drive Culture? The Dilemma of Technological Determinism*, Cambridge, MA: MIT Press, 1994, p. 15.

34 Nicholas Carr, "Zuckerberg's World", *Rough Type*, 18 February 2017, www.roughtype.com/?p=7651.

35 *Field of Dreams*, dir. Phil Alden Robinson, Universal Pictures, 1989.

36 Martin W. Bauer, *Atoms, Bytes and Genes: Public Resistance and Techno-Scientific Responses*, London: Routledge, 2015, p. 140.

37 Tim Jordan, *Hacking: Digital Media and Technological Determinism*, London: Polity, 2008, p. 14.

38 Michael L. Smith, "Recourse of Empire: Landscapes of Progress in Technological America", in Merritt Roe Smith and Leo Marx (eds.), *Does Technology Drive Culture? The Dilemma of Technological Determinism*, Cambridge, MA: MIT Press, 1994, p. 38.

39 Foer, p. 203.

40 Scott Galloway, *The Four: The Hidden DNA of Amazon, Apple, Facebook and Google*, London: Corgi, 2018, p. 38.

41 Brian Winston, *Media, Technology and Society: A History from the Telegraph to the Internet*, London: Routledge, 1998, p. 13.
42 Fernando de la Cruz Paragas, and Trisha Lin, "Organizing and Reframing Technological Determinism", *New Media & Society*, 18.8(2016), pp. 1528–1546.
43 Gibson Burrell, and Gareth Morgan, *Sociological Paradigms and Organizational Analysis*, London and New York: Heinemann, 1979, pp. 26–33.
44 Alphabet, the parent holding company, changed Google's original slogan "Don't be evil" – a reference to Microsoft's monopoly power in the late 1990s – to "Do the right thing" in 2015.
45 Paragas and Lin, p. 1529.
46 Paragas and Lin, pp. 1535–1536.
47 Max Tegmark, *Life 3.0: Being Human in the Age of Artificial Intelligence*, London: Penguin, 2018, p. 18.
48 Tegmark is a member of the Effective Altruism Global forum, and a regular contributor to its events at www.eaglobal.org/speakers/max-tegmark/.
49 Vladimir M. Petrović, "Artificial Intelligence and Virtual Worlds – Toward Human-Level AI Agents", *IEEE Access*, 6(2018), pp. 39976–39988.
50 Warren McCulloch, and Walter Pitts, "A Logical Calculus of the Ideas Immanent in Nervous Activity", *The Bulletin of Mathematical Biophysics*, 5.4(1943), pp. 115–133; Turing Alan, "Computing Machinery and Intelligence", *Mind*, 49(1950), pp. 433–460.
51 Jerry A. Fodor, *The Language of Thought*, Cambridge, MA: Harvard University Press, 1975; Allen Newell, and Herbert A. Simon, "Computer Science as Empirical Inquiry: Symbols and Search", *Communications of the Association for Computing Machinery*, 19.3(1976), pp. 113–126.
52 Daniel Crevier, *AI: The Tumultuous Search for Artificial Intelligence*, New York: BasicBooks, 1993, p. 17.
53 Ray Kurzweil, *The Singularity is Near: When Humans Transcend Biology*, London: Duckworth and Co., 2005.
54 Steve LeVine, "AI Researchers are Halting Work on Human-like Machines", *Axios*, 3 June, 2018, www.axios.com/ai-researchers-are-halting-work-on-human-like-machines-c7c821c2-59b1-40da-bdb4-e2a368b215aa.html.
55 Noam Chomsky, "On Cognitive Structures and their Development: A reply to Piaget", in Massimo Piattelli-Palmarini (ed.), *Language and Learning: The Debate between Jean Piaget and Noam Chomsky*, Cambridge, MA: Harvard University Press, 1980.
56 Turing, pp. 433–434.
57 Hubert Dreyfus, *What Computers Can't Do*, New York: MIT Press, 1972.
58 John Searle, "The Chinese Room", in Robert A. Wilson and Frank Keil (eds.), *The MIT Encyclopedia of the Cognitive Sciences*, Cambridge, MA: MIT Press, 1999, p. 115.
59 "Turing Test Success Marks Milestone in Computing History", *University of Reading*, 8 June, 2014, www.reading.ac.uk/news-and-events/releases/PR583836.aspx.
60 W. Grey Walter, "An Imitation of Life", *Scientific American*, 1 May 1950.
61 Stuart Russell, and Peter Norvig, *Artificial Intelligence: A Modern Approach*, revised edition, London: Pearson, 2016, pp. 4–5.
62 Jerry A. Fodor, *The Modularity of Mind*, Cambridge, MA: MIT Press, 1983.
63 Hubert Dreyfus, *What Computers Still Can't Do: A Critique of Artificial Reason*, revised edition, New York: MIT Press, 1992, p. xviii.
64 Luke Dormehl, *The Apple Revolution: Steve Jobs, the Counterculture and How the Crazy Ones Took over the World*, London: Virgin Books, 2013, p. 411.

65 Dormehl, p. 297.
66 Dormehl, p. 422.
67 John Alderman, *Sonic Boom: Napster, P2P and the Battle for the Future of Music*, London: Fourth Estate, 2001. Had he waited but two more years, Alderman would have been able to share the wisdom of Joseph Menn's, *All the Rave: The Rise and Fall of Shawn Fanning's Napster*, London: Crown Business, 2003.
68 Stephen Witt, *How Music Got Free: The Inventor, the Music Man, and the Thief*, London: Vintage, 2016, p. 84.
69 "2000 Industry World Sales", *IFPI annual report*, 9 April 2001, www.ifpi.org/content/library/worldsales2000.pdf.
70 Witt, p. 156, 189–190.
71 Walter Isaacson, *Steve Jobs: The Exclusive Biography*, London: Abacus, 2015, pp. 400–404.
72 "Annual Music Study 2012", *NPD*, 16 April 2013, www.npd.com/wps/portal/npd/us/news/press-releases/the-npd-group-after10-years-apple-continues-music-download-dominance-in-the-u-s/.
73 Kate Bevan, "Is There Any Good Reason Why I Should Buy an iPhone?" *The Guardian*, 20 September 2007, www.theguardian.com/technology/2007/sep/20/guardianweeklytechnologysection.apple.
74 "Apple iPhone Review", *CNET*, 30 June 2007, www.cnet.com/products/apple-iphone/review/.
75 Guy Kewney, "Why the iPhone is a Success", *The Register*, 12 July 2007 www.theregister.co.uk/2007/07/12/kewney_iphone_magic/; Rob Kelley, "iPhone Mania Hits Flagship Stores", *CNN Money*, 29 June 2007, http://money.cnn.com/2007/06/29/technology/iphone/.
76 Brian Merchant, *The One Device: The Secret History of the iPhone*, New York: Bantam Press, 2017.
77 Luke Westaway, "Samsung Says 2001: A Space Odyssey Invented the Tablet, not Apple", *CNet*, 26 August 2011, www.cnet.com/news/samsung-says-2001-a-space-odyssey-invented-the-tablet-not-apple/.
78 "Apple Launches iPad", 27 January, 2010, www.apple.com/uk/newsroom/2010/01/27Apple-Launches-iPad/.
79 David Carnoy, "Amazon: We have 70–80 percent of e-book market", *CNet*, 2 August 2010, www.cnet.com/news/amazon-we-have-70-80-percent-of-e-book-market/.
80 Scott Westerfield, "Amazon v Macmillan: Free Market Fail", *The Guardian*, 3 February 2010, www.theguardian.com/commentisfree/2010/feb/03/amazon-macmillan-kindle-books.
81 "February 2017 Big, Bad, Wide & International Report: Covering Amazon, Apple, B&N, and Kobo eBook Sales in the US, UK, Canada, Australia, and New Zealand", *Author Earnings*, http://authorearnings.com/report/february-2017/.
82 Galloway, pp. 166–167; Foer, pp. 121–122.
83 Foer, pp. 106–107.
84 Bill Martin, and Xuermel Tian, *Books, Bytes and Business*, London: Routledge, 2010, p. 71.
85 Celeste Martin, and Jonathan Aitken, "Evolving Definitions of Authorship in Ebook Design", in Ana Alice Baptista, Peter Linde and Niklas Lavesson (eds.), *Social Shaping of Digital Publishing: Exploring the Interplay Between Culture and Technology*, Amsterdam: IOS Press, 2012, p. 45.
86 "New Version of iOS Includes Notification Center, iMessage, Newsstand, Twitter Integration among 200 New Features", *Apple Newsroom*, 6 June 2011, www.apple.com/ca/newsroom/2011/06/06New-Version-of-iOS-Includes-

Notification-Center-iMessage-Newsstand-Twitter-Integration-Among-200-New-Features/.

87 "Steve Jobs and the Tablet of Hope", *The Economist*, 28 January 2010, www.economist.com/node/15394190.

88 Rachel King, "Conde Nast Sees 268% Digital Subscription Increase Thanks to iPad", *ZD Net*, 26 October 2011, www.zdnet.com/article/conde-nast-sees-268-digital-subscription-increase-thanks-to-ipad/.

89 Glenn Fleishman, "How Newsstand Failed the Magazine, and what Apple Should Do", *Macworld*, 30 October 2014, www.macworld.com/article/2841061/how-newsstand-failed-the-magazine-and-what-apple-should-do.html.

2 Distribute and Be Damned

It was in the middle of the nineteenth century, on the 1st of November, 1848, that William Henry Smith II opened a bookstore at Euston station, the London terminus for the London North-West railway which itself had opened a little over a decade previously. Smith, who had been born in 1825, was not the first member of the family to enter into the news trade and bookselling business: his grandfather, Henry Walton, operated a small "newswalk" delivering papers in Berkeley Square, while his father, the original William Henry, opened a reading room in the Strand in 1821. In the 1810s, the news trade in Britain had been stagnating, due in part to the imposition of a penny in duty by the government but also rising costs as newspapers grew in size.[1] As the 1820s and 1830s progressed, however, the government and middle classes became increasingly concerned with the wider character of the population. Some, such as Joseph Livesay and Charles Knight, began cheap publications such as the *Moral Reformer* and *Penny Magazine* in order to provide a more wholesome diet of information for the "lower orders" that would both improve their education and promote social harmony; others, such as James Mill, argued that the press could act as a safety valve for popular protests. Both arguments had their appeal to those in power, and by 1836, the government had reduced Stamp Duty before removing it altogether in 1855.[2] Under the increasingly prosperous conditions for the news trade as the nineteenth century progressed, William Henry senior was eventually well placed to prosper, especially as a decline in taxes was accompanied by technological developments which allowed newspaper publishers to increase printing rates from 250 copies per hour to between 1,100 and 1,800 following the invention of Koenig's steam printing press. By 1828, the further improvements introduced by Augustus Applegath for his flatbed printing press installed at *The Times* meant that more than 4,000 sheets could be printed each hour – a rate that increased to 8,000 when he developed a working rotary press.[3] By moving to the Strand, Smith was able to take advantage of a series of factors: proximity to Fleet Street, where the papers were printed, as well as Somerset House where they were stamped and, finally, the General Post Office where copies could be loaded onto mail and stage coaches to be sent to the country at large.[4] It was in such circumstances that Smith began to boast that his activities enabled him to be "first with the news".

Typically, histories of the press and its significance to the development of a public sphere in countries such as the United Kingdom and USA focus on the activities of the writers, editors, and publishers. Craig Calhoun, for example, in *The Roots of Radicalism*, offers a version of the rise of the public sphere that has its origins in the activities of individuals such as Richard Price, Joseph Priestley, and Thomas Paine, while in the more immediate context, Simon Dawes considers the effects of recent legislation and activities such as superinjunctions on newspaper publishers.[5] While the means of distribution have tended to come into play with regard to legacy media, the assumption has often been that it was publishers who were the drivers of innovation. Historically, this was because publishers were often identical with printers, as in the rush of political pamphleteering in the seventeenth century,[6] or were owner-proprietors who were also very active with regard to the content that appeared in their publications, as with E.S. Dallas and W.T. Stead.[7] Habermas's notion of a public sphere as "a realm of our social life in which something approaching public opinion can be formed"[8] has thus tended to focus on the media as producers of public opinion in recent criticism when it has not focussed on the actual *spaces* (town halls, or the use of art in public places[9]). More rarely, commentary dealing with legacy media has concentrated on a technological aspect that has affected the public sphere separate to the content that is seen to shape opinion, such as the rise of cheap wood pulp which, according to Kaplan, had a profound effect on the formation of an American "republic of letters", making available a cheap mass press in the early twentieth century.[10] While avoiding any simplistic notions of technological determinism, as indicated in the previous chapter, it is the role of such technological systems of production and distribution in shaping the public sphere that is of particular significance here.

Returning to the early nineteenth century, as Wilson observes it was the static nature of technological production which hindered the early news trade the most: too few papers were printed.[11] As these difficulties were addressed through innovations in print technology, a second problem emerged as an obstacle to the continued growth of William Henry Smith II's company: distribution. The mail coach system had begun to distribute newspapers in the 1780s and continued unchallenged until the 1830s but the service was slow, with coaches averaging seven to eight miles per hour in summer and only five miles in winter, compared to 40 miles per hour for trains by the mid-century.[12] Not only were trains faster, they could also carry more, whether passengers or freight. As Clarke observes, the expansion of the railways was one factor in the growth of newspaper circulation in the second half of the nineteenth century, contributing to the ecology in which print operated.[13] Other factors, as well as innovation such as faster printing, and the introduction of cheap wood pulp paper (which discouraged lending of papers as well as reducing costs), included the abolition of stamp duty, and the rise of literacy among the lower middle and upper working classes. So important was this trade that special newspaper trains were introduced in 1876 and London publications became national. There was no sudden transformation with the introduction of rail, but slowly the coaching network that had built up during the late eighteenth and early nineteenth centuries was replaced, allowing Smith to extend his bookstores and news outlets across the country. By 1861, a journalist writing in the magazine *Once a Week* could observe that every railway except the Great Western was in "literary possession of Mr W. H. Smith".[14] Such was Smith's monopoly over the trade by the end of the century that when W. T. Stead shocked the nation with his campaigning journalism against child prostitution in the *Pall Mall Gazette*, the company's refusal to handle the newspaper contributed to the editor's undoing.[15]

The impact of railways on print distribution has long been recognised: as Hayes summarises it, "the development of passenger railways combined with the widespread availability of inexpensively-produced books significantly influenced what people read, how they obtained what they read, and, indeed, how they read."[16] As an important part of the media ecology of the nineteenth century, the railway network was a significant component of the public sphere, allowing people to receive news more quickly than before. This system was supplemented by wide road networks in the twentieth century, which, in turn, influenced the growth of print wholesalers. As Wilson notes, by the 1970s, WH Smith had moved from being one retailer among many to being the main distributor for newspapers. This system of distribution for print was still going strong, for magazines at least, at the beginning of the twenty-first century. Certainly, newspaper sales had begun to decline, but this was not the case for most consumer magazines in 2006 and at that point, in the UK, WH Smith continued to dominate the wholesale distributor market with a 39 per cent market share, along with Menzies Distribution (27 per cent, but with a monopoly in Scotland) and Dawson News (19 per cent). These three companies were responsible for shifting large quantities of newsprint around the UK to 185 smaller wholesalers (mostly subsidiaries of these big companies) who would then pack them into vans for distribution to some 53,000 retail outlets.[17]

The system for distributing the news had undergone a vast transformation from 1792 when Henry Walton operated a newswalk in Berkeley Square to the massive enterprise responsible for distributing huge quantities of print across the country and internationally. The only common element linking both ends of the spectrum was that between 1792 and 2006, most consumers who wished to read some form of journalism relied on print. Just about every other aspect of the process had changed beyond all recognition, from the presses on which papers and magazines were printed to the transport systems required to move them in bulk. This point is important: insisting upon the "good old days" of print journalism ignores the fact that the print industry was subject to incredible innovations – but innovations that took place over a period of some two centuries. What is evident in the past 20 years of widespread use of the Internet, and a mere decade since the rise of apps and smartphones, is that the systems of news production have been utterly disrupted and that the economic value of news has shifted unsustainably from production to distribution.

Parasitology: Tech Tapeworms and Clownfish

> There is a collective consciousness among content creators that they are bearing the costs and that others are reaping some of the revenues. Inevitably that profound contradiction will be a catalyst for action and the moment is nigh.
>
> There is no doubt that certain websites are best described as parasites or tech tapeworms in the intestines of the internet.[18]

Speaking to *The Australian* newspaper in 2009, this was how the newspaper tycoon Rupert Murdoch described companies such as Google. A year after the greatest financial crash since 1929, the advertising revenues of News Corp continued to decline even as Google's grew exponentially. The role played by Google (and then Facebook) in the changing economic fate of news production is the main focus of this chapter – but it is also worth considering how big tech companies came to occupy such a position in relation to more traditional media companies, and how much the rapid changes in the economics of journalism were solely the responsibility of digital media upstarts.

First of all, however, it is worth considering what it means to be a tech tapeworm: the analogy might not be the most accurate one available. In the Pacific, for example, especially around the waters of Northern Australia, Southeast Asia, and Japan, lives *Amphiprion ocellaris*, or the common clownfish, easily recognisable by its orange-brown and white stripes. These fish dwell among the tentacles of the Ritteri anemones and have developed a particular mucus that protects them from the stinging poison of the anemones: that poison tends to drive away predators of the clownfish, while *Amphiprion ocellaris*, in turn, protects the anemones from fish that will eat them. Nature is full of such examples of mutual symbiosis, some more dramatic than others, whereby creatures that inhabit different life forms may provide different benefits. Rather in the same way that Jussi Parikka argues that we should consider the essentials of a non-human media, dynamic systems of relations, perceptions, and cohabitations that create new processes of "embodied technics".[19]

Before exploring the tapeworm role of Google and other Big tech firms, I wish, briefly, to rewrite the history of news distribution offered at the opening of this chapter in terms of a media parasitology. The media has always been involved in such symbiosis: in his wonderful book, *Media Parasites in the Early Avant-Garde*, Niebisch draws upon Michel Serres' theory of the parasite to show how avant-garde movements such as Dadaism and Futurism sought to exploit new technologies such as radio and cinema to their own ends, adoring the "increasingly accelerating media ecology" of the early twentieth century and profiting from it like a parasite.[20]

For Niebisch, Dadaists and Futurists were not artist-heroes rejecting the system but subversives who sought to repurpose media channels and re-codify them into art. These parasites, I would argue, were themselves hosts upon another set of activities that were also, in turn, parasitic. In the nineteenth century, publisher-entrepreneurs such as Livesey and Knight sought to educate the masses, to raise them from darkness to enlightenment, but James Mill's scepticism found a different, more nuanced criticism in the writings of his son. John Stuart Mill may have defended the essential freedom of the Fourth Estate, as it came to be known, but he also recognised that it was this freedom that also contributed to tyranny of opinion: "Precisely because the tyranny of opinion is such as to make eccentricity a reproach, it is desirable, in order to break through that tyranny, that people should be eccentric."[21] The myth – and it has always been a myth – of the Fourth Estate has frequently served the press very well, and has been repeatedly deconstructed by academics, whether with regard to the rough and tumble of Chicago journalism in the 1920s or its service in the cause of the French Revolution. It is important to recognise this fact in order to avoid falling into a false dichotomy with regard to the future of journalism in the face of recent technological innovations – which, in the end, merely represent the latest in a long history of disruption from the time of Gutenberg at least. In the service of communicating its message – and, along the way, making money – the media often rides on the back of other social and technological innovations.

To reconsider the media as a parasite – a dangerous tactic in the era of Donald Trump and fake news – is to avoid sentimentality with regard to the disappearance of print and the emergence of new, digital ecologies. The entrepreneur-as-hero model implicit in the opening account of this chapter around Henry Walton and Willam Henry Smith and Sons is much harder to maintain when we recognise these figures as necessarily parasitic in their business model, first of all relying on the business of Fleet Street and Somerset House, and then the mail coaches of the Post Office and the rail network that developed across Britain during the nineteenth century. They are better considered as clownfish than tapeworms: such figures subverted the original intentions of coach and train, to transport people and goods, in the service of transporting news, and if they lived off the industry of such networks so, in turn, London publishers – and indeed the rail networks themselves, maintained a parasitic relationship with the distributors. *The Times* of London and the *Pall Mall Gazette* needed readers, and it was distributors who provided those readers – a factor that Rupert Murdoch gravely had to face when he backed down from his argument with Google in 2012.

Parasite media: in some ways, this is what all media is, a symbiosis with other networks and systems, providing information and entertainment. When the relationship does indeed work as symbiosis, it provides additional services and values that make it sustainable, which is why the current rage for disruption within the distribution of media is so powerfully damaging: it is often hard to see how the shift from production to distribution can be profitable for those who make the news. Yet to recognise that both sides of this ecology – producer *and* distributor – offer a vital part to the media ecology of news is an important step in understanding how the media shapes our public sphere.

The transition from production to distribution did not begin with the big tech companies that dominate this book: rather, they have taken advantage of a situation that emerged in the 1990s out of government and tertiary sector organisations, in particular universities and research institutions. The development of the Internet as an open-source platform – in particular the growth of the web out of the work by Tim Berners-Lee – has been extremely well-documented, but of significance to this chapter is how it became a commercial platform. The importance of business organisations in the spread and development of the Internet should not be underestimated: my own very first encounters with the net in 1990 were via a university account at a time when access to university was limited to a much smaller proportion of the population than today. Commercial Internet service providers began to appear in the late 1980s in the USA, and for online communications to become more than a niche activity for researchers, it was clear that businesses would have to become involved. The initial stages were modest, as with CompuServe's gateway to the National Science Foundation's NSFNet at Ohio State University in 1989, and the American government began slowly approving corporate use from 1988 onwards, but from 1994 onwards, especially as the NSF began to disburse its assets, the Internet became a truly commercial medium.[22]

One of the first commentators to recognise the significance of this was Nicholas Negroponte in his 1995 book *Being Digital*. Negroponte saw that, across a swathe of media, users would eventually shift from relying on networks that shifted atoms (such as newsagents delivering physical newspapers, or shops renting video tapes) to those that distributed bits, the data on the CDs, books, and paper documents that dominated the information society of the mid-1990s. Negroponte's predictions were often correct – in an admittedly somewhat broad and essentially vague way: his notion of the *Daily Me*, for example, foreshadowed mass personalisation of news media, and he correctly assumed that some form of touch technology would replace what he saw as the mediocre interface of mouse and keyboard for the vast majority of users. At this point, however, I wish to concentrate on one particular prediction of Negroponte's which has proved to be much more ambiguous. Discussing the work of *The New York Times* writer, John Markoff (who covered tech reporting for the newspaper until his retirement in 2016), Negroponte suggested that he would be willing to pay Markoff a literal – rather than proverbial – two cents for his copy were it ever to be disintermediated from *The New York Times* and to become part of a personalised *Daily Me*:

> If one two-hundredths of the 1995 Internet population were to subscribe to this idea and John were to write a hundred stories a year (he actually writes between one-hundred-twenty and one-hundred-forty), he would earn $1,000,000 per year, which I am prepared to guess is more than *The New York Times* pays him. If you think one two-hundredth is too big a proportion, then wait a short while. The numbers really do work. Once somebody is established, the added value of a distributor is less and less in a digital world.[23]

Except that the numbers (on the whole) do not work: the distributors simply changed rather than disappeared. Negroponte assumed that technical solutions that were regularly being applied in the field of computer and communication sciences would transfer easily across social and economic boundaries. His major assumption around the possibility of micropayments was optimistic to say the least. By 2004, the IEEE had scathingly attacked micropayments as an idea whose time had passed – twice.[24] While PayPal (originally Confinity) was established precisely as a means to enable seamless transfer of payments, credit systems such as Visa and the major international banks still dominate the process with a series of charges that are designed to make it as profitable to them as possible: as such, 2 cents to John Markoff has really never figured as part of their business plans.

While the economic model does not provide a direct living wage for most writers, bloggers, and vloggers, those who do manage to profit by creating content – in a few cases even becoming millionaires – do so from what are, in effect, micropayments handled via another source. This, in turn, draws attention to the second fallacy of Negroponte's statement that distribution is less and less important in adding value. In 1995, Negroponte made two significant assumptions: first of all, that the future constituency of the Internet would be similar to the tech-savvy audience that had used it from the late sixties until that point, and that secondly his unbounded faith in established capitalism would make it open to change without external disruption. Blockchain technologies offer the possibility of a truly decentralised micropayment system; however, we are not there yet, and at the time of writing, encrypted currencies such as Bitcoin – the main beneficiary of blockchain – operate more as speculative commodities such as gold than authentic trading currencies such as the dollar.[25] And yet, micropayments are possible, not through completely decentralised payment networks for which blockchain offers huge potential, but via the huge tech intermediaries of companies such as Google, Amazon, Apple, and Facebook. Self-publishing via platforms such as Kindle Direct Publishing and YouTube has allowed hundreds of thousands, if not millions of individuals, to create their own works and sell them directly to the public, with the tech companies operating as payment processors.

The effects of this transformative publishing industry lie to one side of the main scope of this book, which is to consider the effect of big tech on journalism, but it is significant enough to deserve a short detour. Because these new publishing industries, such as for e-books and vlogging, are monopolised by the tech giants, so transparent information about the economics of these activities is hard to come by and tends to be bundled with other financial information. According to One Click Retail, Amazon's e-book sales grew 6 per cent to $750 million in the USA in 2017, although that was only a fraction of the growth in physical book sales at the site which rose 46 per cent to $3 billion during the same period.[26] Nonetheless, with revenues to authors up to 70 per cent on title sales, a considerably greater amount of that $750 million made its way to individuals compared to traditional publishing. While Amazon does not release statistics of its bestselling independent authors, *Forbes* has been keeping track of the highest earning YouTubers since 2015, particularly Daniel Middleton who, as gamer DanTDM, had a following of 17 million viewers and earned $16.5 million in 2017.[27] The fact that gamers dominate half of the top ten list – an activity traditionally dealt with poorly by mainstream media – is illustrative of the dramatically changing demographic among younger viewers especially; the fact that another gamer, PewDiePie, does not dominate that list also gestures towards other aspects of the transition from a particular type of (for want of a better word) professional media production to a more amateur aesthetic. PewDiePie, or Felix Kjellberg, used racial slurs and anti-Semitic references on his channel, which has led to a series of scandals – without denting his 61 million and rising audience.

YouTube and the Forbes list tend to focus on a particular aspect of the digital entertainment market which is that it operates according to a "winner-takes-all" approach to economics, whereby the best performers in a market are able to take the lion's share of profits leaving very little to remaining competitors. This is by no means restricted to the digital entertainment: in 2013, Alan Kreuger remarked in a speech responding to the World Wealth Report – which saw the aggregate wealth of the top 12 million richest people in the world rise by 10 per cent to $46.2 trillion – that the world was now dominated by a "rock and roll" economy in which the most talented and lucky made the greatest wealth.[28] As his epithet suggested, this is a phenomenon that has long been recognised in the music industry (and other sectors of entertainment), and the one that has now spread more visibly to parts of manufacturing, whereby Apple could take 87 per cent of smartphone profits in 2017.[29] More troubling for a number of economists, however, Kreuger among them, is that this kind of economy has, for the past decade at least, been associated with a hollowing out of the middle classes. As indicated in the previous chapter's discussion of some of the perceived threats of artificial intelligence more generally, the winner-takes-all approach to economics can produce millionaires for those lucky enough to score the largest audiences, but represents wealth extraction for those millions who have not seen significant increases in income – and in many cases a fall in real terms – since the financial crash of 2008.

The Decline of Legacy Media

In very simple terms, particularly for traditional print newspapers, the past two decades have been a period of steady decline in terms of circulation. This has been well-known and well-commented upon in recent years. The Pew Research Center tracked growth in USA sales during the post-war period from some 40 million daily sales in the late 1940s to more than 60 million in the early 1990s, declining then to 35 million by 2016.[30] While the impact of the Internet and computer-mediated communications in relation to print newspapers has been dramatic, the relationship between print and online has sometimes been more ambiguous than it appears at first. In a 2016 meta-survey of newspapers' circulation from 90 countries between 2000 and 2009 by Cho, Smith, and Zentner, the penetration of digital media affected regional publications much more than national ones. This was almost certainly due to the reliance of the former on classified advertising, and declines in both circulation and number of titles predated the move of publishers online in the late 1990s. Nonetheless, despite this ambiguity, it is also clear from Pew's research that as broadband and mobile phone penetration increased – from an average of 1.21 per cent of the population to 13.15 per cent between 2000 and 2009 in the case of the former, and from 36.71 per cent to 107.84 per cent in the case of the latter (with many users having more than one phone) – 2005–2009 saw a rapid acceleration of the decline of print copies each year. Important consequences of such decline can go far beyond the simple financial health of newspaper organisations, with a wider number of titles being historically linked to the vigour of the democratic system.[31]

Not that the financial decline of newspapers has been minimal. Sridhar and Sriram note that for every $1 gained in digital advertising between 2005 and 2011, newspapers lost $27 in print advertising.[32] The discrepancy is dramatic: while online ad spends for major US newspapers rose from just under $3 million to nearly $6 million during that period, print fell from just below $120 million to approximately $60 million. ROP (run of press) ads within newspapers took the biggest hit in terms of lost revenue, accounting for $20 of the $27 lost, followed by preprint inserts and classifieds. The pattern of advertising habits tends to form a familiar picture: when advertisers increase their digital ad spend, they pump in less money for print, and the promise of digital for a greater return on investment means that they spend considerably less overall for advertising activities. As Fortunati and O'Sullivan observe, print newspapers have come to be seen as the "weakest layer" in the network of personal media, which has important consequences for social participation and sustainable social change.[33]

The impact of digital technologies on legacy news media, whether the web or mobile, has been well-documented over the past decade or more. The Pew Research Center data previously reported that between 2003 and 2014, circulation numbers in the United States were down 27 per cent, with a 35 per cent decline in reporters.[34] In the UK, a report commissioned by the Cairncross Review into the sustainability of high-quality journalism revealed that circulation and print advertising revenues for news titles had dropped by more than a half in a decade, from nearly £7 billion to just over £3 billion, and that the number of journalists had declined by a quarter in the same period, from 23,000 in 2007 to 17,000 in 2017.[35] The *UK Press Gazette* had reported the closure of nearly 200 local and regional titles in the UK between 2005 and 2016,[36] a figure which the Mediatique report raised to more than 300. It noted that the dramatic changes had been "fuelled by shifts in consumer behaviour and facilitated by technological innovation" (p. 4), particularly among younger users, resulting in cost-cutting exercises in newsrooms across the country. While observing that the media ecosystem is much more than print newspapers, one of the reasons for the government commission of both the report and the Cairncross review was because traditionally, it was such newspapers that had been most responsible for social participation and engagement via activities such as reporting local court cases and council meetings. The impact of big tech companies such as Google and Facebook on local news media is a profound one, but there are also further local factors – particularly in the UK – that the Mediatique report glosses over. Long before his father's assault on news aggregators as parasites, James Murdoch criticised the BBC for its role in using public money from the licence fee to fund commercial television and websites.[37] Such was the political sensitivity of this relationship that the BBC created a Local News Partnership (LNP) in 2017, providing access to relevant audio and video via the company's NewsBank, with an additional 150 "local democracy" reporters funded – which, as the *UK Press Gazette* reported, mainly went to three companies: Trinity Mirror, Newsquest, and Johnston Press.[38] This is not to denigrate the activities of the LNP agreements, but 150 new journalists comprised a very small fraction of the 6,000 jobs lost over the preceding decade. The precariousness of such activity was further highlighted when Johnston Press, owner of *The Scotsman* and *The Yorkshire Post* among other titles, was bought out by a consortium of its debt investors at the end of 2018 following a series of financial difficulties.[39]

Research done in the USA by the Mendoza College of Business concluded that when local newspapers close, the cost of local government rises.[40] It had long been known that geographic areas with reduced media coverage had less-informed voters and lower voter turnout, but the research by Gao, Lee, and Murphy suggested that municipal borrowing could increase by 5–11 basis points in the long run. The reasons for this are not necessarily simple: as well as the fact that it tends to be local media that scrutinises local government, the authors of the report expressed concerns that underlying economic conditions within an area could drive both the closure of news organisations and increased borrowing costs as government sought to ameliorate negative conditions. One significant factor contributing to the decline of American local newspapers was the use of Craigslist: the authors found that the entry of Craigslist into an area increased the possibility of closure by about 10 per cent, which fits alongside other research that suggests Craigslist affects advertising revenues negatively.[41] For many local newspapers and sites, classified advertising had long been one of its most effective sources of revenue, with researchers such as Gurun and Butler demonstrating the deleterious effect of competition from Craigslist on property advertising in the Pittsburgh and St. Louis areas.[42]

When talking about the decline of legacy media, this is more accurately described as the decline of a legacy *medium*: print. While we have already considered the significant reduction of print newspapers in the print as a whole, some sample statistics from the UK will also demonstrate the trend. Until 2018, the biggest-selling print newspaper in the UK was *The Sun*. At its height in July 1994, the paper sold an average of 4,305,957 copies daily, which fell over the next six years but still topped 3.5 million in 2000: in March 2018, sales had further declined to 1,465,000 (the free sheet *Metro* narrowly outstripped it for the top position with a circulation of 1,472,437)[43] While dramatic, *The Sun*'s drop was considerably less than those for *The Mirror* and *The Telegraph*, which posted double digit falls in the same period. Yet, this does not tell the entire story of what remains a very robust news service in the

UK (as it is, indeed, in the United States). For example, by cherry-picking statistics, it would be possible to present the entire British news industry as being in decline since 1951, when the *News of the World* was the largest ever selling newspaper with some 8.4 issues being bought every week.[44] Such a narrow view ignores the massive changes that took place over the next 50 years as a greater number of Sunday and weekend titles were launched, increasing the overall number of readers that were, in turn, divided between those titles. Similarly, it is far from the case that fewer people read the news: *Feedspot* tracks the top 50 news titles in the UK, ranking them according to social media followers, with top sites including the BBC (over 45 million Facebook fans and more than 9 million Twitter followers), *The Guardian* (nearly 8 million Facebook fans, over 7 million Twitter followers), and the *Mail Online* (14.5 million fans, 218,000 followers) in May 2018.[45] Similarly, Comscore ranked the BBC in the top three sites visited in the UK with nearly 41 million unique visitors each month, a reach of more than 83 per cent of the population and only behind Google (46.6 million) and Facebook (42.6 million), while legacy news titles such as *Mail Online* (29 Million), *The Guardian* (22.2 million), and *The Telegraph* (20.7 million) also made to the top 20. Such numbers far outstrip traditional circulations (2.6 million for the *Daily Mail* at its height in 1961, which was actually half that of its main rival at the time, the *Daily Express*), and yet they have not brought the rewards typically associated with massive readerships: vastly improved advertising revenues.

Advertising and Disruption

The rise of Craigslist offers one example of the power of disruption in legacy media practices, in this case advertising. Craigslist, founded in 1995 by Craig Newmark, has now been around so long that an article by Mac Ryan in 2017 for *Forbes* magazine referred to it as an "online dinosaur",[46] something that is not often said about Amazon, set up a year earlier. Actually, while Craigslist may indeed be itself ripe for disruption, it is useful to consider the history of media advertising to understand the significance of changes that have taken place in consumption practices over the past two decades.

Beard notes that the typical observation that our conceptions of advertising and branding date from the turn of the twentieth century is a false one, and that earlier histories – far from being irrelevant – may demonstrate how promotional practices among the ancient Greeks, Romans, Chinese, and even Mesopotamian cultures convey a sense of status and power as well as the quality of goods.[47] While that may be true, we shall limit ourselves here to a more conventional understanding of advertising from the end of the nineteenth century insofar as it represented a disruption of consumption practices in the media. As Catherine Harbor observes, the late seventeenth and eighteenth centuries saw an increasing use of advertisements for things such as concerts and entertainments,[48] and Carl Robert Keyes records how periodicals from the time of the American Revolution encouraged patriotic "citizen consumers",[49] but it is approximately one hundred years later that advertising became key to the success of journals and periodicals.

A number of media historians, including Sumner and Schneirov, follow Theodore Peterson in locating the invention of a modern mass media to the turn of the twentieth century.[50] 1893, in particular, was an important year, in that this was when the publisher Frank A. Munsey found himself facing $100,000 in debts and with declining sales of his magazine, *Munsey's Weekly*. While it had originally sold some 40,000 copies a week in 1889 with a cover price of 25 cents, by 1891, sales were starting to fall and the magazine became a monthly one. When Samuel McClure launched *McClure's Magazine* in 1893 with a cover price of 15 cents, in October of the same year, Munsey slashed his magazine to ten cents and saw circulation increase to 500,000 in six months and 700,000 by 1897.[51] While Munsey took advantage of technological advances in printing and paper production, effectively repositioning his magazines as cheap pulp titles that would produce a golden age of genre writing in the early twentieth century, both he and McClure were the first publishers to realise the advantages that advertising could bring. *McClure's, Munsey's,* and John Brisben Walker's *Cosmopolitan* (a conservative literary monthly, very different to the magazine of the same name today) were all sold at below the cost of their production and instead made their profits from advertising revenue. While niche titles, particularly the glossies and more highbrow titles, would buck the trend later in the twentieth century, this funding model would become dominant throughout the next hundred years for the vast majority of newspapers and magazines. In recent years, faced with the decimation of advertising revenues from digital platforms, many publishers have begun to criticise the public for being unwilling to pay for content; yet as Schneirov observed in the late 1990s, advertising made possible a true mass media that, in turn, initiated a scheme of cultural production that become dominant, spreading to other media such as broadcasting.[52] Buchwitz traces the development of radio from a hobbyist medium in the late nineteenth century to a commercial entity that relied on sponsorship rather than subscriptions from the 1920s onwards to make money, developing an overlapping four-stage model that she also applies to the initial stages of Internet commercialisation:[53]

- Phase 1: Technology (Radio, 1899–1923; Internet, 1990–1995). At this point, the medium is largely controlled by technicians and hobbyists who are more concerned with testing and improvement than content.

- Phase 2: Content (Radio, 1912–1925; Internet, 1993–1998). Consumers are established as a new class of user and production of content starts to become an industry.
- Phase 3: Advertising (Radio, 1922–1929; Internet, 1994–2001). Consumers now form a large enough audience to attract marketers and advertising is eventually accepted, often grudgingly, as a practical solution to the question of who will pay for content.
- Phase 4: Advertising becomes content (Radio, 1930–1949; Internet, 2001–2008). As consumers seek to avoid advertising, advertisers blur the boundaries between content and marketing.

Buchwitz herself points out that this model should not be applied too precisely, and that the interactions between content and advertising can be very flexible in different circumstances, but this brief history of media advertising draws attention to two very significant points: the first, that digital media fits very much with consumer patterns of behaviour over the past hundred years in that audiences rarely wish to pay the full price (or, indeed, *any* price) for content if they can avoid it, and that advertising itself produced a disruption of media production at the end of the nineteenth and beginning of the twentieth centuries.

Jonathan Taplin, in *Move Fast and Break Things*, observes that history is often marked by abrupt transitions, as in the Gilded Age of the 1890s when J. P. Morgan and John D. Rockefeller began their influence of the US economy and political scene.[54] Taplin himself argues that the current wave of digital disruption which is breaking apart the media innovations of the twentieth century has moved from a process of democratic decentralisation to absolute monopolies, singling out Google in particular as the company which has come to dominate a market more completely than at any other time since Rockerfeller's Standard Oil.[55] The term disruptive innovation was first used by Clayton Christiansen and Joseph Bower in 1995 to describe the process by means of which new entrants to a market could eventually displace established competitors.[56] As companies tend to innovate faster than their customers' needs evolve, they typically charge more for those innovations to early adopters and more sophisticated consumers; disruptive innovation comes when a competitor – usually new to market – implements a process that opens up such developments to the bottom end of the market, allowing more consumers access to products or services that previously had been limited to customers with either a lot of money or skill. By taking lower gross margins or targeting smaller markets that are unattractive to established companies, such start-ups can take away market share. For Christiansen and Bower, disruption is entirely normal in markets where, rather brutally, leading companies consistently fail to stay at the top of their industries and give way to late entrants: Xerox was replaced by Canon, Sears by Walmart.

The role of technology has always been important in such disruption and for del Rosal, its starting point is the exponential computing power growth, as exemplified by – but not limited to – Moore's Law, the heuristic that the number of transistors that can be added to a piece of silicon doubles every 18 months or so. Writing in 2015, del Rosal argued that the ability to include the power of 30 mobile phones in one case by 2025 would lead to novel forms of interaction – eye wear as an interface, augmented reality, motion sensing, and haptic feedback.[57] Some of those technologies, AR in particular, seem to be progressing in a way that fits del Rosal's schema, but perhaps the most impressive interface development in the three years since he wrote his book – voice – is barely mentioned by him at all, while Google Glass, an innovation discussed in some detail, looks set to be relegated to a niche product. This is not to mock del Rosal's futurology *per se*, but to draw attention to a common mistake made by techno-evangelists who operate within a limited mode of technological determination and ignore social or cultural parameters. The demise of Google Glass was much less to do with technological considerations (which, so the argument goes, can always be overcome by exponential computing power growth) than the fact that other people became increasingly confrontational when faced with the possibility of being recorded by Glass wearers, as well as that such wearers tended not to like being referred to as "glassholes": sometimes, fashion sense has as important role to play as technology, otherwise, we would have long been driving Sinclair C5s.

A focus on technology alone, then, is always a mistake when considering the impact of disruptive technologies. Dobbs, Manyika, and Woetzel are more effective in determining underlying macro forces driving large-scale changes in the world.[58] They list these four categories as: the rise of emerging markets; technology as a means of accelerating the "natural" forces of the market; an ageing world population; and accelerating flows of trade, capital, and people. These categories – of which technology is but one part – are effecting huge transformations, such as the shift of markets from the west to the east, a greying workforce that can no longer retire at such an early age, and increasing globalisation. Writing in 2016, Dobbs, Manyika, and Woetzel do not take into account reactions against such globalisation as expressed in events such as Brexit, the populist policies of Donald Trump, or anti-immigration trends throughout the advanced economies; it is too early to write off corrective effects within such populist expressions, but the fact that in the decades ahead half of the world's economic growth will come from massive cities such as Kumasi in Ghana or Santa Catarina in Brazil – largely ignored by western political elites today – indicates that the centre of gravity will inevitably shift away from the West. This, then, is a part of the socio-economic shift that is taking place now across the globe that will indeed transform all parts of the economy, the media included. Dobbs,

Manyika, and Woetzel, in my opinion, do not pay sufficient attention to a fifth factor – environmental change – that will have an equally important effect on how we live and work in the future, but their other four categories are important examples of the driving forces behind world change over the next century. We live in disruptive times, but then we have always lived in disruptive times since the period of the industrial revolution at least. A comparison of the 1955 Fortune 500 firms to their 2016 counterparts shows that only 12 per cent of the earlier companies survived and prospered: while Boeing, IBM, Proctor and Gamble, and Kellogg went from strength to strength, American Motors, Studebaker, and Detroit Steel were replaced by Facebook, Microsoft, and Apple, what Mark Perry refers to as "creative destruction".[59]

There is a raft of titles that seek to encourage CEOs and organisations to embrace this creative destruction, ignoring the fact that for the vast majority of people news of the impending demise of their relative prosperity is always a painful prospect. Gans observes that "as a concept disruption has become so pervasive that it is at risk of becoming useless",[60] and instead he focusses on Christiansen and Bower's original problem: how is it that great companies, doing what made them great, fail? Gans begins with the compelling example of *Encyclopedia Britannica*, a company that devised an entire sales technique that served it extremely well for decades: consumers became convinced (or convinced themselves) that paying hundreds of dollars was a signal that they cared about their children's education, purchasing this symbol in a format – a series of printed volumes – that often would be opened no more than once or twice a year. Having refused to licence their content to Microsoft in 1985, *Britannica* fell victim to a far cheaper but more accessible format – the *Encarta* CD-ROM – which, in turn, was replaced by Wikipedia, "an encyclopedia that wasn't a business at all".[61] *Britannica* had first been marketed in the United States in the 1790s, and in the 1930s over 2,000 sales people were employed to promote the title door to door (I even applied for – and failed to become – just such a salesman upon completing my first degree in 1990). With the rise of CD-ROM and then the Internet, the once-successful strategy that *Britannica* had been committed to for the best part of a century made no sense anymore so that, in 2012, the print edition came to an end and, with it, the door-to-door sales force.

The very notion that someone would come to your door and *try to sell you an encyclopaedia* is utterly preposterous in the twenty-first century, as relevant to modern life as a village blacksmith to shoe a horse or log drivers to manoeuvre cut trees down the river to treatment plants. There are plenty of other examples of companies that have fallen foul of technological advances – Kodak's success as a producer of film for cameras was simply too great for it to invest properly in digital cameras, while Blockbuster closed its last stores in 2013. Disruption that has taken place in the digital media marketplace is painful, and its consequences for the production of journalism in particular must, I believe, be challenged – very simply, distributors are taking too much capital at the expense of producers in current forms. Yet, the notion that disruption is something new is a fallacy. In the sphere of the media, disruption has followed on new technological formats in broadcast and developments in print. What is new in this iteration is that the profits of media consumption have transferred to distributors who, in turn, have incredible control over what information can or cannot be accessed in the new public sphere. Two are especially important in terms of shaping our modern lives online: Facebook and Google.

The Distribution Duopoly

Thanks to David Fincher's 2010 movie, *The Social Network*, Facebook probably has the most famous origin story of any tech company, and the film demonstrated the love affair that many users had with big tech in the early part of the twenty-first century. Apple (although not Microsoft) had blazed a trail to the notion of tech's innate coolness, but it was Facebook and, to a lesser extent, Google that were able to capitalise most on this public perception. Facebook, founded in 2004 by Mark Zuckerberg and other students at Harvard, rose quickly over the next decade to dominate social media and, as we have already seen, was the largest IPO of its time when the company was listed publicly in 2012. Google, initially founded as a research project by Larry Page and Sergei Brin at Stanford in 1996, grew more slowly but achieved dominance of another market search at the same time that Facebook was beating all competitors. For Google in particular, its emergence just at that moment when Microsoft was facing increased attention from the Department of Justice for potential abuses of its monopoly position meant that the company could grow in a way that was not possible for Netscape, the earliest Internet-based company that had posed the biggest threat in the mid-1990s. This space that the relative withdrawal of Microsoft provided allowed Google to flourish in ways that would not necessarily have been possible had it begun life half a decade earlier: Microsoft would almost certainly have intervened in some shape or form before Google's IPO in 2004 and it is more than likely that, for the better part of the decade, users could have been googling inside Internet Explorer as the Seattle company's search engine of choice rather than its later, somewhat unloved child, Bing. Had Microsoft made a multibillion dollar bid for Google at the turn of the new century, similar to the $7.5 billion deal by which it acquired Github, the software development platform, in the summer of 2018, the development of big tech would have been very different.

At its IPO in 2004, Google sold nearly 20 million shares for $1.67 billion, giving it a market capitalisation of $23 billion. A decade later, that market capitalisation had risen to \$397 billion.[62] The secret to its remarkable financial success is extremely simple: advertising. In 2001, Google's advertising revenue amounted to some \$70 million; by 2010, that figure had risen to \$28.24 billion, and in 2017 it was \$95.38 billion.[63] The company's total revenues in 2017 – from sales of devices and other services in addition to advertising – were \$110.9 billion. The message is clear: without advertising, Google would be an impressive company of the size of Adobe or Chanel (which finally hit the \$10 billion revenue mark in 2018, some 135 years after its formation); with advertising, it is one of the largest companies in the world. Its growth has historically been driven by search (between 2010 and early 2018, Google accounted for between 86 and 90 per cent of searches across the globe), supplemented in recent years by the rise of Android. Indeed, so important has Android become in terms of monopolising the mobile market that, in July 2018, it was hit with a record €4.34bn fine (exceeding the previous record €2.42bn fine it received for perceived abuse of its dominant position in the search market in 2017). When Page and Brin founded Google, they famously included the motto "Don't be evil" as a reminder not to repeat the abuses of Microsoft in the nineties. As a subsidiary of Alphabet, that motto was quietly removed from the company's code of conduct in May 2018,[64] although the warning signs had been in place much earlier than that. In a widely cited article in *InfoWorld* from March 2014 entitled "Google? Evil? You have no idea", Robert X. Cringely humorously outlined some of the ways in which the organisation's plans for world domination were progressing in a manner that made Microsoft appear the model of restraint, including financial transactions, shopping, and all forms of entertainment.[65]

Since Cringely's article, it is quite clear that Google's *plans* for domination are not the same as reality: the company is as notorious for not following through on technological innovations such as Jaiku and Dodgeball (the latter eventually succeeding separately as Foursquare) as it is for dominating the small number which it controls almost completely. For every Google search engine, Maps, or Android, there are dozens of failed social media platforms or hardware non-starters. The recent fine for Android, however, does offer some insight into how the company has, in a few key areas, managed to achieve such complete domination. Work on Android began in 2003, although it was following the company's buyout by Google in 2005 and the launch of the iPhone and iOS that substantial transformations took place so that, by the time the first public version was released on the HTC Dream in 2008, Steve Jobs thoroughly believed that the company *was* evil, vowing to go "thermonuclear" on Google.[66] This rancour, which lasted at least until Jobs's death in 2011, erased the previous closeness between the two companies: Stephen Levy even remarked that in Google's early years, there was so much similarity between the executive teams of both organisations that they even seemed to operate as one company.[67] However, when Apple began secret development of the iPhone in 2004, Google's equally secretive purchase of Android led to an all-out war for control of the mobile market place in the subsequent decade.

In terms of sheer volume, Android appears to have easily won the battle: by the first quarter of 2018, devices powered by Google's operating system – effectively given away for free (hence the EU fine) – accounted for 85.9 per cent of all sales, with iOS being a distant 14.1 per cent.[68] By this time, all other potential competitors – Microsoft, Symbian, or Blackberry's RIM operating system – had disappeared. Yet, this absolute control in terms of volume of sales is completely reversed when it comes to profits: in some respects, the competition is a false one – aside from its Pixel devices, Google is not in the mobile market to make a profit, but the device manufacturers it leases its operating system to are, and in terms of making money, all of them apart from Samsung are struggling. In the same quarter where Android accounted for nearly 90 per cent of all devices sold, Apple – even with a slight dip in sales – managed to take 86 per cent of all smartphone profits. This massive disparity between Android and iOS obscures a fundamental similarity between the two companies: that essentially, for all the talk of innovation, they have become behemoths dependent on one service or product. For Apple, it is the iPhone, accounting for more than 60 per cent of its revenue by the beginning of 2018 (a slight decline from nearly 70 per cent in 2015); for Google, it is advertising. Without advertising, Google and its parent company, Alphabet, are respectable, medium-sized tech companies; from 2001 to 2010, Google's revenue was almost entirely dependent on web searches. Google does not need to make money on sales of its Android operating system: what it does need is to ensure that its services are fully available on every device. As people moved from desktop and laptop computers to mobile, so it needed to ensure that they would still use Maps, Gmail, Docs, and, of course, Google Search to provide a constant stream of information. Thus far, we have strayed from the subject of Google's impact on journalism, but understanding the organisation's dominance of advertising is crucial to understanding the commercial environment in which much journalism thrives or fails. In a decade, Google had supplanted the original innovators of web search such as Yahoo!, Excite, and Altavista, but the rise of Apple's mobile operating system threatened, in turn, to supplant Google as the search engine of choice. By exercising market share dominance via Android, Google looks set to maintain its primacy for the foreseeable future, and today search is one of the primary means by which we encounter the news.

Yet, it is not the only way to find the news: while this chapter concentrates more on Google as a distribution network, the second route to finding information is via the serendipity of social media. While some platforms such as Twitter have a crucial role to play in this regard, the clear market leader is Facebook. As Google rose to prominence over early innovators, Facebook emerged to take market share from predecessors such as MySpace and Friendster. Kirkpatrick traces the early – and now famous – rise of Facebook from Mark Zuckerberg and Eduardo Saverin's Harvard dorm project to a company worth $15 billion in the space of half a dozen years,[69] and by the time of its IPO in 2012, the company was valued at $104 billion, the largest for a new public company at the time (though subsequently surpassed by that for Alibaba in 2014). By the end of that year, the site had passed a billion users (although later counts would question how many of those were authentic accounts), growing to 1.86 billion by the beginning of 2017. For a period of time between 2013 and 2015, it was the largest website in the world according to Alexa.com (a position it has since ceded to Google and YouTube), during which time it transformed its relations with users' consumption of media via the News Feed.

Initially, Facebook had concentrated on allowing users to comment on each other's' profiles or walls, but as it began to concentrate on providing a steady stream of new stories, it categorised these as a newsfeed, a basic aggregator of posts that members of the site would like based on their preferences expressed through likes and connections to friends and other users. In March 2013, the company announced that it intended to redesign the site "to reduce clutter and focus more on stories from the people you care about".[70] Initially, the focus of the blog was on friends – their photos as well as posts they made or ones that arose from pages that users followed. The redesign was particularly important in terms of making the site more mobile friendly, and it was rolled out slowly over subsequent months. According to Lars Backstrom, the engineering manager for News Feed at the time, the average user's feed had 1,500 possible stories per day in 2013 but only 20 per cent were served up by Facebook's algorithm.[71] The commercial appeal of the changes was easily demonstrable in the form of autoplay adverts, which became much more common in the revised feed and contributed to Facebook's increased profitability, while larger photos gave the feed more impact and the algorithm was modified to include more "high quality" news stories, that is content from commercial and other suppliers.

The effects of the revised News Feed were profound, although the full implications would not be recognised immediately. In its efforts to create what Zuckerberg referred to as the "perfect personalized newspaper" for every person in the world,[72] Facebook appeared to have consolidated almost two decades of digital mass-customisation. The very earliest news websites in the mid-1990s, such as Hotwired and Time Pathfinder, sought to use the power of digital over print to allow end users to focus on the content that mattered to them. In these earliest instances, the intention of publishers was to maintain users within their own sites, but very quickly portals developed such as MSN, AOL, and

Excite which aimed to become the personalised front page of the web for the increasing number of users, aggregating content from multiple sources including news that would be offered via customised feeds. Facebook's particular refinement (which effectively demolished competitors) was to combine news sources from more official sources with high personal ones from friends and family. The results were controversial even in 2014: a number of reports, such as one from *The Guardian* in June of that year, reported that Facebook had contravened ethical guidelines in seeking to manipulate users' emotions when it conducted experiments in 2012, hiding a number of emotive words from approximately 1 in 2,500 users without their consent to see whether it would affect their behaviour on the site.[73]

Although the company claimed to be much more open about such experiments by the time that the News Feed was in full flow, suspicions continued to linger, and in the next chapter, we shall consider the implications of the Cambridge Analytica scandal and how Facebook was monetising user information. In his book *The Filter Bubble*, Eli Pariser discussed how companies such as Facebook and Google were more effectively reflecting user's interests and reinforcing their prejudices, demonstrating its origins in attempts to collaboratively filter the flood of information that was starting to emerge in the digital domain as early as the late 1980s.[74] In many respects, the filter bubble is simply an update of older concepts of echo chambers or experiments into confirmation bias conducted by Peter Wason in the 1960s. What made the Facebook News Feed so effective was that it brought together information from official or semi-official sources alongside stories from friends and family. Alongside cat videos or photos of your best friend's new daughter, News Feed would display articles about events in your local town, information about pages of business, and brands you followed – or news about presidential candidates. All the time, Facebook's algorithm – the Algorithm, as Zuckerberg and Facebook evangelists referred to it – selected which stories appeared in the feed, seeking to make the site as addictive as possible and maintain a constant flow of data to advertisers. None of this is new to Facebook: the consumer/publisher triangle, whereby publishers serve content to attract readers, who will then provide an audience for advertisers, has been a stock element of the publishing industry. What Facebook was able to do – at least for a short time – was to enable third-party sources such as advertisers and news (or fake news) producers to piggyback on the trust that came from sharing more intimate stories with relatives and close friends.

The effect of this flattening of relations between third-party sources and friends was dramatic. By August 2017, according to research by the Pew Research Center, two-thirds of Americans obtained their news from social media, with a majority relying on Facebook.[75] And yet, as Vaidhyanathan has pointed out, in 2017 the organisation conceded that an emphasis on news – as well as leading to extremely damaging effects in the 2016 election that will be considered in the next chapter – had led to increasing anxiety and unhappiness as people were subject to a constant barrage of "human misery and news of the world",[76] leading the company to reduce the frequency of news content from January 2018 onwards. Not that such changes could prevent a series of woes for Facebook during 2018: if it had been the largest IPO ever in 2012, then in 2018, it suffered the largest ever stock market drop as it lost 20 per cent of its value, or $119 billion. In part, this drop was caused by a shift in focus away from the News feed to its Stories feature: the fallout from the Cambridge Analytica scandal, along with the realisation that it was increasingly alienating its users, led Facebook both to pay more attention to user privacy and to de-emphasise the flow of news stories, two features that contributed to projected declines in Facebook's earnings.[77] The fact that Mark Zuckerberg could lose $16 billion personally as a result of this fall and yet only drop from fourth to sixth on the Forbes list of the richest people in the world demonstrates just how significant his company has become to the global economy.

Mark Ritson has described the impact of Google and Facebook as a "digital duopoly" that emerged in 2016 and which he expected to become even more influential in subsequent years. While discussing the effect of the two media giants in terms of marketing, the impact of such spend extended through a multitude of media outlets. Writing in December 2017, Ritson observed that together these two companies were anticipated to account for 84 per cent of all digital media investments for the year: this does not, it must be admitted, include China – which operates in its own, restrictive system – but the effects on legacy media have been dramatic. In the field of marketing agencies, Ritson expressed particular concern that an entire industry would be swept away by disruption as the two companies removed the need for a middleman, but the effects had only been slightly less dramatic in other areas of media production. As he observes, traditional media "have no option than to play ball with the duopoly", and when those two companies are effectively vacuuming up nearly all digital media spends, it makes it extremely difficult for other organisations to run their businesses profitably.[78] Evans and Schmalansee have argued that "winner-takes-all thinking does not apply to the platform economy",[79] but Barwise and Watkins disagree: in the past decade, the rise of these two means that for any advertiser who wishes to reach both hyperlocal audiences and to have a chance (China aside) of scaling up to global readerships, there are only real options: Google and Facebook.[80]

Ritson presents a compelling example of how Google's platform dominance had an immediate effect on media producers for the best part of a decade: in 2008, Google implemented a policy called "first click free" (FCF), first on news searches and then on general web search. Prior to this, the search engine had only crawled and indexed pages that were available publicly, but as its search bots were increasingly being blocked by paywalls that were being established, it affected Google's efficacy as a search engine and thus its business model. When faced with this conflict of interests, media producers were now forced to make a choice. Essentially, publishers had to offer up to three articles per day for free before users encountered a paywall if they wished to improve their rankings in the search engine. Unsurprisingly, as publishers sought to monetise their content online, this policy was almost universally hated, and yet such was the power of Google that they generally had to comply if they wished to attract readers. Axel Springer SE and News Corp had described it as "toxic", with Robert Thompson, Chief Executive of News Corp observing that "if you don't sign up for 'first click free,' you virtually disappear from a search."[81] The *Wall Street Journal* was one of the first to boycott the feature in February 2017 and by October, shortly before Ritson's warning of the dangers of the duopoly, Google had replaced "first click free" with another policy that allowed greater flexibility to publishers who were seeking to implement paywalls. The backlash had been growing for some time, however. Originally, the purpose of FCF had been, ostensibly, to improve the "user experience", but major publishers began to impose their own limits of articles – typically half a dozen or so free articles a month that were technically in breach of Google's guidelines. As we shall see in a later chapter, however, the search behemoth found itself in a bind: to enforce its own strictures and degrade search engine results for mainstream media publications seems to have contributed, at least in part, to a rise in fake news websites. The power of distribution was threatening to completely distort the potential for content creation, whereby a blog in Macedonia – which did not care a damn about paywalls as a small group of users relied entirely on advertising for revenue – could outstrip the major journalism sites in every country at least for a short time.

Google announced its replacement of FCF as a process of "enabling more high quality content for users", observing in a blog post that:

> Over the past year, we have worked with publishers to investigate the effects of FCF on user satisfaction and on the sustainability of the publishing ecosystem. We found that while FCF is a reasonable sampling model, publishers are in a better position to determine what specific sampling strategy works best for them.[82]

While a number of commentators remarked that this is a useful first step in rectifying Google's dominance of the market for the distribution of news, it still presents two problems for publishers. The first, as noted by Ritson, as well as Moore and Tambini, is that a decade of "first click free" has conditioned readers to receive free content, at precisely that time when the growth of mobile and apps offered potential relief from a decade of reading for free on the web. Even here, Google's growth was not entirely benign: while Apple had begun pushing a business model from the very beginning that would encourage app developers to charge for content, Android's app store tended to foreground free apps instead. Putting such user behaviour to one side, the replacement to FCF was also an extension of Google's underlying policy: it offered publishers some flexibility over how many articles could be offered but, as Critchlow observes, to maintain search visibility, even content behind paywalls must be clearly marked as machine-readable text – meaning that it is also clearly labelled in the search engine as subscription-only.[83] FCF is dead: long live the first free click.

Distribution and the New Public Sphere

The digital duopoly of Google and Facebook has been a defining factor in shaping the media landscape since 2010. Taplin refers to the effects of this duopoly as a process of "digital destruction", observing that the Big Four's jealous guardianship over their own technological monopolies is matched only by a scant regard for creative intellectual property:

> What we have been witnessing since 2005 is a massive reallocation of revenue from creators of content to owners of platforms ... More people than ever are listening to music, reading books, and watching movies, but the revenue flowing to the creators of that content is decreasing while the revenue flowing to the four big platforms is increasing.[84]

The relations between media and technologies of distribution have always been, at best, a symbiotic one: content creators require an audience to be successful, and distributors require something to disseminate. The danger posed by Facebook and Google in their current format is that they are *too* successful, and thus threaten the very content that they require to drive their own business models. The modifications that took place in Facebook's News Feed were intended to deliver "high-quality" stories alongside personal flows of information – for all that, Facebook may have unintentionally contributed more than any other organisation to the growth of fake news which is the subject of the next chapter. Such was Google's concern that, in 2017, it established the Digital News Innovation Fund to disburse €150 million over three years to support journalism across Europe. It would be very easy to dismiss this as a PR stunt in the light of its €2.7 billion fine by the EU. Nonetheless, such sponsorship – while raising all sorts of questions about how a private company may effectively influence the development of future journalism via what is, in effect, patronage – is a recognition of how the balance has shifted between content creators and distributors: having disrupted the model by which most media had been funded in the twentieth century and, in the process, sucking up nearly all of the revenue attached to digital advertising, Google and Facebook pose a very real threat to commercial journalism in its current form.

It should be emphasised that this threat does *not* lie entirely in the hands of these two companies. Google's Digital News Innovation Fund shares many similarities to the LNP of the BBC which, for very different reasons, also posed a serious threat to commercial news organisations in the United Kingdom. Indeed, the very notion of media monopolies was being warned against by Ben Bagdikian in his influential 1983 book, *The Media Monopoly*, and when he updated that title in 2004, he observed that the majority of news production and media entertainment in the United States was dominated by five groups: Time Warner, The Walt Disney Company, News Corporation, Viacom, and Bertelsmann.[85] Bagdikian, unsurprisingly, failed to see much of the future in that book: Facebook did not even exist when he revised the title, but he gives no mention to Google nor Amazon (although Microsoft makes frequent appearances). What is more astonishing is how completely different the media landscape looks just 15 years later: all Bagdikian's corporations still exist, and are still responsible for much of the content creation in the USA – it is simply that the real money has shifted to the platforms.

However, it would be entirely foolish to assume that the current state of affairs is a permanent one. Taplin makes just such an observation when he remarks that, while writing *Move Fast and Break Things*, he had assumed he was living in a period similar to Rockefeller's complete domination of the economy via Standard Oil in the 1890s, rather than 1906 when the antitrust case was filed against the company, leading to its eventual breakup in 1911.[86] Such a breakup looks very unlikely in the United States – as has been mentioned previously, the big tech companies have been very effective at enlisting the consumer on their side via discounted or even free products. Nonetheless, in Europe, such companies are looking increasingly threatened by legislation and fines that seek to divert dollars heading into offshore accounts into the coffers of the EU, an activity that appears to be more likely to be stimulated by Donald Trump's "America First" agenda. In any case, all of this ignores China: in 2010, Google China closed down following the cyberattacks on its servers as part of Operation Aurora, an extremely sophisticated attack by hackers with apparent ties to the People's Liberation Army;[87] Facebook was simply blocked the preceding year under the excuse that Xinjiang independence activists were using the network.[88] With an estimated 772 million Internet users in 2017, China alone accounted for 20 per cent of the global digital population and, despite all their attempts to create censorship tools that will be amenable to the Chinese authorities, both Google and Facebook had utterly failed to make their mark in the country. At the time of writing, Google at least has been attempting to make inroads, although its censored search engine, "Project Dragonfly", has also come under intense pressure from the Trump administration.[89] The current digital duopoly is very much a USA-centric story, just as previous media monopolies focussed on Europe and America, and it is by no means impossible that a future media monopoly platform could be Chinese in origin.

Leaving to one side such speculation, in terms of the immediate circumstances for media production, it is clear that the aggressive tactics of Facebook and Google over the past decade are forcing a re-evaluation of how content providers operate. This chapter has spent a great deal of time discussing advertising because that has been the primary means of commercialising activities such as journalism for a period of a century or more: beginning in the late nineteenth century and exploding in the twentieth century, especially via broadcast media, advertising became the magical model by means of which to provide content to an audience for (virtually) free. While print publishers bemoan – rightly – the effect that the Internet has had upon their business models, it was broadcast which first educated its audience that it was possible for the news to be given away. In the digital era, Facebook and Google have simply been more effective at implementing the advertising model, providing a wider reach to advertisers at greatly reduced costs. The relationship between media and advertising had, for Habermas, been instrumental in the transformation of the public sphere away from its liberal role of providing a voice for wider audiences: citing Bücher, he remarked sourly that "the paper assumes the character of an enterprise which produces advertising space as a commodity that is made marketable by means of an editorial section".[90] Such cynical manipulation had already weakened the open discourse that Habermas believed characterised the early stages of the public sphere well before the rise of digital technologies, but these have even presented difficulties for the continuation of an attenuated form precisely because platforms have grown into such significant monopolies. Boeder's observation that the public sphere might be close to complete collapse is probably, as he himself admits, something of an exaggeration;[91] yet, trust in mediated communications – as frequently expressed as a hatred of the mainstream media – has never seemed so prevalent.

It is far too simplistic to place the blame for such distrust entirely at the feet of the digital duopoly discussed here, but one reason for it stems from the frenetic pace at which media producers have left behind many previous norms of "objective" reporting in the struggle to gain readers who can be monetised. It is becoming clear that advertising – at least as a sole source of revenue – is failing such companies as a business model. Victor Pickard predicted in 2009 that advertising-supported journalism would soon be dead.[92] One reaction, entirely understandably, has been to focus on paywalls: while that will definitely work for a number of organisations, however, it is highly unlikely to succeed for all. A number of commentators such as Chritchlow and Dixon[93] have recently begun to discuss how media "bundling" may offer a better way forward, a technique that has more recently been tried (with limited success for content providers, it must be said) in the sphere of music via Spotify, Google Play, and Amazon and Apple Music, but with greater apparent opportunities for video via Netflix, Apple, and Amazon Prime. Bundling is by no means new to the digital era, and in many respects represents a simple evolution of the services previously offered by technologies such as cable and satellite subscriptions. Chritchlow even suggests that Google itself could provide the framework for some kind of bundling in the form of a Spotify for publishers.

Bundling may offer one route out for media companies to make money from journalism, although for the best part of a decade various commentators have discussed whether journalism online can ever be profitable and sustainable.[94] Jeff Jarvis has suggested that the future for journalism is to establish new relationships between writers and readers, and that the business ecosystem of news production will indeed use automation to make greater efficiencies, but that this needs to come after a transformation of the ways in which journalists see themselves as organisers, educators, and collaborators with their readers, as well as revolutionising the format of copy using data, hyperlocalised stories, and curating information online.[95] Jarvis offers some sensible observations about the need for journalism to change, but it still remains the case that although the demise of news in the service of a public sphere is prematurely announced, yet the consolidation of flows of capital and finance into a digital duopoly has contributed to a severe weakening of that public service in a way that William Henry Smith II could never have envisaged.

Notes

1 Charles Wilson, *First With the News: The History of W.H. Smith, 1792–1972*, London: Jonathan Cape, 1985, p. 13.
2 Hannah Barker, *Newspapers and English Society, 1695–1855*, Abingdon: Routledge, 1999, p. 21.
3 Lauren Wallace, "19th Century Print Visionaries", *Printweek*, 3 April 2008, p. 21.
4 Wilson, p. 18.
5 Craig Calhoun, *The Roots of Radicalism: Tradition, the Public Sphere, and Early Nineteenth-Century Social Movements*, Chicago, IL: University of Chicago Press, 2013; Simon Dawes, "Press Freedom, Privacy and the Public Sphere", *Journalism Studies*, 15.1(2014), pp. 17–32.
6 Jason Peacey, *Print and Public Politics in the English Revolution*, Cambridge: Cambridge University Press, 2013.
7 Graham Law, and Matthew Sterenberg, "Old v New Journalism and the Public Sphere; or Habermas Encounters Dallas and Stead", *Interdisciplinary*

Studies in the Long Nineteenth Century, 2013, www.19.bbk.ac.uk/articles/10.16995/ntn.657/.

8 Jürgen Habermas, "The Public Sphere: An Encyclopedia Article (1964)", transl. by Sara Lennox and Frank Lennox, *New German Critique*, 3(1974), pp. 49–50.

9 Miles Malcolm, "A Game of Appearances: Public Spaces and Public Spheres", *Art & the Public Sphere*, 1.2(2011), pp. 175–188.

10 Richard L. Kaplan, "Press, Paper and the Public Sphere: The rise of the cheap mass press in the USA, 1870–1910", *Media History*, 21.1(2015), pp. 42–54.

11 Wilson, p. 14.

12 Duncan Campbell-Smith, *Masters of the Post: The Authorized History of the Royal Mail*, London: Penguin, 2011, pp. 96–97.

13 Bob Clarke, *From Grub Street to Fleet Street*, London: Revel Barker, 2010, p. 254.

14 Wilson, p. 100.

15 Clarke, p. 261.

16 Kevin J. Hayes, "Railway Reading", *American Antiquarian Society*, 106 (1997), pp. 301–326.

17 Jason Whittaker, *Magazine Production*, London: Routledge, 2008, pp. 51–53.

18 Cited in Siva Vaidhyanathan, *The Googlization of Everything (And Why We Should Worry)*, Berkeley: University of California Press, 2012, p. 33.

19 Jussi Parikka, *Insect Media: An Archaeology of Animals and Technology*, Minneapolis: University of Minnesota Press, 2010, p. 200.

20 Arndt Niebisch, *Media Parasites in the Early Avant-Garde: On the Abuse of Technology and Communication*, London: Palgrave, 2012, p. 28.

21 John Stuart Mill, *On Liberty, Utilitarianism and Other Essays*, Mark Philp and Frederick Rosen (eds.), Oxford: Oxford University Press, 2015, p. 66.

22 Banks, Michael, *On the Way to the Web: The Secret History of the Internet and Its Founders*, New York: Apress, 2008, pp. 181–183.

23 Nicholas Negroponte, *Being Digital*, New York: Alfred A. Knopf, 1995, p. 84.

24 Michael Lesk, "Micropayments: An Idea Whose Time Has Passed Twice?" *IEEE Security & Privacy*, 2.1(2004), https://ieeexplore.ieee.org/document/1264856/.

25 Ole Bjerg, "How is Bitcoin Money?" *Theory, Culture and Society*, 33.1(2015), pp. 53–73; Jon Baldwin, "In Digital We Trust: Bitcoin Discourse, Digital Currencies, and Decentralized Network Fetishism", *Palgrave Communications*, 4(2018), www.nature.com/articles/s41599-018-0065-0.

26 Natasha Onwuemezi, "Amazon.com Book Sales Up 46% in 2017, Says Report", *The Bookseller*, August 21 2017, www.thebookseller.com/news/amazon-book-sales-45-616171.

27 Madeline Berg, "The Highest-Paid YouTube Stars 2017: Gamer Dan-TDM Takes the Crown With $16.5 Million", *Forbes Magazine*, 7 December 2017, www.forbes.com/sites/maddieberg/2017/12/07/the-highest-paid-youtube-stars-2017-gamer-dantdm-takes-the-crown-with-16-5-million/#49d2ed601397.

28 Chrystia Freeland, "The Rise of the Winner-Take-All Economy", *Reuters*, 20 June 2013 www.reuters.com/article/us-column-freeland/column-the-rise-of-the-winner-take-all-economy-idUSBRE95J0WL20130620.

29 "Apple Passes Samsung to Capture the Top Position in the Worldwide Smartphone Market While Overall Shipments Decline 6.3% in the Fourth Quarter, According to IDC", *IDC*, 1 February 2018, www.idc.com/getdoc.jsp?containerId=prUS43548018.

30 "The Pew Research Center Looks at the United States Newspaper Industry Today", *The Seybold Report*, 17.11(2017), pp. 2–5.
31 Deagon Cho, Michael D. Smith, and Alejandro Zentner, "Internet Adoption and the Survival of Print Newspapers: A Country-Level Examination", *SSRN*, 2015, p. 14.
32 Shrihari Sridhar, and Srinivasaraghavan Sriram, "Is Online Newspaper Advertising Cannibalizing Print Advertising?" *Quantitative Market Economics*, 13.4(2013), pp. 283–318.
33 Leopaldina Fortunati, and John O'Sullivan, "Situating the Social Sustainability of Print Media in a World of Digital Alternatives", *Telematics and Informatics*, 10.9(2018), pp. 1–42.
34 Pew Research Center, pp. 3–5.
35 Department for Digital, Culture, Media & Sport, *Overview of Recent Dynamics in the UK Press Market*, London: Mediatique, 2018, pp. 7–8.
36 Jasper Cox, "New Research: Some 198 UK Local Newspapers Have Closed Since 2005", *PressGazette*, 16 December 2016, www.pressgazette.co.uk/new-research-some-198-uk-local-newspapers-have-closed-since-2005/.
37 Dan Milmo, "James Murdoch Attacks BBC", *The Guardian*, 19 January 2001, www.theguardian.com/media/2001/jan/19/broadcasting2.
38 Freddy Mayhew, "Most of 150 New BBC-Funded Local Democracy Reporters Go to Trinity Mirror, Newsquest and Johnston Press", 7 December 2017, www.pressgazette.co.uk/most-of-150-new-bbc-funded-local-democracy-reporters-go-to-trinity-mirror-newsquest-and-johnston-press/.
39 Stuart Turner, Richard, "£150m Bid Was Made for Johnston Press During Sale Process", *PrintWeek*, 26 November 2018, https://www.printweek.com/print-week/news/1166250/gbp150m-bid-was-made-for-johnston-press-during-sale-process.
40 Pengjie Gao, Chang Lee, and Dermot Murphy, "Financing Dies in Darkness? The Impact of Newspaper Closures on Public Finance", 2018, *SSRN*, https://papers.ssrn.com/sol3/papers.cfm?abstract_id=3175555.
41 Gao, Lee, and Murphy, pp. 21ff.
42 Umit G. Gurun and Alexander W. Butler, "Don't Believe the Hype: Local Media Slant, Local Advertising and Firm Value", *The Journal of Finance*, 67.2(2012), pp. 561–598.
43 Charlotte Tobitt, "National Newspaper ABCs: Metro Climbs above The Sun's Total Circulation as Mirror and Telegraph Titles Post Double-Digit Drops", *PressGazette*, 15 March 2018, www.pressgazette.co.uk/national-newspaper-abcs-metro-climbs-above-the-suns-total-circulation-as-mirror-and-telegraph-titles-post-double-digit-drops/.
44 "News of the World Circulation Data: Who Read it and How Many Bought it?" DataBlog, *The Guardian*, www.theguardian.com/news/datablog/2011/jul/08/news-of-the-world-circulation-data.
45 "Top 50 UK News Websites to Follow in 2018", *Feedspot*, 29 May 2018, https://blog.feedspot.com/uk_news_websites/.
46 Ryan Mac, "Can Craigslist be Killed? These Startups Are Taking Aim", *Forbes*, 2 May, 2017, www.forbes.com/sites/ryanmac/2017/05/02/offerup-letgo-killing-craigslist/#74a7cf8e6ff7.
47 Fred K. Beard, "The Ancient History of Advertising: Insights and Implications for Practitioners, *Journal of Advertising Research*, 57.3(2017), pp. 239–244.
48 Catherine Harbor, "'At the Desire of Several Persons of Quality and Lovers of Musick': Pervasive and Persuasive Advertising for Public Commercial Concerts in London 1672–1749", *Journal of Marketing Management*, 33.13/14(2017), pp. 1170–1204.

49 Carl Robert Keyes, "History Prints, Newspaper Advertisements, and Cultivating Citizen Consumers: Patriotism and Partisanship in Marketing Campaigns in the Era of the Revolution", *American Periodicals*, 24.2(2014), pp. 145–186.
50 David Sumner, *The Magazine Century: American Magazines Since 1900*, New York: Peter Laing, 2010; Matthew Schneirov, *The Dream of a New Social Order: Popular Magazines in America, 1893–1914*, New York: Columbia University Press, 1994; Theodore Peterson, *Magazines in the Twentieth Century*, Chicago, IL: University of Illinois Press, 1956.
51 Sumner, pp. 21–22.
52 Schneirov, p. 4.
53 Lilly Anne Buchwitz, "A Model of Periodization of Radio and Internet Advertising History", *Journal of Historical Research in Marketing*, 10.2(2018), pp. 130–150.
54 Jonathan Taplin, *Move Fast and Break Things: How Facebook, Google and Amazon Have Cornered Culture and Undermined Democracy*, London: Pan, 2018, p. 279.
55 Taplin, p. 21.
56 Clayton Christiansen, and Joseph Bower, "Disruptive Technologies: Catching the Wave", *Harvard Business Review*, 73.1(1995), pp. 43–53.
57 Victor del Rosal, *Disruption: Emerging Technologies and the Future of Work*, Dublin: Createspace, 2015, pp. 3–4.
58 Richard Dobbs, James Manyika, and Jonathan Woetzel, *No Ordinary Disruption: The Four Global Fources Breaking all the Trends*, New York: PublicAffairs, 2016.
59 Mark Perry, "Fortune 500 Firms 1955 v. 2016: Only 12% Remain, Thanks to the Creative Destruction that Fuels Economic Prosperity" *AEIdeas*, 13 December, 2016, www.aei.org/publication/fortune-500-firms-1955-v-2016-only-12-remain-thanks-to-the-creative-destruction-that-fuels-economic-prosperity/.
60 Joshua Gans, *The Disruption Dilemma*, Cambridge, MA: MIT Press, 2016, p. viii.
61 Gans, p. 2.
62 Ranesh Kumar, *Strategic Financial Management Casebook*, Amsterdam, London and New York: Elsevier, 2017, p. 206.
63 Google's ad Revenue from 2001 to 2017 (in billion U.S. dollars), *Statista*, 2018 www.statista.com/statistics/266249/advertising-revenue-of-google/.
64 Anthony Cuthbertson, "Google Quietly Removes 'Don't be Evil' Preface from Code of Conduct", 21 May, 2018, www.independent.co.uk/life-style/gadgets-and-tech/news/google-dont-be-evil-code-conduct-removed-alphabet-a8361276.html.
65 Robert X. Cringely, "Google? Evil? You Have No Idea", *InfoWorld*, 13 March 2014, www.infoworld.com/article/2610434/cringely/google–evil–you-have-no-idea.html?page=2.
66 Walter Isaacson, *Steve Jobs: The Exclusive Biography*, London: Abacus, 2015, p. 472.
67 Stephen Levy, *In The Plex: How Google Thinks, Works, and Shapes Our Lives*, New York: Simon and Schuster, 2011, p. 218.
68 Global Mobile OS Market Share in Sales to End Users from 1st quarter 2009 to 2nd quarter 2018, *Statista*, 2018, www.statista.com/statistics/266136/global-market-share-held-by-smartphone-operating-systems.
69 David Kirkpatrick, *The Facebook Effect: The Real Inside Story of Mark Zuckerberg and the World's Fastest Growing Company*, London: Virgin Books, 2011, p. 235.

70 "A New Look for News Feed", *Facebook Newsroom*, 7 March 2013, https://newsroom.fb.com/news/2013/03/a-new-look-for-news-feed/.

71 Kurt Wagner, "Here's How Your Facebook Feed Works", *Mashable*, 6 August 2013, https://mashable.com/2013/08/06/facebook-news-feed-works/.

72 Eugene Kim, "Mark Zuckerberg Wants to Build the 'Perfect Personalized Newspaper' For Every Person in the World", *Business Insider*, 7 November 2014, http://uk.businessinsider.com/mark-zuckerberg-wants-to-build-a-perfect-personalized-newspaper-2014-11.

73 Charles Arthur, "Facebook Emotion Study Breached Ethical Guidelines, Researchers Say", *The Guardian*, 30 June 2014, www.theguardian.com/technology/2014/jun/30/facebook-emotion-study-breached-ethical-guidelines-researchers-say.

74 Eli Pariser, *The Filter Bubble: What the Internet is Hiding from You*, London: Penguin, 2012, pp. 27–28.

75 Elisa Shearer, and Jeffrey Gottfried, "News Use across Social Media Platforms, 2017", *Pew Research Center: Journalism and Media*, 7 September 2017, www.journalism.org/2017/09/07/news-use-across-social-media-platforms-2017/.

76 Siva Vaidhyanathan, *Antisocial Media: How Facebook Disconnects Us and Undermines Democracy*, New York: Open University Press, 2018, p. 33.

77 David Goldman, "Facebook Just Had the Worst Day in Stock Market History", *CNN Tech*, 26 July 2018, https://money.cnn.com/2018/07/26/technology/business/facebook-stock-drop/index.html.

78 Mark Ritson, "Why You Should Fear the 'Digital Duopoly' in 2018", *Marketing Week*, 5 December 2017, www.marketingweek.com/2017/12/05/ritson-digital-duopoly-2018/.

79 Cited in Patrick Barwise, and Leo Watkins, "The Evolution of Digital Dominance: How and Why We Got to GAFA", in Martin Moore and Damian Tambini (eds.), *Digital Dominance: The Power of Google, Amazon, Facebook, and Apple*, New York: Oxford University Press, 2018, p. 41.

80 Barwise and Watkins, pp. 41–42.

81 Graham Ruddick, "Google to Ditch Controversial 'First Click free' policy", *The Guardian*, 2 October 2017, www.theguardian.com/technology/2017/oct/02/google-to-ditch-controversial-first-click-free-policy.

82 "Enabling More High Quality Content for Users", *Google Webmaster Central Blog*, 1 October 2017, webmasters.googleblog.com/2017/10/enabling-more-high-quality-content.html.

83 Will Critchlow, "First Click Free is Dead, but is its Replacement Really any Better for Publishers?" *Distilled*, 2 October 2017, www.distilled.net/resources/first-click-free-dead-is-replacement-better/.

84 Taplin, p. 102.

85 Ben Bagdakian, *The New Media Monopoly*, Boston, MA: Beacon Press, 2004, p. 3.

86 Taplin, pp. 279–280.

87 Ellen Nakashima, and Ashkan Soltani, "FBI Warns Industry of Chinese Cyber Campaign", *The Washington Post*, 15 October 2014, www.washingtonpost.com/world/national-security/fbi-warns-industry-of-chinese-cyber-campaign/2014/10/15/0349a00a-54b0-11e4-ba4b-f6333e2c0453_story.html?utm_term=.fafd3226d874.

88 Alice Kirkland, "10 Countries Where Facebook has been Banned", *Xindex*, 4 February 2014, www.indexoncensorship.org/2014/02/10-countries-facebook-banned/.

89 Chaim Gartenberg, "White House Calls on Google to Abandon Controversial Chinese Search Engine Project", *The Verge*, 4 October 2018, www.theverge.com/2018/10/4/17938376/google-china-search-engine-white-house-vp-mike-pence-criticism.

90 Jürgen Habermas, *The Structural Transformation of the Public Sphere: An Inquiry into a Category of Bourgeois Society*, transl. by Thomas Burger, London: Polity, 1989, p. 184.
91 Pieter Boeder, "Habermas' Heritage: The Future of the Public Sphere in the Network Society", *First Monday*, 10.9(2005), http://firstmonday.org/article/view/1280/1200.
92 Victor Pickard, "Take the Profit Motive Out of News", *The Guardian*, 23 July 2009, www.theguardian.com/commentisfree/cifamerica/2009/jul/23/newspapers-internet-adverstising.
93 Chritchlow, "First Click Free is Dead"; Chris Dixon, "How Bundling Benefits Buyers and Sellers", *cdixon blog*, 8 July, 2012, http://cdixon.org/2012/07/08/how-bundling-benefits-sellers-and-buyers/.
94 See for example, Derek Thompson, "How Will Online Journalism Ever Make Money?" *The Atlantic*, 15 March 2010, www.theatlantic.com/business/archive/2010/03/how-will-online-journalism-ever-make-money/37504/; Umair Haque, "Can Good Journalism Also be Profitable?" *Harvard Business Review*, November 2009, https://hbr.org/2009/11/can-good-journalism-also-be-pr.
95 Jeff Jarvis, *Geeks Bearing Gifts: Imagining New Futures for News*, New York: CUNY Journalism Press, 2014.

3   Zombie Media
Alt-Journalism, Fake News, and Robot Editors

On November 13, 2016, five days after the close of the bitterly contested 2016 US presidential election, the top link in Google presented readers with the following story regarding the outcome of the vote:

> To all the liberal loonies still rioting because you claim Trump did not get the popular vote, get your meds now and prepare to be shocked because the finals results are in. Trump got 306 Electoral College vote while Hillary Clinton got 232. For #PopularVote: #Trump: **62,972,226** #Clinton: **62,277,750**[1]

Although the final popular vote was still being finalised on November 13, already at this stage, it was being reported by the mainstream media that Hillary Clinton was on her way to winning that vote (the eventual number was to be Clinton over 65 million, Trump slightly less than 63 million). What is most significant about this story is not necessarily its content, provocative as that was, but the fact that a majority of people searching for the term "final election result" would have almost certainly clicked on a link not to one of the major media organisations covering the election assiduously, such as *The New York Times*, *The Washington Post*, or CNN, but rather an anonymous WordPress blog at 70news.wordpress.com. Published under the headline "FINAL ELECTION 2016 NUMBERS: TRUMP WON BOTH POPULAR (62.9 M -62.2 M) AND ELECTORAL COLLEGE VOTES (306-232)HEY CHANGE.ORG, SCRAP YOUR LOONY PETITION NOW!", certainly this "news" story had neither a particular concern with either factual accuracy or the typical rhetorical conventions of news reporting.

Philip Bump, writing in *The Washington Post* on November 14, drew attention to the position of the 70news story in Google, as well as the supposed source for its figures – a tweet by @Koxinga8 and another spurious site, USASupreme.com, with the repeated, pithy observation on the content of these and other assertions, "That's not true".[2] In the weeks following the surprise election of Donald Trump as the 45th president of the United States, the role of fake news in the outcome of the election became a source of considerable concern for a large number of commentators, particularly in the light of assertions that Russian-backed propaganda efforts may have had an important role to play in the final result.

While the election of Trump has presented the most dramatic example of the role of digital and online technologies in the dissemination of clearly false information, this chapter is more concerned with why such technologies are perceived now as especially important for such propaganda. Indeed, if we replace the term fake news with propaganda (as indeed many commentators have done), then it is clear that, on one level, there is nothing especially original about the (dis)information campaign of 2016, which will undoubtedly take its place alongside other Presidential skulduggery, whether Lyndon B. Johnson's 1964 denunciation of the unprovoked attack on U.S. vessels in the Gulf of Tonkin, Ronald Reagan's 1985 obfuscation of facts surrounding the sale of missiles to Iran with cash then funding the *contras* in Nicaragua, or the lie by James Polk in 1846 that Mexicans had killed Americans on U.S. soil, an assertion that helped begin the Mexican–American War. Although fake news may appear to be a twenty-first century phenomenon, spin is at least as old as Julius Caesar's portrayal of the Gauls as lawless barbarians or the defence of actions of the state by Roman historians such as Titus Livius and Quintus Fabius Pictor. What is important about the contemporary phenomenon of fake news is that it draws attention to the dissemination of an alternative network of supposed "journalistic" sources that have flourished outside the more traditional structures of state-mediated or other public organisations. Alternative publications – such as the *samizdat* journals in Soviet Russia – are not new, but historically they have tended to be more limited in their reach than the mainstream media. As Leona Toker has observed, in the case of the Russian journalist, writer and Gulag prisoner, Varlam Shalamov, *samizdat* journals offered a fragmented – and often frustrating – route to publication for politically sensitive views that were banned by authorities.[3] The new breed of alt-journalism operates under very different circumstances than that of post-war underground soviet publications and it does not automatically supplant more traditional sources of the news, but what is clear is that, as with the example of the 70news site cited earlier, it is possible for it – if only momentarily – to eclipse mainstream media for many consumers.

With the inauguration of Trump in January 2017, the term "fake news" began to take on a very new life of its own, essentially becoming a clarion call for Trump and his followers to attack any story that does not satisfy their own agenda. What is important here is the means by which technological changes to the dissemination of journalism in the past two decades have created those conditions in which a substantial proportion of readers are no longer certain of their sources, thus contributing to the conditions in which fake news – both as false information purporting to be journalism and the denunciation of bona fide journalism as potentially false – can proliferate. Prior to 2016, the term fake news was barely used, but 12 months later was named Word of the Year by the Macquarie Dictionary. As an example of the intersections between journalism, readers, and technology, it offers an illustrative case study of the unintended consequences of disruptive innovation, as well as a counter to deterministic views of the role played by technology which tend to ignore the social and cultural contexts in which such technology operates. Reductionist accounts of technological determinism, as Fernando de la Cruz Paragas points out, are rightly critiqued for their simplistic conclusions but that, drawing on Burrell and Morgan's four paradigms of sociological analysis (functionalist, interpretive, radical humanist, and radical structuralist) it is possible to provide much complex accounts of the impact of technology on social, cultural, economic, and political systems.[4] As such, this chapter will explore the role that changes in social media and the online distribution of news, particularly the effects of automation of screening stories, had to play in the recent election and the latest alternatives to mainstream media.

A Genealogy of Alt-Journalism

In April and May 2017, self-defined "New Right" journalist, Mike Cernovich, and Washington, D.C. bureau chief for the website Infowars, Jerome Corsi, were granted White House press passes shortly before petitions began online to revoke the credentials for CNN. Cernovich, who had previously found some notoriety as an advocate of the MRA (Men's-Rights Activists) movement and author of the self-help book, *The Gorilla Mindset*, pivoted towards political commentary during 2016, describing himself as a "national security reporter" and "documentary maker", while Infowars, which lists itself the "#1 Internet News Show in the World", has emerged as a popular successor to the right-wing talk radio shows of the 1990s and early 2000s. Both Infowars and Cernovich have had a significant role to play in recent years in promoting various conspiracy theories, most bizarrely the "Pizzagate" conspiracy that placed leading Democrats at the centre of a child sex-abuse ring centred on the Comet Ping Pong pizzeria in Washington. The award of such press passes to these figures was seized on as evidence of President Trump's favouring unconventional alt-journalists, as they were increasingly being referred to, especially in the light of (as it turned out) hoax stories that press credentials were being revoked from more traditional outlets such as CNN, NBC, ABC, and the *New York Times*. As ever, the actual truth of such claims was considerably more complex: the press passes awarded to Cernovich and Corsi were of a temporary nature, much more readily available than the permanent credentials awarded following security clearance and approval for congressional press passes by the Standing Committee of Correspondents. As with so many of the Trump administration's activities in the first six months, heat generated by an apparent willingness to break with standard conventions was often frustrated by other checks and balances, but the admission of such figures was an indication that Trump had often looked to alternative sources of news to report on him favourably during and after the election, most notably Breitbart, whose executive chair, Steve Bannon, was appointed by Trump as the White House Chief Strategist.

Rather like the term "fake news", alt-journalism is a phenomenon that has a much longer history before coalescing into a particular form associated with online commentary and reporting from a typically right-wing, even far right, bias. The ease with which individuals could set up news sites (if not necessarily attract attention and readership) was evident since the launch of the *Drudge Report* in 1995, aggregating news with a conservative bias during the presidency of Bill Clinton. Cernovich's own website, Danger and Play, had effectively begun life as a men's rights blog before including political commentary, and since the end of the 1990s, the news reporting landscape has shifted from a more highly centralised cluster of print publishers and broadcasters into a much more diverse, even chaotic, scattering of blogs, alternative news services, and social media feeds – a few of them, such as Donald Trump's own Twitter account – sometimes reaching an audience of millions.

Yet while the technological means for disseminating information to phones and computers worldwide was different, this breaking of the monopoly of mainstream media illustrated that the monopoly itself was in many respects a historical anomaly. As historians such as Conboy, Curran and Seaton, and Chapman have frequently observed, many of the earliest broadsheets emerged as something closer in status to that of an underground press, unloved and unwanted by those in authority.[5] The metamorphosis of the Fourth Estate into the mainstream media, part of that "structural transformation" of the public sphere into part of the public relations and communications infrastructure that is frequently neglected by journalists who prefer to think of themselves as the watchdogs of the state, had led to a demand for alternatives since the 1960s at least, and not simply restricted to the Soviet bloc. In the 1970s, observers such as Roger Lewis and Robert Glessing were reporting on countercultural and clandestine publications such as *The Los Angeles Free Press* and the Liberation News Service, providing coverage of events which were neglected by the main outlets.[6] Such alternative sources were generally part of the New Left and suffered in that movement's general decline following the end of the Cold War, but by the early 2000s, the possibilities offered by the Internet offered the potential for new forms of alternative journalism. As Chris Atton, John Downing, and Clemencia Rodriguez argued, the emergence of amateur media producers coincided with the simplification of distribution online to create a new category of citizen journalism.[7] As Dan Gillmor commented, however, technology brought with it other dangers:

> Technology has given us a world in which almost anyone can pub-lish a credible-looking web page. Anyone with a computer or cell phone can post in online forums. Anyone with a moderate amount of skill with Photoshop or other image-manipulation software can distort reality. Special effects make even videos untrustworthy.
> We have a problem here.[8]

The rise of citizen journalism coincided with a major breakdown in pub-lic relations as a result of political decisions made following the 9/11 ter-rorist attacks. Although the left especially had tended to look critically at the mainstream media since the Vietnam War at least, a particular blow to its credibility with a wider public was caused by the aftermath of the invasion of Iraq in 2003. It is worth considering the differences in terms of the role of the media following the events of 2003, including much greater public distrust, in contrast to the Gulf conflict of 1991.

There had been considerable criticism of the media coverage of Opera-tion Desert Storm, as the 1991 conflict was code-named. The 2003 inva-sion of Iraq was very different, however. William Hutchinson observes that while there were many similarities between the first and second Iraq campaigns – most notably a willingness of reporters generally to portray weapons and technology as heroes of each war, as well as to only deal with "official" rather than independent reporters – the "embedded" journalists attached to the second war were frequently seen as even more in the service of military propaganda than in 1991. As Hutchinson re-marks, the behaviour of the media in both campaigns "did not display balanced, dispassionate, or objective coverage of the violence taking place",[9] but that in 2003 "embeds" were given preferential treatment entirely while independent journalists, "unilaterals", were treated with hostility. By embedding journalists with military teams, reporters were more compliant, censoring their own output because, as they ate, slept, and moved with soldiers, they increasingly bonded with their military protectors to whom they increasingly felt a deep sense of loyalty. As Hutchinson remarks, the attitudes of reporters in both conflicts were not substantially different – if merely more marked and existing for a longer period in 2003 than in 1991. However, a substantial difference he notes is that if, citing Carruthers (2000), the 1991 conflict was the first televi-sion war, then the second, after Schwartz (2004), was the first Internet war. If the mainstream media was almost entirely compliant during the Second Gulf War, not wishing to write anything anti-government in the wake of the September 2001 terrorist attacks, there was considerable public dissent and this began to make itself felt in the proto-blogosphere that had begun to emerge at the turn of the millennium. Social media was, at this stage, merely a nascent factor, but in subsequent years, the fact that mainstream media had not represented wider dissent with the 2003 invasion would come to be viewed as a contributing factor to increasing distrust in its role.

This was perhaps most poignantly felt at first not in the case of US media but in Britain, where the preparation of a dossier entitled *Iraq – Its Infrastructure of Concealment, Deception and Intimidation* was used by both American and British governments to bolster the case for war in Iraq. The British media was not entirely compliant – a Channel 4 news item presented by Julian Rush in February 2003 used the phrase "dodgy dossier" (first employed by *Spiked* magazine) to draw attention to the fact that much of the information in the dossier had been plagiarised from a PhD student's article. As Ibrahim Al-Marashi, whose article was the source of much of the British government's information, wrote in 2006, the role of a government being caught in the act of such plagiarism was unprecedented, although the media consistently misreported what had been plagiarised and what its effects were.[10] Yet, the Blair government doubled down on the importance of its intelligence in supporting the 2003 invasion. When the BBC defence correspondent Andrew Gilligan reported in May of that year that the dossier had been "sexed up", particularly with regard to a claim that Saddam Hussein could deploy weapons of mass destruction in 45 minutes (adding in an article for *The Mail on Sunday* that it had been Number 10's Director of Communications, Alistair Campbell, who had been responsible for inserting that claim), the government began to systematically attempt to discredit BBC sources, such as Dr David Kelly, who had provided Gilligan with important information. In the subsequent judicial inquiry into the suicide of Kelly, chaired by Lord Hutton, the government was cleared of wrongdoing and the BBC severely criticised.

And yet, while the British government had been ostensibly cleared, the British public remained sceptical in many instances. As the first Internet war, there were increasing opportunities to present alternative views more easily than in previous conflicts, and online sources such as the Dr David Kelly blog (http://dr-david-kelly.blogspot.co.uk) began to offer contrasting views to official sources (albeit often drawing on mainstream media reports by those correspondents who were themselves critical of the government's role). While the mainstream media in the UK at least did offer potential resistance to the British government's official line, the chilling effect of the Hutton Inquiry following its castigation of the BBC (with the resignations of the Chairman of Governors, Gavyn Davies, and the Director General, Greg Dyke) was felt much more widely.[11] The more immediate effect was a loss of trust in Tony Blair and his Labour government, but the fact that respectable news organisations were also bruised in this encounter contributed to their diminishment in the public eye. Very few, if any, mainstream news outlets emerged with much honour from the 2003 invasion of Iraq, preparing the way for accusations of fake news a decade later.

The relative compliance of many media outlets (either willingly or because of the fear of government coercion) increasingly saw willingness among consumers to try alternative sources. The fact that traditional print media and even broadcasters to a lesser degree were in decline was reflected in part in a vituperative and, ultimately, irrelevant argument in the USA regarding the status of journalists versus bloggers. For the better part of a decade, some established media outlets criticised the proliferation of online-only sites – some of which, such as the Huffington Post, were growing into substantial publishing operations, for all that they relied upon armies of amateur rather than professional bloggers. As newspapers in particular, willingly or otherwise, adopted many of the techniques of blogging, the distinction became increasingly irrelevant: by 2012, Huffington Post contributors, alongside another online-only site, Politico, were awarded Pulitzer Prizes for articles relating to life for soldiers returning from conflict and Matt Wuerker's political cartoons. Similarly, in 2014, the Ninth Circuit ruled in *Obsidian Finance Group vs. Crystal Cox* that even if not working for the institutional press, bloggers were entitled to First Amendment protection. Events such as the court ruling and Pulitzer Prizes indicated just how dispersed the influence of the "institutional press" had become in the decade and a half following the emergence of citizen journalism.

Until this point, the emergence of alternative journalism deploying new technologies to reach wider audiences with their versions of the facts could still probably be considered to share some similarities with the countercultural approaches of the underground press of the 1960s. There were some signs, however, that the new grassroots journalism – which now had very good reasons not to trust the mainstream media – would not be confined to the left. The *Drudge Report*, one of the first political scandal sheets online, was devoted to undermining the Democrats, while the establishment of the Fox News Channel – hardly grassroots in the way described by Gillmor and others – would provide a template for reporting that would reinvigorate the right in the twenty-first century. The final step for the emergence of the alt-right, however, emerged in an extremely surprising form: that of computer games journalism.

The very loose confederacy of hacktivists, trolls, and game player that operated under the tag, "Gamergate," has been extremely important as a testing ground for many of the techniques that were later to be deployed in the 2016 election. Its ostensible origin lies in a blog post (later discredited) written by Eron Gjoni in August 2014, claiming that a former girlfriend of his, Zoe Quinn, had gained favourable reviews for her 2013 game *Depression Quest* by sleeping with a journalist, Nathan Grayson, who worked for the gaming website Kotaku. The pitiably trivial events described by Gjoni, and initially labelled the "Quinnspiracy" began to snowball during the summer of 2014 after Adam Baldwin applied the label "Gamergate", arguing that the nascent online movement was a backlash against political correctness and part of a wider discussion around culture and ethics.[12]

Many of the somewhat squalid events surrounding Gamergate, such as the misogyny and harassment directed against Quinn and other women game developers and commentators (such as Brianna Wu and Anita Sarkeesian), are less relevant to this chapter. It will be clear from my own, brief comments, that my own attitude towards the online phenomenon was largely negative, although not completely: one ostensible target of Gamergate's ire – that gaming journalism is frequently unethical and corrupt – is very clearly true. Unfortunately, one of the clearest examples of such corruption – the regularly high marks awarded to the game *Assassin's Creed: Unity*, that was clearly released in an unfinished state while the wider controversy was raging – was largely ignored by many of the most active Gamergaters who preferred to concentrate on the apparent depredations of a small group of alternative, largely independent developers who were producing games aimed at a different constituency to that targeted by the large publishers of AAA console games. It was clear that this was the real target of many of those who organised the push for Gamergate on sites such as 4chan and the Reddit subgroup "Kotaku in Action": labelling opponents as SJWs (Social Justice Warriors), much of the activity in the name of Gamergate was an attempt to discredit and drive away those seen as, at best, arguing for greater progressivism and inclusivity in games or, at worst, seeking to close down and censor any gaming perspective that did not agree with their own left-wing agendas. The fact that the effects of much Gamergate-related activity were an attempt to enforce its own crude censorship on those it opposed, through despicable activities such as doxxing opponents (revealing personal details that could open them to physical assault) and making rape or death threats was an irony that was not lost on those commenting on Gamergate from the mainstream media.

It is, indeed, this relation to the mainstream media that is most pertinent to the rise of alt-journalism as an activity associated with the alt-right. Throughout the late summer, Gamergate raged across social media with the vast majority of participants on sites such as Twitter blissfully unaware that flame wars were taking place a mere hashtag away. When major news publications began to pay attention in October 2014, they were almost universally hostile to the phenomenon. Thus, for example, in the UK, news organisations such as *The Guardian* and *The Telegraph* ran stories with titles such as "Gamergate is loud, dangerous and a last grasp at cultural dominance by angry white men" (by Jessica Valenti) or "#Gamergate: the misogynist movement blighting the video games industry" (Bob Stuart). Titles across the Atlantic tended a little more towards circumspection, although the dominant trend was to reject the claims of pro-Gamergate activists as spurious, as with "Feminist critics of video games facing threats in 'Gamergate' campaign" (Nick Wingfield, *The New York Times*) or "What is #Gamergate and why are women being threatened about video games?" (Ellana Dockterman, *Time*). Almost without exception, the notion that Gamergate was anything other than a misogynist movement (one, for example, actually concerned with ethics in computer games journalism) was dismissed completely by the mainstream media.

By contrast, activities on social media – most notably Twitter – as well as forums and bulletin boards displayed a much more diversified set of opinions, ones which moved quickly to antagonism and hate on both sides to a lesser or greater degree. Andy Baio at *The Message* conducted an analysis of 72 hours of Gamergate-related activity on Twitter in October 21–23, 2014, culling over 300,000 tweets collected at a time when Gamergate and its related hashtag NotYourShield (a reference to not being able to use other minorities as a shield to attack pro-Gamergaters) were trending.[13] Of the not-inconsiderable morass of tweets some two months into what Baio – expressing his own bias very clearly – called a "train wreck", approximately 69 per cent were retweets leaving just under a hundred thousand as original tweets, with some 17,410 users posting original messages over three days. Baio noted that the most retweeted users were pro-Gamergate, with ten times as many tweets being reposted by a larger, veritable army of pro-Gamergate supporters (although, Baio also pointed out, the most popular individual tweets were by anti-Gamergate individuals such as the former NFL player and gamer, Chris Kluwe). Baio's final estimate was that between 90 and 95 per cent of tweets took a very clear stance for or against the movement, and that there was virtually no crossover between the two sides, indicating a clear polarity that made this a microcosm of culture wars in the United States.

It is worth repeating that support for Gamergate does not indicate any intrinsic link to what would be more clearly labelled alt-right two years later. Many of those involved were against certain types of progressivism though not automatically for white supremacism (and, indeed, anti-feminism seems to have been a much more immediate target, hence #NotYourShield), a few may indeed have been concerned with ethical questions, and an indeterminate number were trolls in it for the lulz. Likewise, questionable tactics such as doxxing and death threats (if not rape threats) were to be found among both pro- and anti-Gamergate supporters, although they seemed more common among the former – perhaps because the former was a more vocal group on social media. While bearing both these points in mind, however, it is significant that some of the patterns that emerged during the Gamergate controversy, most notably the mobilisation of opinion against a mainstream media that was perceived as hostile to the cause (and in the vast majority of cases clearly was), presaged similar patterns that emerged during the Trump presidential campaign of 2016. Indeed, for one publication – Breitbart – it could even have served as a dry run. The technological editor of Breitbart, Milo Yiannopoulos, was initially contemptuous of the gaming community, announcing in a tweet from 2013 that "Few things are more embarrassing than grown men getting over-excited about video games".[14] By the second half of 2014, however, Yiannopoulos had quickly realised that writing pro-Gamergate pieces attacking some of his favourite SJW targets was an easy way to build up a huge following. Depicting Gamergate as a "consumer revolt against shoddy standards in games journalism and wacky feminist critiques of popular titles",[15] Yiannopoulos not only extended his reach greatly but also meant that Breitbart provided – as in the later Trump campaign – a clear alternative home to Gamergate supporters in the face of almost uniform media opposition.

Gamergate ultimately failed in almost all of its objectives: if anything, it prompted a surge in support of extending diversity into video games as publishers seek to avoid the accusations of misogyny that surrounded it by the end of 2014. Indeed, without any clear central organisation, without any notable leaders, its demands were perhaps inherently contradictory (demanding a removal of censorship, for example, while actively seeking to censor alternative voices; demanding greater ethics in journalism while frequently behaving in an unethical fashion). Indeed, those contradictions themselves would become the hallmarks of "post-truth" journalism a mere two years later. As well as clearly exposing a divide between mainstream media and anti-progressive voices which had been bubbling away since the 1990s, however, Gamergate was also extremely important in terms of demonstrating that a technologically savvy network, one hiding in plain sight, could often achieve a great deal despite mainstream hostility. The actual number of pro-Gamergate supporters was not necessarily that large, although clearly larger than the number of journalists who turned their attention briefly to the topic in the summer of 2014. What is more, many of these supporters were *activists*, fully engaged in combating what they saw as antagonistic perspectives rather than occasionally surfing the crest of a wave when a publication realised that this Gamergate-thing actually was a thing. Activities such as "Operation Disrespectful Nod", a mailing campaign that, briefly, convinced major advertisers such as Intel to pull their ads from Kotaku and other anti-Gamergate sites, demonstrated a peer-to-peer, crowdsourcing approach to tactics that could be extremely effective from time to time even if the movement as a whole failed to convince a wider audience.

As a movement, then, Gamergate was doomed to remain on the margins, but as an example of how to mobilise digital technologies to support marginal activities and force them into the mainstream – as, for example, in providing additional PR activity to a reality TV star who was considering running for president – it was one of the most remarkable training grounds to have emerged in recent years. The involvement of Yiannapoulos as virtually the only major journalist to actively support Gamergate meant that Breitbart became an ally of this technology savvy segment of the alt-right audience, and figures such as Mike Cernovich – who latched onto the protest as a means to combat feminism – were increasingly politicised by it. As with other forms of alternative journalism, neither Gamergate nor the alt-journalism movement it influenced was simply caused by newly available technologies in the form of social media channels, but the social, cultural, and political forces that shaped Gamergate were able to exploit those channels first of all to try and re-shape gaming journalism and then move against the mainstream media.

Post-Truth Journalism: Epistemology and Gatekeeping

The inauguration of Donald J. Trump as the 45th President of the United States saw a remarkable proliferation of epithets for the relationship between journalism and truth. Trump's own favourite was "fake news", as in his notorious tweet on 17 February, following a highly unusual press conference (ostensibly to notify the media of the appointment of his labour secretary, Alexander Acosta, but which actually turned into an assault on the press assembled at the White House), in which he declared:

> The FAKE NEWS media (failing @nytimes, @NBCNews, @ABC, @CBS, @CNN) is not my enemy, it is the enemy of the American People! 1:48 pm -17 Feb 2017

Within the first month of Trump's inauguration, his administration appeared to be in a constant battle not merely with the media but with how to represent basic facts of the transition to power. Among various other conflicts in the first six months of Trump's presidency, disagreements included the size of his inauguration crowd, whether or not he called the White House a "dump", various polls as to his popularity ratings and many, many stories regarding the investigations into Russia interference in the 2016 election.

As Danielle Kurtzleben noted, Trump used the epithet "fake news" seven times in one of his press conferences on Thursday, 16 February.[16] What was particularly significant about Trump's use of the term, Kurtzleben continued, was that it represented a shift of usage within a very short space of time. Prior to Trump's inauguration, fake news entered mainstream circulation in reference to stories that were deliberately intended to ignore or distort the truth. Trump, however, began to use the term to refer to any unfavourable stories, seeking to use Twitter in particular to circumvent traditional media distributions to address his followers directly. The aforementioned message about the "FAKE NEWS media" had been retweeted nearly 40 thousand times and liked by some 115 thousand followers by the end of Saturday, 18 February, demonstrating some of the reach by which, according to Kurtzleben, Trump would attempt to rebrand fake news in order to pursue his own agenda.

It has long been a truism surrounding theories of the Fourth Estate that an important task of journalism is to serve as a watchdog on those in power. Tom O'Malley offers a clear summary of the power of the press as playing "a central, if unofficial, role in the constitution. It could, through the articulation of public opinion, guide, and act as a check on, government."[17] Likewise, Brian McNair observes that a political media is important because, citing Anthony Sampson, "a mature democracy depends on having an educated electorate."[18] But McNair also notes the many problems even at the turn of the century with this politics in the modern world, that as a largely mediated phenomenon it has been subject to a number of crises, whether the dumbing down of political information in the service of infotainment or the rise of spin. More recently, Bob Franklin has offered an excellent summary of the problems facing legacy media, with declining audiences and revenues, but also the various challenges and opportunities to be viable in the future.[19] As was indicated in the brief summary of alt-journalism, this crisis has been at least two decades in the making, and indeed journalism has regularly experienced similar crises.

In *The People Vs. Tech*, Bartlett proposes a framework of six pillars of democracy, extending the constitutional notion of four branches of government – executive, legislative, judiciary, and media – that protect four principles based on equity, representation, freedom, and justice. For Bartlett, democracy depends upon the following: active citizens; a shared culture; free elections; stakeholder equality; a competitive economy and civic freedom; and trust in authority.[20] Each of these pillars, suggests Bartlett, is threatened by technology – for example, economic participation is facing challenges via mass automation, or the enforcement of tribal politics via social media bubbles leads to a breakdown of shared cultures – yet, this should not be reduced to a simplistic tech versus people that Bartlett chooses as his eye-catching title. For example, he also points out that there is also a "tech arms race" between democratic societies and more authoritarian regimes such as those in Russia and China, one that democracies need to win – and one in which Russia and China, for very different reasons, have invested huge efforts, often seeking to undermine the very notion of democracy through activities around the election of Donald Trump.

The ability of Trump to hijack fake news and manipulate it as a rallying cry allowed him to distract attention away from what his Chief

Strategist Steve Bannon identified as one of the most effective sources of opposition to Trump in terms of an independent media, calling the mainstream media the "opposition party". In an interview with *The New York Times* at the end of January 2017, Bannon told editors of the paper that they failed to understand how the country had elected Donald Trump as the president and needed to "keep their mouth shut".[21] As such, the constant epithet of fake news functions very simply as propaganda, coming close even to the simple assertion of the Big Lie (as refined by Goebbels), whereby if something is repeated enough times it will be believed by a substantial portion of the populace. In a more sophisticated use of the term, the redefinition of fake news follows Jowett and O'Donnell's definition of propaganda as deliberate and pre-meditated communications, systematically carried out with organised regularity in an attempt to shape perceptions.[22] As propaganda, such redefinitions of fake news as have been set forth by the Trump administration can and should be resisted, and yet there remains the point that the ready acceptance of at least parts of the wider public to accept these redefinitions arises from a series of structural problems that affect journalism more widely.

Perhaps the most fundamental of these, and the most difficult for both journalists and the wider public to understand, is the essential difficulty regarding objectivity itself. For a great many professional journalists, objectivity has been held up as an essential tenet of journalism, the reporting of facts that can be verified by demonstrable evidence. The skein of such evidence, however, tends to be a difficult one to completely comprehend; much of it relies on the testimony of witnesses or documentary evidence that requires interpretation and thus the possibility of bias. As Megan Knight and Claire Cook observe, objectivity is a myth that has been

> thoroughly unpicked and discredited among the media theorists... [yet] remains firmly entrenched in the professional practice of journalism, and the more the profession comes under fire, the more objectivity is defended as a necessary part of the contribution that news organisations make to society as a whole.[23]

Such things as statutory obligations upon broadcasters in the UK to remain impartial do not mitigate the epistemological problems of objectivity as a concept. For example, as Stuart Hall observed back in the 1970s, there is a tendency to depend on those officials in positions of power, those "primary definers" such as judges, police, teachers, doctors, to provide an authenticated version of the truth, and who have in the past 15 years too often shown themselves willing to manipulate the media for their own ends. For Hall and other cultural theorists of journalism, news is an activity based around social production, but for journalists themselves, there is clearly a practice that often seems to self-evidently depend on knowing the facts (and, by extension, the truth and reporting these in an unbiased manner). Theories of social production deny the possibility of that self-evident truth, although this is not by any means to defend the kind of *laissez-faire*, anything goes attitude towards facts currently on display in sectors of the political establishment. Facts should and must be checked wherever possible, but the very conditions as to which facts are important – and what efforts then must be expended on them to verify their truth or falsehood – are more complex than the positivist assumptions made by many practitioners. Indeed, as Alfred Hermida observes, social media has questioned the top-down, individualistic ideology of traditional journalism and forced writers to explore networked, iterative forms of verifying their information.[24]

A very real (if until recently unlikely and somewhat esoteric) consequence of this positivist assumption of journalists towards the truth of their trade has been that increasingly large segments of the population have been unwilling to trust them. If the task of journalism is to verify the truth of the world (which is in and of itself an impossible assertion), then the failure to do so makes journalism itself suspect. A Gallup Poll from September 2016 recorded the lowest level of public trust since 1972 among Americans in media organisations, with only 32 per cent of them expecting the mainstream media to "report the news fully, accurately and fairly".[25] The biggest change at the time was among Republicans (with a drop to 14 per cent). This contrasted to roughly half of the population having trusted the media between the 1950s and early 2000s, although the fact that only half of adult Americans believed the news they read in the final decades of the twentieth century is hardly a cause for celebration among journalists and editors. Underlying this erosion of trust was a growing realisation, particularly following media reporting of the Iraq invasion, that at best the press was capable of being mistaken. More drastically in other areas such as climate change, dedicated activists had long engaged in disruptive programmes of disinformation. Because there is always the possibility of interpretation of the facts, because even the highest levels of professional practice must work with models of the real world, then so as with theories of climate change, a determined and systematic attempt to change perceptions through propaganda always has fertile ground upon which to operate. If we are told enough times by a profession that it is operating to the highest standards of truth – and yet those standards are impossible to achieve – then confusion always remains a possibility.

In addition, it is also demonstrable that journalists and media organisations always operate with some kind of bias, even though this is not always apparent to them and may not be what the wider public always believes. A common opinion of conservatives in America in recent years, for example, has been that the mainstream media operates with a liberal preference, and this can often the case in terms of social issues such as LGBT or women's reproductive rights; yet in terms of economics and underlying assumptions about American primacy in the world, they are often much more conservative. Matthew Gentzkow and Jesse Shapiro demonstrated that common assumptions regarding the imposition of ideological constraints on publications by their proprietors or even editors rarely happen in practice, but rather journalists tend to respond to economic signals and incentives – that is, if their readers want certain stories with a certain slant, that is what they will provide.[26] In recent years, this has resulted in an increasing polarisation of the media between liberals and conservatives, driven even more by the realisation that analytics can offer even greater levels of feedback into which stories are more successful and thus highly incentivised.

In the post-war media landscape of the twentieth century, certain models of gatekeeping emerged that came to be seen as self-evidently true but which now are beginning to seem as quaint as steam engine enthusiasts in the age of self-driving vehicles. As news production became increasingly expensive, not simply in terms of broadcast media but also for the production and distribution of print, so the tendency was to monopolise and professionalise that production. A smaller number of outlets worked hard to establish trust with their respective audiences, and as theorists such as David Manning White (1950) and Pamela Shoemaker (1991) demonstrated, their knowledge of which facts were worthwhile and which were not depended on a series of factors – organisational structure, production cycles, editorial "instinct", sometimes even overt political beliefs – that were treated as self-evidently true but were not.[27] This is by no means to categorise such gatekeeping as propaganda: it was not a systematic and deliberate attempt to change public perception in many cases, but because there were relatively few outlets, it was much easier to create a common understanding of what constituted good journalism. This is not as straightforward as it first appears: as Shoemaker has noted more recently, a fundamental tenet of American media law and policy assumes that "more media outlets are better than few", which is one reason why in the USA (as opposed to Europe at certain points in its history) there has been a reluctance to adopt state-sponsored outlets.[28]

Even before the Internet became widely available for most users, however, for political journalism, there were a series of crises emerging that were indicators of underlying structural problems. McNair, writing at the turn of the century, identified the relative failure of traditional media organisations to deal with political spin as a determined activity to shape news cycles, while outmoded models of impartiality had become restricted to the attempt to "tell both sides of the story" (whether Labour versus Conservative, or Republican versus Democratic) without a deeper understanding of the increasing plurality of social and political views. As with disruption, which was considered in the previous chapter, the Internet and digital media has almost completely disrupted the gatekeeping consensus that dominated late twentieth-century monopolies. It is not so much that it is necessarily cheaper to produce the news – to actually produce anything remotely resembling quality journalism still requires teams of reporters and fact checkers, an unfortunate truth in the cost-cutting environment in which an increasing number of newspapers are forced to operate. Rather, the distribution of information has radically changed, whereby social media and search engine algorithms become the new gatekeepers for the dissemination of stories.

Shoemaker and Vos offer perhaps the most coherent theoretical approach to gatekeeping to have appeared in recent years, although their book was published at the beginning of the period of social media disruption that has changed so much of the way that we consume the news in less than a decade. In many respects, it is the relationship between algorithms and *fake* news that greatly concerns this chapter and, as such, this is largely neglected by Shoemaker and Vos: after all, media organisations that straightforwardly lie (rather than simply offering a biased view of events) tend not to survive long in contemporary open societies due either to regulation or being challenged in the courts. With regard to journalistic production, and where an emphasis is on producing verifiable news, the gatekeeping models proposed by Shoemaker and Vos have been disrupted but by no means entirely demolished. It remains very much the case that it tends to be people – journalists – who decide on the newsworthiness of events (a factor that will be returned to in the next chapter when considering automated journalism), responding in particular to "vivid" as opposed to "pallid" recollections of events, and giving those recollections traction insofar as they can be converted into narratives.[29] In addition, while digital technologies have greatly disrupted news production and distribution, the idea that was fashionable for a brief period of time in the late 1990s and early 2000s, that the Internet would free up individuals to radically transform media via such things as personal websites and blogs, is simply untrue: in the vast majority of cases, the major sources of information – whether as news or entertainment – tend to be produced by organisations and, as such, Shoemaker and Vos's matrix of the levels of analysis for gatekeeping remains valid. After individual decisions about the newsworthiness of a story, it remains the case that information has then to be converted into a narrative or genre that is recognisable by an audience to gain traction (what Shoemaker and Vos refer to as the "communications routine level of analysis") as well then as conforming to organisational levels (is this story consonant with our business or organisational mission?), social institutional levels (such as whether it will be profitable in a market-oriented publication), and social system levels (the wider social and cultural values that shape our relations with each other). From this, they adopt Kurt Lewin's field theory as an approach to gatekeeping (adapted from Manning White and Shoemaker's earlier work), whereby multiple gates operate within and outside organisations, creating various pressure points in which messages are transmitted, discarded, or shaped according to various levels of individual, organisational, or social activity.[30] The value of this approach to the social media age is that it is highly networked: there is never one gate but multiple ones, with distributed agency across organisations.

Shoemaker and Vos mention Facebook only once – rather blandly observing that the site, alongside others such as Reddit and YouTube, "allow anyone to become a gatekeeper by passing along news items and commenting on them".[31] In this approach, they clearly see social media users as, at best, individual gatekeepers or forces operating largely outside the organisation: this ignores the effect that large social media sites such as Facebook have in actually creating the news (which, as noted in the previous chapter, Zuckerberg explicitly wished to achieve when he drove the redesign of Facebook's news feed). While useful, then, gatekeeping theory as developed for late twentieth-century media monopolies has its limitations, and Vos has suggested the need to "reimagine gatekeeping as a concept in the digital era".[32] More recent work, such as that by Myers West, and Welbers and Opgenhaffen, extends Shoemaker's and Vos's field theory approach. Myers West demonstrates how, by ranking, channelling, promoting, and deleting posts, social media sites such as Facebook act as networked gatekeepers,[33] and we shall explore an extended case study of such activity in the final chapter of this book when turning to the role of big tech in suppressing Infowars. Welbers and Opgenhaffen concentrate on the significance of Facebook in particular for news sites, offering as it does one of the most important means today for them to connect with an audience: by mapping shares and likes as part of the engagement with a story, they are able to demonstrate how social media is able to boost the diffusion of that story, although they still tend to treat Facebook as a fairly transparent medium for transmission of information across the network.[34] What the election of 2016 showed very clearly was that social media was anything but a transparent medium.

The Algorithm of Truth in a Post-Truth Age

In February of that year, four months before Donald Trump announced that he would enter the election as a Republican contender, a group of engineers at Google published a paper that created a considerable stir in engineering circles. Titled "Knowledge-Based Trust: Estimating the Trustworthiness of Web Sources", the eight engineers explained their work in attempting to compute the trustworthiness of 119 million web pages against a database of 2.8 billion facts and thus influence its page ranking in Google's search engine.[35] Observing that most attempts to rank pages depended on exogenous signals such as hyperlinks to a site, indicating its popularity, the authors based their work on assessing trustworthiness as defined by accuracy and shared some links with work undertaken by Ray Kurzweil, Director of Engineering, to create a form of artificial intelligence that could understand content without relying on such third-party inputs. While the authors identified the possibility that accuracy could be ranked (at least when dealing with the database of facts to hand), several obstacles remained in the way of its implementation: irrelevant noise, trivial facts, and a high percentage (some 15 per cent) with regard to false positives for accuracy. In the end, the authors concluded, algorithms would be able to determine the truth of a page based on the accuracy of its facts, but such accuracy was nowhere near good enough for release into the wild.

As such, and leaving aside for one moment Hume's distinction between matters of fact and relations of ideas in *An Enquiry Concerning Human Understanding* (to which truth as generally accepted reasoning may be said to belong), this leaves us with a trade-protected page ranking system that depends on elements such as popularity as determined by hyperlinks or aggregated searches, the exogenous links referred to by Google's engineers. Similarly, such aggregated data inform Google's autosuggest feature, helping searchers by beginning to complete their search terms.

Carole Cadwalladr, writing in *The Guardian* in 2016, described her experience of undertaking a thoroughly mundane, twenty-first-century task: googling a search term. Entering the letters a-r-e j-e-w-s, Google autocomplete offered a range of suggested questions: "are jews a race?", "are jews white?" "are jews christians?" and "are jews evil?"[36] Alongside a range of suggested answers to the questions (including that "Jews are demonic souls from a different world"), Cadwaladr discovered that the direct answer autocorrect suggestion to the word "women" was "are women evil?". In 2006, Google had been subject to a lawsuit by the Anti-Defamation League because the first result for "jew" had been a link to the anti-Semitic website, jewwatch.org, leading Google to emphasise that the page ranking system was automated. Over the next few years, the processes involved in generating Google results continued to attract attention from time to time, as when Tom Chatfield drew attention to the search engine's disturbing trend of suggesting that women shouldn't work, shouldn't vote, and shouldn't even have rights.[37] In general, Google had taken a lofty role with regard to its position, exonerating itself as a company with regard to its duties of overseeing its algorithmic curators. In December 2016, however, Google was one of a small handful of tech companies being blamed for the surprise outcome of the American election. Cadwalladr's story was published on

December 4. By December 5, Google had removed autosuggestions for women and Jews being evil, the need to eradicate Muslims, and the suggestion that Hitler was one of the good guys.

These particular suggestions indicated very clearly to Cadwalladr and other commentators that Google's page ranking system had been successfully gamed by the alt-right. By deploying tactics that had proved so successful with Gamergate, tech-savvy figures on the alt-right had constructed a shadow Internet of blogs, web pages, and social media pages that could be linked to and searched for via automated processes, driving up the popularity of such page rankings. The exogenous verifiers blindly followed by the undead army of Google's search bots had created a distorted vision of the world, one in which the simplest understanding of truth – a correspondence of words to the world or, as Aristotle remarked, "to say of what is that it is, or of what is not that it is not"[38] – was defined by the far right. A knowledge-based trust algorithm is designed to combat such manipulations, although of course it would depend on also trusting Google's own factual database: who, after all, would watch the watchmen?

Although there are plenty of other sites that offer routes into journalism online, alongside Google the other increasingly effective monopoly consists of Facebook that, in recent years, has sought to increase the number of users accessing news through its pages. As David Kirkpatrick observed in 2011, Facebook then was seeking to redefine news into something produced by users and consumed by their friends,[39] but this user-generated content approach to news (which perhaps had some tangential connections with the popularisation of citizen journalism during the previous decade) began to demonstrate more sinister aspects during the 2016 US election. The significance of Facebook's contribution is due in part because of the changing means by which American consumers in particular get their news: a Pew Research Center survey from 2016 found that the majority of US adults, 62 per cent, received their news from social media.[40] The original premise of Facebook, as a means to connect friends and family, has an important impact on how we view relations with other organisations. Vaidhyanathan makes the ironic observation that "Facebook lowers the transaction costs of maintaining relationships across great distances,"[41] reducing friendships to a cost–benefit analysis that can be maintained with a minimum of effort and expense. Yet, the determination to preserve social relations – which extend also to those larger, political efforts such as participating in a polity – often requires much greater effort.

In part, the popularity of Facebook (along with, to a lesser extent, Twitter) represents a logical consequence of the much-observed phenomenon of the acceleration of news, which began with the introduction of 24/7 cable news channels in the 1980s, their proliferation in the 1990s, and, of course, rapid advances in Internet and digital communications from the late 1990s onwards. As Emily Bell remarks, increasingly "media organizations are ranked on their ability to pivot toward new formats and revenue sources with decisive speed",[42] but while this has resulted in users of social media sites being able to receive information more quickly than ever before, at the same time it means that the constant push to break news continuously leads to less fact-checking and accurate detail, even from respected sources. At the same time, Facebook itself finds itself being pushed increasingly into the role of a sometimes-unwilling gatekeeper: while Zuckerberg may have repeatedly emphasised the user-generated aspect of the news feed, a kind of citizen journalism of our daily lives and friendships, the indiscriminate use of that news feed by Facebook users to share all kinds of news stories means that increasingly the company is seen as a media provider, with the responsibilities that attend that position. As a number of commentators observed, by the end of 2016, Zuckerberg was finally starting to admit that Facebook was a media company, although clearly not a conventional one.[43] Facebook's eagerness to avoid being labelled a publisher was, as Ansgar Koene pointed out, due to its desire to avoid the regulations and libel laws constraining such organisations.[44]

What is increasingly clear is that the role taken by more traditional news organisations with regard to gatekeeping in the past has now shifted decisively to technology companies such as Google and Facebook. Facebook in particular, as Nahon and Hemsley observe, exercises gatekeeping through channelling news feeds: the power of traditional gatekeepers such as CNN, NBC, and ABC has declined with the emergence of social media and thus "today's gatekeepers are gatekeepers partly because people pay attention to them".[45] Increasingly, it has faced criticism over the opaque techniques that it uses to monitor and control the flow of information, such as the accusations of censorship that followed the removal of the famous photograph of a young, naked Phan Thi Kim Phuc, photographed by Nick Ut as she fled a napalm attack in Vietnam, because the image did not comply with child pornography guidelines, Similarly, outside of the United States, the company has come under fire for failing to follow local regulations, as when it was rebuked by the German government for failing to remove quickly enough hateful or illegal materials. Where the experiment has been the boldest, however, is in terms of Facebook's attempt to automate the process of gatekeeping that, traditionally, has been the preserve of editors and journalists.

As we shall see in the next chapter, the phenomenon of robot journalism is increasingly important in areas such as financial reporting, but at the time of writing, it is perhaps robot editing or curation that has a greater impact upon our consumption of the media. The process has not been fully automated on Facebook by any means. Most notably, a filter bubble study in 2015 sought to examine the effects of withholding or promoting certain types of news by modifying the algorithms that presented certain stories in the news feed. As Koene observes,

> how visible the site makes the content has a huge impact on how far it spreads beyond the account of the original contributor. The way an algorithm works can have a similar effect to a newspaper editor selecting a piece for the front page.

As such, the filter bubble, by following people's preferences, makes it very hard, in the words of Eric Schmidt, for people "to watch or consume something that has not in some sense been tailored for them". Pariser has called this the "passing of the torch from human gatekeepers to algorithmic ones",[46] but the failure of that algorithmic gatekeeper became evident in August 2016 when, having fired human content curators, fake news began to trend on the site, with the top story featuring a false headline that Fox News had fired "traitor" Megyn Kelly for backing Hillary Clinton.[47] Although human editors were reinstated three days later, the commitment to ensuring that curation takes place through algorithms remains very clearly at the forefront of Facebook's operations. According to the digital marketing site Zephoria, with more than 1.86 billion active users worldwide and more than half a million comments per minute, any chance of collating that information through human intervention is completely impossible. Processing vast quantities of data is something where computers have a clear advantage over humans.

And yet, as we have already seen, this is only true in terms of a quantitative advantage. In terms of quality, the benefits are far from clear. Throughout the 2016 election, a plethora of fake news stories began to trend on Facebook, clearly intended to shape the vote in one direction or another, as with a false allegation that Barack Obama had signed an executive order banning the Pledge of Allegiance in schools, or that Pope Francis had endorsed Trump, or that Trump had claimed previously that he would run as a Republican because they were the "dumbest group of voters in the country".[48] As the majority of American adults now get their news from social media sites, such fake news could easily proliferate – not merely in the USA but also in European countries such as the UK, Italy, France, and Germany.[49] Sometimes, fake news stories have outperformed legitimate stories by the most popular media companies due to the fact that organisations such as Facebook have outsourced the gatekeeping of such information to end users and software: if the primary function of an algorithm is to judge a story on its popularity (a relatively simple and easily quantifiable exercise) as opposed to its verifiability (which, as we have already seen, is almost impossible to quantify), then fake news that appeals to more readers will quickly become even more popular than unpalatable real reporting.

In an analysis of top performing news stories from the final three months of the 2016 campaign, Craig Silverman found that headlines from hoax sites and hyperpartisan blogs outperformed those from major news outlets such as *The New York Times* and *Washington Post,* generating more than 8.7 million shares, reactions, and comments compared to nearly 7.4 million for the mainstream media. Until that phase of the campaign, traditional media sources had easily outperformed fake news sites, but headlines such as those claiming Hillary Clinton sold weapons to ISIS or the apparent murder of an FBI agent investigating her email leaks proved far more tempting.[50] While a number of these stories shared similar roots in 4chan and related sites to attempt to influence the outcome of the election by using an alt-right shadow Internet, the issue was given a greater impact by the apparent intervention of Russian, state-sponsored hackers to cloud the democratic process. By mid-2017, it was becoming evident that Russian interference was even more widespread than previously believed, with deliberate attempts to spread fake news in an attempt to discredit American democracy if not necessarily support the election of Donald Trump.[51]

Even without the intervention of outside powers, the presidential election demonstrated just how important social media companies had become during a scandal that came to light in 2018. In May of that year, Cambridge Analytica, a political consulting firm that had done work for the Trump campaign, announced that it was closing amidst allegations of misuse of voters' data. Cambridge Analytica was founded as a data mining company in 2013 and was partly owned by the family of Robert Mercer who, among other activities, was a funder of Breitbart news. In 2016, it collated data for the Brexit and Trump campaigns, especially after Steve Bannon (as the vice president of Cambridge Analytica as well as the editor of Breitbart) joined Trump's campaign. SCL Group, the public relations and messaging firm that used data provided by Cambridge Analytica (and for which CA may have been a shell company), took pride in its ability to target and persuade people of its clients' preferred messages, describing its techniques as "psychological warfare".[52] As part of its activities to support Trump, Cambridge Analytica CEO Alexander Nix reached out to WikiLeaks founder Julian Assange about emails hacked from the Democratic National Committee's servers, but more significant activity came in the form of its relations with Facebook. Aleksandr Kogan, an American-Russian researcher at Cambridge University, built a Facebook app that was a quiz called thisismydigitallife. This app not only harvested data from the 270,000 users who took part in the quiz (based on an earlier myPersonality psychometric test) but, by exploiting a loophole in Facebook's API, was able to gather information about other accounts linked to theirs. By 2015, Cambridge Analytica was claiming that they had a data set of over 40 million users to work with, a number that had grown to an estimated 87 million by the time the scandal broke in 2017.[53]

Christopher Wyllie, the ex-Cambridge Analytica employee who blew the whistle on the company's operations, revealed how this data set could be used to influence peoples' decisions. First of all, a "training set" would be created, collecting data via personality tests to see how their responses to questions would tend to reflect things such as political orientation. Once completed, this could then refer to the data collected in its entirety, the "feature set" against which those target variables – how people tend to vote – could be measured. The training set was not necessarily thisismydigitallife: to provide viable target variables, users generally have to complete very extensive questionnaires and were more often paid by Cambridge Analytica. Once that set was completed, however, having such a huge data set made available from Facebook allowed the company to target political advertising much more effectively.[54] The public relations disaster for Facebook that emerged in the wake of these revelations was that it allowed so much of the data collected from its users to be served up to third party's so easily. Cambridge Analytica was, in many respects, engaging in the kind of political manoeuvring that was common to political PR firms across the developed world, although never with such huge amounts of personal data collected unwittingly from users. Russian influence in the 2016 election, however, was of a very different order.

On October 31, 2016, then President Obama warned the Russian President, Vladimir Putin, not to seek to interfere in the US election or to face the consequences.[55] At that point, the primary concern was related to hacked emails from the DNC servers that were being disseminated via WikiLeaks, but it transpired that the operations apparently sanctioned by Putin were much larger. The Russian government had sought to interfere in the elections to damage Hilary Clinton's campaign but also, more generally, to undermine confidence in the US election system. Using a company founded in 2013, the Internet Research Agency (IRA), based in Saint Petersburg, the government sought to proliferate the amount of fake news and propaganda that was available via social media, sometimes by simply using advertising on networks such as Facebook, but also by employing a "troll army" to mould American public opinion. According to documents later leaked by *Buzzfeed*, workers at the IRA would be instructed to post some 50 articles a day on social media, maintaining multiple Facebook and Twitter accounts as well as blogs. As people wrote those articles and posts, so an army of automated bots would share and proliferate them, causing them to rise up the rankings and so gain wider traction across social networks.[56] Snyder has also explored extensively how Vladimir Putin encouraged the establishment of a web of human and digital propagandists who not only sought to undermine faith in the democratic process, but also gave overt support to European separatists and pro-Russian factions.[57] In such circumstances, Russian propagandists faced a system of automated, algorithmic gatekeepers which were increasingly replacing human editors and journalists: as such, the communications network of the United States of America proved itself incredibly easy to infiltrate.

The crisis represented by fake news during 2016 and 2017 was particularly poignant because, as the former Director of the FBI, James Comey, confirmed in a response to questions from Senator Martin Heinrich during his testimony to Congress in May 2017, it in part stemmed from "a hostile act by the Russian government" against the USA.[58] The intervention of Russian hackers, however, represented only symptom of the transformation of the media landscape that has taken place in the first two decades of the twenty-first century. As we have seen in the previous chapter, the disruption of the distribution and economics of older media monopolies by big tech has led to a rush to gain new readers, with one effect being a polarisation of audiences who tend to respond to "vivid" rather than "pallid" news: one consequence of this is a push towards more partisan language which, in turn, influences political divisions and helps to break down a sense of shared culture. Alongside the physical remediation of news away from print and broadcast into digital formats, social media has had a crucial role to play in the establishment of new forms of gatekeeping, ones where automated algorithms fulfil the functions once undertaken by human editors. The fact that this clearly resulted in a system error does not, by any means, mark the end of this transformation: by the end of 2016, for example, Facebook was handling 300 petabytes of data on its servers (or the equivalent of about 120 billion smartphone photos). The transition from small, centralised production by professional publishers to huge amounts of user-generated content in the form of digital shares and posts on social media represents a system that has scaled far beyond traditional forms of human gatekeeping. For the immediate future, it is clear that the algorithms of truth are not yet able to prevent zombie media overrunning its users. In the next decade, however, we will almost certainly witness step changes in automation that will see robot editors fulfilling much more efficiently a task that we once considered all-too-human.

Notes

1 'Final Election 2016 Numbers', *70News*, Posted on November 12, Updated on November 13, 2016, https://web-beta.archive.org/web/20161114005316/https://70news.wordpress.com/2016/11/12/final-election-2016-numbers-trump-won-both-popular-62-9-m-62-7-m-and-electoral-college-vote-306-232-hey-change-org-scrap-your-loony-petition-now.
2 Philip Bump, "Google's Top News Link for 'Final Election Results' Goes to a Fake News Site with False Numbers", *The Washington Post*, November

14 2016, www.washingtonpost.com/news/the-fix/wp/2016/11/14/googles-top-news-link-for-final-election-results-goes-to-a-fake-news-site-with-false-numbers/?utm_term=.f1993e68ccdf.

3 Leona Toker, 'Samizdat and the Problem of Authorial Control: The Case of Varlam Shalamov', *Poetics Today*, 29.4(2008), pp. 735–758.

4 Fernando de la Cruz Paragas, 'Organizing and Reframing Technological Determinism', *New Media and Society*, 18.8(2016), pp. 1528–1546.

5 Martin Conboy, *Journalism: A Critical History*, London: Sage, 2004; James Curran, and Jean Seaton, *Power Without Responsibility: Press, Broadcasting and Internet in Britain*, 7th edition, Abingdon: Routledge, 2009; Jane Chapman, *Comparative Media History: An Introduction, 1789 to the Present*, London: Polity, 2005.

6 Roger Lewis, *Outlaws of America: The Underground Press and its Contexts*, London: Penguin, 1972; Robert Glessing, *Underground Press in America*, Bloomington: Indiana University Press, 1972.

7 Chris Atton, *Alternative Media*, London: Sage, 2002; John Downing, Tamara Ford, Genève Gil, and Laura Stein, *Radical Media: Rebellious Communication and Social Movements*, Thousand Oak, CA: Sage, 2001; Clemencia Rodriquez, *Fissures in the Mediascape: An International Study of Citizen's Media*, Cresskill, NJ: Hampton Press, 2001.

8 Dan Gillmor, *We the Media: Grassroots Journalism By the People, For the People*, North Sebastopol, CA: O'Reilly Media, 2004, p. 174.

9 William Hutchinson, 'Media, Government and Manipulation: The Cases of the Two Gulf Wars', *Australian Information Warfare and Security Conference*, 2008, http://ro.ecu.edu.au/cgi/viewcontent.cgi?article=1027&context=isw, p. 36.

10 Ibrahim Al-Marashi, 'The "Dodgy Dossier": The Academic Implications of the British Government's Plagiarism Incident', *Middle East Studies Association Bulletin*, 40.1(2006), pp. 33–43.

11 Simon Rogers, *The Hutton Inquiry and its Impact*, London: Politico's publishing Ltd, 2004.

12 Gregory Perreault, and Tim Vos, 'The Gamergate Controversy and Journalistic Paradigm Maintenance', *Journalism*, September 30 2016, doi:10.1177/1464884916670932; Shira Chess, and Adrienne Shaw, 'A Conspiracy of Fishes, or, How We Learned to Stop Worrying About Gamergate and Embrace Hegemonic Masculinity', *Journal of Broadcasting and Electronic Media*, 59.1(2015), pp. 208–220.

13 Andy Baio, '72 Hours of #Gamergate', *The Message*, October 27 2014, https://medium.com/message/72-hours-of-gamergate-e00513f7cf5d#.hxhvydyv1.

14 Xavier Glitch, 'The GamerGate-Supporting Journalist Who Hates Gamers', https://storify.com/x_glitch/the-gamergate-supporting-journalist-who-hates-game.

15 Milo Yiannopoulos, 'I've Been Playing Video Games for Nearly a Year: Here's What I've Learned', *Breitbart*, July 16 2015, www.breitbart.com/big-hollywood/2015/07/16/ive-been-playing-video-games-for-nearly-a-year-heres-what-ive-learned/.

16 Danielle Kurzleben, 'With "Fake News", Trump Moves from Alternative Facts to Alternative Language', *NPR*, February 17 2017, www.npr.org/2017/02/17/515630467/with-fake-news-trump-moves-from-alternative-facts-to-alternative-language.

17 Tom O'Malley, 'Labour and the 1947–9 Royal Commission on the Press', in Michael Bromley and Tom O'Malley, (eds.), *A Journalism Reader*. London: Routledge, 1997, pp. 126–158.

18 Brian McNair, *Journalism and Democracy: An Evaluation of the Public Sphere*, London: Routledge, 1999, p. 1.
19 Bob Franklin, 'Introduction', in Bob Franklin (ed.), *The Future of Journalism: In an Age of Digital Media and Economic Uncertainty*, Abingdon: Routledge, 2017, np.
20 Jamie Bartlett, *The People Vs Tech: How the Internet is Killing Democracy (and How We Save It)*, London: Ebury Press, 2018, pp. 1–3.
21 Michael M. Grynbaum, "Trump Strategist Stephen Bannon Says Media Should 'Keep its Mouth Shut'", *The New York Times*, January 26 2017, www.nytimes.com/2017/01/26/business/media/stephen-bannon-trump-news-media.html?_r=0.
22 Garth S. Jowett, and Victoria J. O'Donnell, *Propaganda and Persuasion*, 6th edition, London: Sage, 2014, pp. 7–8.
23 Megan Knight, and Claire Cook, *Social Media for Journalists: Principles and Practice*, London: Sage, 2013, p. 106.
24 Alfred Hermida, 'Tweets and Truth: Journalism as a Discipline of Collaborative Verification', *Journalism Practice*, 6.5–6(2011), pp. 659–668.
25 Art Swift, 'Americans' Trust in Mass Media Sinks to New Low', *Gallup*, September 14 2016, www.gallup.com/poll/195542/americans-trust-mass-media-sinks-new-low.aspx.
26 Matthew Gentzkow, and Jesse Shapiro, 'Media Bias and Reputation', *Journal of Political Economy*, 114.2(2006), pp. 280–316.
27 David Manning White, 'The "Gate-Keeper": A Case Study in the Selection of News', *Journalism Quarterly*, 27(1950), pp. 383–390; Pamela J. Shoemaker, *Communication Concepts 3: Gatekeeping*, Newbury Park, CA: Sage, 1991. See also D. Charles Whitney and Lee B. Becker, '"Keeping the Gates" for Gatekeepers: The Effects of Wire News', *Journalism Quarterly*, 59.1(1982), pp. 60–65 and Stephen D. Reese and Jane Ballinger, 'The Roots of a Sociology of News: Remembering Mr Gates and Social Control in the Newsroom', *Journalism and Mass Communications Quarterly*, 78.4(2001), pp. 641–658.
28 Pamela J. Shoemaker, and Tim P. Vos, *Gatekeeping Theory*, New York: Routledge, 2009, pp. 1–2.
29 Shoemaker and Vos, pp. 26–27.
30 Shoemaker and Vos, pp. 113–116.
31 Shoemaker and Vos, p. 124.
32 Tim P. Vos, "Revisiting Gatekeeping Theory During a Time of Transition", in Tim P. Vos, and François Heinderyckx (eds.), *Gatekeeping in Transition*. London: Routledge, 2015, pp. 3–24.
33 Sarah Myers West, "Raging Against the Machine: Network Gatekeeping and Collective Action on Social Media Platforms", *Media and Communication*, 5.3(2017), pp. 28–36.
34 Kasper Welbers, and Michaël Opgenhaffen, "Social Media Gatekeeping: An Analysis of the Gatekeeping Influence of Newspapers' Public Facebook Pages", *New Media and Society*, 20.12(2018), pp. 4278–4747.
35 Xin Luna Dong, Evgeniy Gabrilovich, Kevin Murphy, Van Dang, Wilko Horn, Camillo Lugaresi, Shaohua Sun, and Wei Zang, 'Knowledge-Based Trust: Estimating the Trustworthiness of Web Sources', *Proceedings of the VLDB Endowment*, 2015, https://arxiv.org/pdf/1502.03519.pdf.
36 Carole Cadwaladr, 'Google, Democracy and the Truth about Internet Search', *The Guardian*, December 4 2016, www.theguardian.com/technology/2016/dec/04/google-democracy-truth-internet-search-facebook.
37 Tom Chatfield, 'Is Google Autocomplete Evil?' *BBC Future*, November 6 2013, www.bbc.com/future/story/20131106-is-google-autocomplete-evil.

38 Aristotle, *Metaphysics*, transl. by William D. Ross, Oxford: Clarendon Press, 1928, 1.7.27.
39 David Kirkpatrick, *The Facebook Effect: The Real Inside Story of Mark Zuckerberg and the World's Fastest-Growing Company*, London: Random House, 2011, pp. 219–220.
40 Jeffrey Gottfried, and Elisa Shearer, 'New Use Across Social Media Platforms 2016', *Pew Research Centre*, May 26 2016, www.journalism.org/2016/05/26/news-use-across-social-media-platforms-2016/.
41 Siva Vaidhyanathan, *Antisocial Media: How Facebook Disconnects Us and Undermines Democracy*, New York: Oxford University Press, p. 33.
42 Emily Bell, 'Facebook Is Being Taken Somewhere It Never Wanted to Go', *Columbia Journalism Review*, September 26 2016, www.cjr.org/tow_center/facebook_zuckerberg_napalm_video_palestine.php.
43 See Samuel Gibbs, 'Mark Zuckerbuerg Appears to Finally Admit Facebook is a Media Company', *The Guardian*, December 22 2016, www.theguardian.com/technology/2016/dec/22/mark-zuckerberg-appears-to-finally-admit-facebook-is-a-media-company; Josh Constine, "Zuckerberg Implies Facebook is a Media Company, Just 'Not a Traditional Media Company'", *TechCrunch*, December 21, https://techcrunch.com/2016/12/21/fbonc/; Matthew Ingram, 'Mark Zuckerberg Finally Admits Facebook is a Media Company', *Fortune*, December 23 2016, http://fortune.com/2016/12/23/zuckerberg-media-company/.
44 Ansgar Koene, 'Facebook's Algorithms Give it More Editorial Responsibility – Not Less', *The Conversation*, September 14 2016, http://theconversation.com/facebooks-algorithms-give-it-more-editorial-responsibility-not-less-65182.
45 Karine Nahon, and Jeff Hemsley, *Going Viral*, Cambridge: Polity Press, 2013, p. 53.
46 Eli Pariser, 'Beware Online Filter Bubbles', *TED Talks*, www.ted.com/talks/eli_pariser_beware_online_filter_bubbles/transcript?language=en.
47 Abby Ohlheiser, 'Three Days After Removing Human Editors, Facebook is Already Trending Fake News', *The Washington Post*, August 29 2016, www.washingtonpost.com/news/the-intersect/wp/2016/08/29/a-fake-headline-about-megyn-kelly-was-trending-on-facebook/?utm_term=.878f35fd6904; Sam Thielman, 'Facebook Fires Trending Team, and Algorithm Without Humans Goes Crazy', *The Guardian*, 29 August 2016, www.theguardian.com/technology/2016/aug/29/facebook-fires-trending-topics-team-algorithm.
48 Evann Gastaldo, 'These Are the 5 Biggest Fake News Stories of the Year', *Newser*, December 30 2016, www.newser.com/story/236204/these-are-the-5-biggest-fake-news-stories-of-the-year.html; Tom Cheshire, 'Sky Views: Facebook's Fake News Threatens Democracy', *Sky News*, 2017, http://news.sky.com/story/sky-views-democracy-burns-as-facebook-lets-fake-news-thrive-10652711.
49 Kate Connolly, Angelique Chrisafis, Poppy McPherson, Stephanie Kirchgaessner, Benjamin Haas, Dominic Phillips, Elle Hunt, and Michael Safi, 'Fake News: An Insidious Trend That's Fast Becoming a Global Problem', *The Guardian*, December 2 2016, www.theguardian.com/media/2016/dec/02/fake-news-facebook-us-election-around-the-world.
50 Craig Silverman, 'This Analysis Shows How Viral Fake Election News Stories Outperformed Real News on Facebook', *Buzzfeed News*, November 16 2016, www.buzzfeed.com/craigsilverman/viral-fake-election-news-outperformed-real-news-on-facebook?utm_term=.ttXJ2z592#.lmo6BWd4B.
51 Massimo Calabresi, 'Election Hackers Altered Voter Rolls, Stole Private Data, Officials Say', *Time*, June 22 2017, http://time.com/4828306/russian-hacking-election-widespread-private-data/; Liz Stark, 'Russian Hackers Tried

Altering US Election Data. Now What?' *CNN*, June 15 2017, http://edition. cnn.com/2017/06/15/politics/russia-hacking-election/index.html.

52 Carole Cadwalladr, "'I Made Steve Bannon's Psychological Warfare Tool': Meet the Data War Whistleblower", *The Guardian*, 18 March 2018, www.theguardian.com/news/2018/mar/17/data-war-whistleblower-christopher-wylie-faceook-nix-bannon-trump.

53 Aja Romano, "The Facebook Data Breach Wasn't a Hack. It Was a Wake-up Call", *Vox*, 20 March 2018, www.vox.com/2018/3/20/17138756/facebook-data-breach-cambridge-analytica-explained.

54 Alex Hearn, "Cambridge Analytica: How Did It Turn Clicks into Votes?" *The Guardian*, 6 May 2018, www.theguardian.com/news/2018/may/06/cambridge-analytica-how-turn-clicks-into-votes-christopher-wylie.

55 William H. Arkin, "What Obama Said to Putin on the Red Phone about the Election Hack", *NBC News*, 19 December 2016, www.nbcnews.com/news/us-news/what-obama-said-putin-red-phone-about-election-hack-n697116.

56 Max Seddon, "Documents Show How Russia's Troll Army Hit America", *Buzzfeed News*, 2 June 2017, www.buzzfeednews.com/article/maxseddon/documents-show-how-russias-troll-army-hit-america; Simon Shuster, and Sandra Ifraimova, "A Former Russian Troll Explains How to Spread Fake News", *Time*, 14 March 2018.

57 Timothy Snyder, *The Road to Unfreedom: Russia, Europe, America*, London: Bodley Head, 2018, pp. 159–175.

58 'Full Transcript and Video: James Comey's Testimony on Capitol Hill', *The New York Times*, June 8 2017, www.nytimes.com/2017/06/08/us/politics/senate-hearing-transcript.html.

4 Turing's Test
Automated Journalism and the Rise of the Post-Human Writer

In his 1961 short story, "Studio 5, The Stars", set in the louche, pseudo paradise of Vermilion Sands, J. G. Ballard presented a vision of the near future in which poets no longer needed to work at their craft but instead, via their verse transcribers (VTs), could automatically generate endless reams of perfect prosody. The story, a meditation on the ability of writing to express something essentially human, ends with the narrator, having been challenged by a sociopathic muse, Aurora Day, writing poetry by hand after she destroys his VT. This act is repeated by all the poets across Vermilion Sands.

Ballard's story, concluding with the narrator rejecting a new order to replace his VT via the Red Beach branch of IBM (which detail alone dates this tale), ends with a particularly humanistic vision of a numinous act: Aurora Day, the "insane" afflatus who disappears as mysteriously from Vermilion Sands as she appeared, has literally inspired the decadent poets of the idyllic resort to take up their pens once more. Ballard's visions of the near future (which would almost certainly, like Stanley Kubrick's panoramas of *2001*, have existed in our near past) offer a particularly quaint account of the technology of the VT which – with its buttons and dials – seems to operate as an analogue machine rather than a truly digital one. The focus on poetry is not accidental: for Aristotle, along with music, it was poetry which had the greatest effect upon our psyche, and since the Romantics, it has become normal to assume that poetic language is the spontaneous overflow of powerful feeling. Leaving to one side the various assertions by many cultures outside the Romantic movement that poetry can often serve much more prosaic or mundane features (preserving genealogies, for example), poetry has frequently been denoted as a sign of human ingenuity. Yet in the "mechanical age" of the nineteenth century, as Jason Hall has demonstrated in great detail, Victorian theorists were deeply concerned with what we would perhaps consider the algorithms of poetry. John Clark (1785–1853) went so far as to invent the "Eureka", a "Latin Hexameter Machine" that could automatically generate Latin verses and which, in 1845, problematised "the division between the creative capacities of humans and machines".[1] The Eureka machine, on display in the Egyptian Hall at Piccadilly, had words encoded on turning cylinders which pins would cause to drop: the verses themselves were random, but they followed a set grammatical pattern.

Clark's device was something of an anomaly in the history of automated writing and a machine intended purely for entertainment. In the twenty-first century, the algorithm of writing has not – thus far – bothered itself much with the activity of composing poetry: a character in "Studio 5, The Stars" may say at one point that "poetry is a serious business" but, Rupi Kaur aside, there are few today who make serious money from it. The industrial automation of writing, however, has become increasingly important, with automatic journalism in particular becoming big business for a number of organisations. Consider the following two stories:

Rite Aid posts 3Q profit

CAMP HILL, Pa. (AP) _ Rite Aid Corp. (RAD) on Wednesday reported fiscal third-quarter net income of $81 million.

The Camp Hill, Pennsylvania-based company said it had profit of 8 cents per share. Earnings, adjusted to account for discontinued operations, came to less than 1 cent on a per-share basis.

The drugstore chain posted revenue of $5.35 billion in the period.

In the final minutes of trading on Wednesday, the company's shares hit $2.11. A year ago, they were trading at $8.18.[2]

Buffett's Berkshire Hathaway reports a $12B 2Q profit

Berkshire Hathaway Inc. on Saturday reported a $12 billion second-quarter profit.

Warren Buffett's conglomerate reported a profit of $4.87 per Class B share. A year ago, Berkshire reported $4.3 billion in net income, or $1.73 per Class B share.

Buffett has long said Berkshire's operating earnings offer a better view of quarterly performance because they exclude investments and derivatives, which can vary widely.

By that measure, Berkshire reported operating earnings of $6.9 billion, or about $2.79 per Class B share. That's up from $4.1 billion, or about $1.67 per B share, a year ago.[3]

The second story has a byline for Josh Boak, an economics journalist writing for Associated Press. The tag for the first story, however, is much more significant: "This story was generated by Automated Insights (http://automatedinsights.com/ap) using data from Zacks Investment Research." A very cursory search on Google News in August 2018 for the phrase "This story was generated by Automated Insights" returned about 85,900 results for the preceding year. A very small number of top page hits are clearly news stories written by humans about the links between companies such as AP with Automated Insights, but most – with titles such as "Strong travel demand lifts Boeing in first quarter" or "PepsiCo beats earnings forecasts" – are generated by software. The VT of Vermilion Sands does exist – it's just that there is more serious money in journalism than poetry.

Robo-Writers and the Algorithm of News

As we saw in a previous chapter, the Turing Test was devised by Alan Turing as a means of determining whether humans would be able to differentiate between machine and human responses. While John Searle among others has criticised whether this would demonstrate true artificial intelligence – or, more accurately artificial consciousness, what is often referred to in this book as general artificial intelligence – for practical considerations, this is much less important than the intentional stance of readers and audiences. What matters most in practical terms is whether those readers can distinguish (or, indeed, even care) as to whether the author of a story is a human or algorithm. Writing in 2013, Spyridou *et al* argued that technological innovation was viewed at that time in the newsroom as a means of improving professional practice – that indeed such professional culture articulated as skills, ideas, and practices worked to weaken the potential impact of such innovation.[4] In the space of five years, following even more rapid closures across multiple newsrooms than had even been witnessed in the first decade of the twenty-first century, it is probably not unfair to suggest that this professional culture has been severely attenuated and that publishers – if not journalists and editors – are more willing to experiment with software-generated content, so-called robo-writers or algorithmic journalism. Certainly, a study by Young and Hermida in 2015 found that the *Los Angeles Times* was engaging in what the authors called "computational journalism", the use of the newspaper's Homicide Report and Data Desk to generate material for news stories, if not always the final copy.[5]

The activities at the *LA Times* are part of a much wider phenomenon, what Örnebring and Conill refer to as the "outsourcing of newswork".[6] This includes a wide range of activities, some of which – such as a reliance on external press agencies or using PR agencies – have their roots in twentieth-century practices, but steep challenges to newsroom budgets also push for increased automation of all aspects of the news production process wherever possible.[7] The conditions that would enable the next step away from merely using technology networks to better manage freelancers, for example, towards moving towards full-scale software-generated content represent not solely a technical issue. As Flew *et al* have observed regarding algorithmic journalism proper (what he, like Young and Hermida, refers to as "computational journalism"), fully automated processes will require large government data sets becoming more widely available, more sophisticated software, and a developing digital economy that would allow organisations to make cost savings through new, and initially expensive, technologies.[8] Since that paper's publication, most of these conditions are finally falling into place although it remains the case that in the case of investigative journalism, software is still better placed in the service of human reporters, as we shall see towards the end of this chapter. What Anderson (ironically) referred to as "the future of news" in 2012 still remains, with regard to sourcing many news stories, some way off,[9] but computer-generated news production is beginning to take over in some fields. As Montal and Reich point out in their survey of literature on algorithmic journalism, algorithms should no longer be thought of as precise recipes for step-by-step instructions, but rather as computational actions that can operate at high levels of uncertainty. It is this increased sophistication of computational power that finally enables software to begin creating automated journalism, which they define as "algorithmic processes that convert data into narrative news texts with limited to no human intervention beyond the initial programming".[10] Automated journalism is finally with us, but just as the word "computer" originally referred to humans carrying out iterative processes, so the algorithm of news is a much older invention.

The comparison between Automated Insights and Josh Boak at the start of this chapter is not intended to insult his work at all. Again and again, Automated Insights – one of a number of companies such as Narrative Science using artificial intelligence to generate copy – makes it clear that the AP style guide is a standard for their work, not simply because of the business link between them but because (along with Reuters and the BBC) Associated Press is one of the globally recognised standards for how to *write* journalistic prose. Concise sentences, direct statements, judicious use of the "5 Ws", and the news pyramid – anyone who has ever taught how to write news will understand this approach: very simply, there is a great deal of news writing that has been governed by algorithms (or, as we have preferred to call them, style guides) for the better part of a century. While much of the process of newsgathering (interviews, asking questions, dealing with truculent or awkward people, and so on) cannot yet be done by machines, where highly structured, machine-readable information exists, much of the writing of the news is ripe for automation.

For the past 20–30 years, there has been a prevalent tendency among some academics to view a particular model of journalism and news reporting as having been "invented" within America and the United Kingdom. Rather than tracing the fairly disparate roots of journalism to the sixteenth and seventeenth centuries, authors such as Chelaby, Downing, and Williams have shown that a particular format of writing became prevalent from the nineteenth century onwards.[11] Chelaby goes furthest in this regard, explicitly calling journalism "an Anglo-American invention",[12] while Williams offers a more critical examination of the hegemony of this model, also referred to as the "professional" or "liberal" model.[13] While agreeing with Williams's disparagement of the parochialism of much academic research in the late twentieth century, which tended to fix upon this Anglo-American model as self-evidently correct, Chelaby's observed that the "professionalisation" of journalism in the late nineteenth century had important contributions to make to a notion of the algorithm of news. Most notable was the refusal of a new generation of journalists to engage in political processes (which was very different from the careers of early writers a century or more before), which, in turn, led to an emphasis upon objectivity and impartiality in the public sphere, that the task of the journalist was to report the news and no more.[14] So pervasive is this notion that journalism *is* news – and thus there is a right way and a wrong way to be a journalist – that Hamilton and Tworek have recently produced an extremely useful analysis of the Anglo-American model, drawing upon epigenetics to argue that a better way of thinking of journalism is as a "coating" on the DNA of news: "The types of news and the conventions for providing news, the chemical or protein packaging, have been in flux, changing depending on environmental factors and coated by past experience."[15] As such, rather than considering the Anglo-American model as something essential to the nature of journalism, it should instead be seen as the product of a particular set of historical circumstances. For a number of reasons, I am more sanguine than some commentators about the intervention of automated journalism: while it most definitely does represent a threat to the fate of a number of writers who were involved in particular aspects of producing the news (and whose jobs were under threat for a variety of reasons prior to the rise of automated journalism), nonetheless that kind of objective, fact-reporting news does not by any means represent *all* journalism and that is to leave aside how such facts are collected in the first place. This is not to downplay the difficulties of the current transition: I feel huge sympathies for many journalists who face increased competition from software, but also believe that software is simply incapable, for the foreseeable future, of achieving many of the tasks required of human writers. Automation works where data are supplied in a structured format and an algorithm can be applied – and this does not apply to the vast majority of writing. At the same time, a shift from the Anglo-American model does not mean an acceptance of "anything goes" in its place: as we have seen in the previous chapter, it is precisely the *laissez-faire* attitude of the new tech media companies that has resulted in some of the most egregious errors taking place in reporting around the world. Automated journalism, however, is not a threat to journalism *per se*.

The most extensive survey of automated journalism at the time of writing is Andreas Graefe's *Guide to Automated Journalism* for the Tow Center for Digital Journalism at the Colombia University School of Journalism. Graefe considers the various means by which the use of algorithms to gather news from highly structured sources offers an ability to produce copy more quickly and with fewer errors than human journalists, while also noting how it fuels those same journalists' anxieties about their own futures. Some of the latter issues are returned to by Carlson, who sees in the example of the company Narrative Science a competition to automate most if not all news content against journalists' definitions of their own labour: very simply, software can produce a much greater number of stories, but only when the news is defined within a strictly limited compositional form.[16] Carlson runs through a series of headlines from a variety of publications in 2014 to 2015, such as "The Robot Journalist: Heralding an Apocalypse for the News Industry?" (*Guardian*) and "Can Robots Run the News?" (*Mashable*)[17] – demonstrating that, for the next few years at least, human writers are safe as a much better source of clickbait titles than the software they claim will replace them. What is important to Carlson, however, is that many of these stories are *narratives*, speculative accounts of the possible future of the news industry, and very far from the kind of stories that software is capable of producing at present. Also touched upon, but largely nascent in Carlson's article, is the fact that underlying anxiety is very much driven by the collapse of the "traditional" model of funding media production – advertising – that we have considered previously. Automation is set to replace certain human tasks as it has been doing on a regular basis since at least the beginning of the industrial revolution: the cause of anxiety is whether there are enough complementary industries and activities to soak up an excess of human labour.

Carlson's article is thoughtful in dealing with the rhetoric of automation rather than many of its actual practices, although the example of Narrative Science draws attention to one recurring factor: the move to niche audiences. While the tendency from the nineteenth century has been to engage with mass audiences, the shift from print and broadcast to digital media means that although any one report may receive few hits, the ability to produce such reports in quantity leads to increased web traffic in aggregate.[18] Cohen notes the tendency to refer to such output as "pink slime journalism", after the practice in fast-food restaurants of passing off meat byproducts – "pink slime" – as the real thing.[19] Cohen's own case study is of a failure – a media company called Journatic which floundered when it was revealed that it was using fake bylines against its automated content for "journalists" in the Philippines – but her observation that it "serves as an important harbinger for the future of journalism" is a significant one, even if it really refers to the fast-food, algorithmic news end of journalism.[20] She cites Bill Ryan's argument that cultural work such as journalism had represented the limits of the rationalisation of labour because such practices result in a degradation of the quality of the content when separated by the writer, although Ryan himself had also demonstrated the very means by which professionalisation of the cultural industries themselves could lead to such a very degradation, by enabling professional editors to rewrite contributions and add their own byline.[21] The author's intrinsic link to their copy has often been a tenuous one in the field of journalism, and there have always been exceptions to the moral rights of authors, when reporting on current events, for example. That ability to anonymise and rewrite copy has already, as Cohen observes with reference to Ross, seen a "fast-food revolution in content" in the first years of the twenty-first century.[22]

Authors such as Carlson and Cohen present a rather pessimistic view of the future of journalism in the time of automation. The fast-food revolution in content is certainly with us, but then it always has been, just not in such easily accessible quantities. The yellow press, muckraking journalism, sensationalism – such terms were not invented in the digital age, and humans have always proved themselves capable of producing content that makes readers salivate at the mouths while leaving their minds empty. Indeed, it would be tempting to argue that in the field of automated journalism at least if not automated gatekeeping (which, as we have seen in the last chapter, is currently too easily gamed), it is too labour-intensive to create the data required to feed robot writers. Only a small proportion of news types can currently be automated, but in those areas, it could be that a reliance on algorithmic journalism converting data into narratives without spin could provide a welcome return to more authoritative material. Even then, editors have an important role to play: one of the fundamental ethical questions of automated journalism – the decision as whether or not to reveal the full byline of software-generated stories (which had led to the decline of Journatic) – is a question of human judgement. As Montal and Reich point out, disclosure transparency – who wrote the story – and algorithmic transparency –the processes and data sources that feed into such content – lie in the hands of media organisations to disclose or not.[23] In the short term, companies have been tempted to be opaque because of the perceived disquiet on the part of their audiences, but such a strategy, as the example of Journatic demonstrated, can lead to disastrous consequences in the longer term. As such, Montal and Reich are correct to identify what they call the *occupational* threats offered by automated journalism, but other elements are not so clearly negative.

The Tow Center report by Graefe attempts to map out as comprehensively as possible the ways in which automated journalism could affect the next generation of content production by considering the following areas:

- **Market phase**: The arrival and deployment of automated journalism, in particular by Associated Press, which indicates that it will remain a factor in content provision for the foreseeable future.
- **Conditions and drivers:** The circumstances that enable automated journalism, in particular with regard to the requirement for structured data.

- **Potential**: This especially relates to the ability of software to generate significant amounts of content and on demand.
- **Limitations**: Algorithms cannot query the data that are provided, and at present the writing capabilities of software are limited although likely to improve considerably over the next decade.[24]

In addition, the Tow Center report considers the implications for journalists – especially with regard to employment, what Montal and Reich and other commentators have outlined as the occupational risk – but also the possible benefits that could come through the automation of routine tasks. Interestingly, while Montal and Reich considered algorithmic transparency as an essential moral question for organisations, Graefe's own research did not indicate whether there was a significant demand for such transparency on the part of consumers,[25] although that research was conducted prior to the 2016 Presidential election and the subsequent raising of public awareness with regard to fake news. It is possible, however, that although consumers are – as Graefe observes – less likely to enjoy reading automatically generated content, they may still believe it more credible if it is labelled as such. Transparency does become crucial for organisations when errors emerge, but the bigger questions – largely unanswered by Graefe – revolve around the role of journalism as a watchdog of the state if it becomes increasingly automated.

With regard to the drivers and conditions for the increase of automation within the industry, Dörr in an article published in the same year as Graefe's report highlights the reasons for publishers' keen interest: the struggle for profitability, market share, and readers.[26] As with so many other areas, the primary driver for increased automation is to cut costs, but the relations between journalism and technology have always been close and, as we shall see, I believe that automation offers potential advantages to journalists as well as news organisations. In any case, the limitations of algorithms should not be neglected, especially with regard to their requirements for highly structured data to be effective. We have already seen that a search over a period of a year for the phrase "This story was generated by Automated Insights" returned just under 90,000 stories: in the same period, there were more than 29 *million* stories and articles referencing Trump, none of which appeared to have been written by an algorithm. In the field of journalism, at least, Donald Trump has kept his promise to bring back jobs to American workers.

Machine Learning and Language

A common refrain as Trump's presidency began has been to comment on how irregular the White House's operations were under his tenure. Francine Prose, writing for *The Guardian*, criticised his activities under the headline "Nothing about the Trump presidency is normal",[27] while Walter Shapiro observed wryly: "Never Normal Is the New Normal at the White House".[28] The unexpected behaviour on the President's part means that any attempt to provide a form of regular news algorithm is doomed to failure. This is not to say that there are not generic codes and patterns that have emerged in terms of reporting the White House, for example the almost religious close reading that has taken place whenever Trump tweets. Nonetheless, without even thinking of artificial automation of journalism, if the task of human-driven news algorithms is to – in the famous words of Gaye Tuchman – "routinize the unexpected",[29] then the activities of the 45th President have made that a much more difficult procedure. Writing in 1973, Tuchman's insight was that journalists were expected to give accounts of a wide range of unexpected activities on a routine basis, and that the two important elements of this activity revolved around how they identified such events as newsworthy and how the rituals and routines of their workplace enabled them to produce their reports.[30] Drawing upon well-recognised categories such as "hard" and "soft", as well as "spot" and "developing", news, Tuchman demonstrated a basic formal structure by means of which organisations could schedule non-timely (usually "soft" news) and prescheduled events such as debates and press conferences. This semi-structural approach to the production of news had been taken a stage further in Galtung's and Ruge's 1965 paper on the structure of foreign news,[31] which produced a famous list for classifying the newsworthiness of events that is much debated and even frequently used today, for example Harcup and O'Neill[32] and Joye, Henrich, and Woehlert.[33] Such structuralist and organisational approaches to the production and dissemination of the news by people remain important, as when Moon and Hadley discuss the routinisation of Twitter as a source for gathering stories[34] or Hartley demonstrates how Danish breaking news is regularly categorised.[35] While the responses of Trump may be less easily predictable than former presidents, even to the extent that White House press briefings have taken a very different form since his inauguration in 2017, nonetheless there remains a press corps attached to the White House, with prescheduled events occurring even if it is not always clear what will be said or done in advance. The unpredictability of Trump has been extremely good in terms of injecting brio into North American journalism (and, indeed, for that in many other places around the world), but that unpredictability is also made possible because so much of what happens still takes place in the orbit of Washington.

Overall, it seems unlikely that political reporting in the United States is likely to be automated any time soon. Indeed, as we shall see in the next chapter, the fact that editorialising in relation to the President rather than simply reporting his actions has become the new norm makes such automation extremely difficult if not impossible. The kinds of highly structured news stories considered previously in this chapter simply lack the format of data required to convert them into copy, leaving aside Trump's propensity for distorting facts to suit his current agenda or mood. Recognising, therefore, the important limitations of machine learning, it is helpful to consider some of the factors that have contributed to the current state of automated journalism, employing algorithms as a "finite series of precisely described rules or processes to solve a problem".[36]

The idea of teaching computers to understand human language emerged as a field in the 1950s as part of machine translation, as when IBM and Georgetown University demonstrated a computer that could translate Russian sentences into English in 1954. Although the researchers believed that the problem of machine translation would be solved in a few years, their own device was extremely limited, with a lexicon of only 250 words and a set of six grammatical rules.[37] The demand for translation, however, drove research throughout the 1970s and into the 1990s, with statistical data analysis providing an early methodology for formalising the rules of language so that they were machine-readable and thus, potentially, capable of generating text. An early example of such machine-generated information was weather forecasting in the 1990s, with a Forecast Generator (FOG) producing routine text forecasts from weather maps.[38] Such developments then moved into sports,[39] medical data,[40] and simple forms of storytelling.[41] Dörr offers a useful summary of recent developments in Natural Language Generation (NLG), a subset of Natural Language Processing (NLP), defined by Reiter and Dale as the ability of computer systems to automatically produce human (natural) language from computational information.[42] The contribution of NLG to algorithmic journalism has the potential, as has already been noted in this chapter, to change greatly the role of journalists – but only in restricted areas. The role of algorithmic journalism, as considered by Dörr, follows what he refers to as an input-throughput-output (ITO) model, taken from Latzer *et al*, in which electronic data are taken from private or public databases (input), organised into relevant semantic structures (throughput), and then published to a platform (output): the technology behind NLG is what enables algorithmic journalism to take place, and obviously depended on considerable advances in the ability of machines to read such data in the first instance.[43]

Significant advances appeared to be in place when, in 2015, stories surfaced that Google had taught an AI, DeepMind, to read. The parent company of DeepMind had been founded in London in 2010 and was acquired by Google in 2014, having built a neural network that could be taught to perform cognitive actions such as learning to play games or to read text. In contrast to IBM's Deep Blue and Watson, which were developed to advance one clearly defined function (applying advanced natural language functioning processes in the case of Watson), DeepMind claimed that its system was not pre-programmed but could learn from experience, and it was put to the test against computer games – for example, quickly mastering the video game *Breakout* and playing it more efficiently than any human could, and also defeating a human professional Go player in 2015. Unlike chess, which had demonstrated itself capable of exercising iterative heuristics – being able to process an increasing number of moves ahead – Go was believed not to be amenable to such a process. With regard to reading, however, the best technique turned out to be feeding huge data sets of information to the algorithm, with experts at DeepMind feeding large quantities of *Daily Mail* and CNN articles to learn to read. To demonstrate that comprehension was possible, Karl Moritz Hermann and a team of engineers working at Google set up the system to allow it to extract bullet points from text without simply repeating sentences within the data set.[44]

With regard to such machine comprehension, in early 2018, teams from Microsoft and Alibaba claimed independently that they had created AIs that could match human performance on the Stanford Question Answering Dataset (SQuAD). SQuAD, currently at iteration 2.0, comprises 150,000 questions which require the reader to comprehend a corresponding passage of text before they can be answered. To make the task more difficult, 50,000 of those questions are deliberately unanswerable to ensure that human and machine readers are clear about what they don't know as well as what they do. Microsoft, in a blog post in January 2018, announced that it had achieved a SQuAD score of 82.6 per cent (comparable to 82.3 per cent for humans) and that it was jointly tied with Alibaba.[45] This post led to a slew of headlines about machines replacing humans, with *Newsweek* estimating "millions of jobs at risk",[46] but more critical commentators noted that the SQuAD scoring system relied on Mechanical Turk workers paid $9 an hour to answer questions, who would probably be less motivated to find correct answers than machine systems,[47] and that while the data set looks challenging (with questions on Reformation theology or the concept of civil disobedience), in practice answers rely not on any knowledge of the subject but instead being able to match patterns. For example, as James Vincent remarked in *The Verge*, while a question such as "Whose authority does Luther's theology oppose?" may seem tough, the fact that a reading passage includes the sentence "[Luther's] theology challenged the authority and office of the Pope" makes it clear that this entire test operates around a restricted notion of comprehension.[48] As an expert in NLP, Yoav Goldberg, told Vincent, the test was designed as "a benchmark for machine learning methods", not as for comparisons to human readers. Researchers believed in the 1950s that automated translation was just around the corner: today, we can see some very effective results from machine translation, but NLP and NLG generally work better within clearly defined parameters rather than entirely unsupervised on completely open texts. Likewise, there have been considerable advances in automated or algorithmic journalism, in the past half-decade – but the successes are clearest when dealing with story generation in limited frameworks. Dörr discusses a number of ways in which automated journalism is currently being integrated into media operations, remarking that such companies are still "evaluating whether products match the standards and quality of their brand and how users and journalists react".[49] The most extensive example of such an experiment is the one being conducted by Associated Press and Automated Insights.

AP and Ai

The beginnings of automated journalism were modest. In 2007, Robbie Allen, an engineer at the networking hardware and software company Cisco, set up an online sports network called StatSheet. As he later remarked in a post for Automated Insights, Allen was a fan of basketball and started the company to keep track of – and publish – information on basketball teams.[50] As well as providing detailed statistics for NCAA basketball, StatSheet began serving data reports for college football, NASCAR racing, and the NBA basketball league, as well as providing access to its visualisation tools so that sports enthusiasts could generate such things as historical and real-time reports of such things as injury times or scores. Since the 1990s, most sports had begun to accumulate digital data on events – building on analytics that, in sports such as football, dated back to the 1950s and 1960s; a decade later, such data were becoming significant enough to provide big data analysis, as in the work of Coleman, Bothner, Kim, and Smith, and Waguespack and Salomon.[51] An earlier, famous example of the power of data to revolutionise a sport had been set out by Michael Lewis in his book *Moneyball*, which detailed how the Oakland A team made use of information to transform their position in the baseball league. The ability to identify top players in American football games or track the statistical likelihood of superior performance during Olympic events drew upon highly structured data that could also be output to graphs, charts, and reports as StatSheet did – all without any human intervention. Once templates were coded and set up, software drew information from the huge tranches of data being made available online and published results that were drawn upon heavily by companies such as Yahoo! and ESPN. While sports provided an accessible market for data-driven publishing, in 2011 StatSheets changed its name to Automated Insights, securing $4 million in new funding to help it to specialise in "realtime content automation" in areas such as real estate, finance, and weather reporting.[52]

As with its initial venture into sports automation, at this stage, Automated Insights (Ai) was concentrating on areas where there was a demand for information to be provided in a way that could be easily digested by people, but where there were not enough writers available to produce content. From November 2010 to September 2011 when it changed its name, StatSheets had generated over 100,000 articles with only a staff of 12; in 2013, that number would rise to 300 million pieces of content, greater than the combined output of all media companies according to Lance Ulanoff.[53] By this time, Ai had refined its software as Wordsmith, creating a platform-based service that could be licenced to other companies, using Amazon Web Services to draw upon thousands of servers when required to generate millions of stories in a short space of time. In an interview with Ulanoff, Allen observed that the task of the human team at Ai was to improve sentence and paragraph structure to ensure that content did not sound automated. This, in turn, influenced how stories were published with bylines: while some clients were very clear in terms of the source for content, others did not wish readers to know that stories were produced by Wordsmith.

With its NLG tools having been refined enough to begin offering its resources to third parties, Ai signed a deal with Associated Press in 2014 to begin automating corporate finance stories. In this, it was following the lead made by Narrative Science which provided its Quill software to *Forbes* in order to summarise earning reports. In an interview with *Forbes* in 2015, co-founder of Narrative Science, Kris Hammond, stood by his 2012 claim that the company's software would write Pulitzer-prize-winning journalism within five years:[54] 2017 came and went without any such event, thus proving that the claim was clearly nonsense. Yet in many respects, a more fundamental shift was taking place. The title of the article in which Hammond's interview appeared asked a simple question: "Can big data algorithms tell better stories than humans?" In the period since media organisations such as *Forbes* and AP have started using such algorithms, the answer is yes – if by this are meant very restricted circumstances and conditions to measure such success. Indeed, in a study conducted by Clerwall in 2014, readers of a number of stories generated by software or human journalists often responded that although they found the computer-generated stories more boring and descriptive, they also considered them more objective.[55] The software of companies such as Narrative Science and Automated Insights has produced both many more stories than could be handled by human journalists and the ones which handle only the facts in a fashion that seems to follow the Anglo-American model to the absolute letter. In 2015, Ai and AP released a joint press statement in which they described how Wordsmith had helped them produce 4,400 quarterly reports in the space of one year, a twelve-fold increase over manual efforts. As has been suggested before, there would be little difference between the reports produced by an algorithm and a person because Wordsmith was programmed to follow the AP style guide as closely as possible. Such reporting also had at least one other noticeable effect: prior to adopting Wordsmith, AP tended to concentrate its reporting on the top 300 firms trading on the American and world stock exchanges, but after using Ai's software, that number increased to some 4,500 firms. A study by Blankespoor, deHaan, and Zhu discovered that there was a correlation between this increased reporting and the volume of trade taking place as more and more readers started to take interest in previously neglected companies.[56]

The benefits to Associated Press from their use of Wordsmith were very clear as well: the amount of time required to analyse quarterly reports, as well as restricting the number of stories that could be published, tied up journalists who would otherwise be engaging in other activities. Within two years, AP was reporting that 20 per cent of their time had been freed up from such reports:[57] more significantly, considering the twelvefold increase in reporting covered by AP, rather than simply replacing journalists with software, they appear to have been used to fine-tune the algorithm and templates as data are used to generate copy. In a report from early 2018, Laura Pressman from Ai observed that a great deal of work had been involved in setting up Wordsmith to fit into both AP's workflows and to be able to use data from Zacks Investment Research, which provided Associated Press with the raw information it required for its stories.[58] Both AP and Ai were keen, at least in the first years of the project, to emphasise that no job losses followed this move into automated journalism.

Wordsmith operates according to rule-based instructions that operate on highly structured data that can branch into several choices of sentence and paragraph structure depending on the format of the input. Thus, for example, information from a three-month period (common for quarterly reports) will generate sentences remarking on upward or downward trends in share prices depending on whether percentage changes are greater than or lesser than zero. As the system was being set up with AP, its journalists constantly monitored output for a period of two months, making suggestions to improve sentences to improve the quality of auto-summaries. As Wordsmith is now more widely available, it is possible to engage with the software as a service online at wordsmith.automatedinsights.com. When automating stories, the workflow breaks down into the following categories:

- The source of data that will be used: if this is not being generated in-house by researchers or data scientists, but instead pulled from a variety of third-party sources or via APIs, then it is important to have a developer who can ensure that such data are formatted and presented consistently for Wordsmith to work with.
- Those responsible for preparing the template: in this instance, it is recommended that the writer(s) of a template are familiar with the data being used so that they can understand how it will be employed to create particular narratives.
- Those responsible for publishing the narrative: typically, there will be a developer responsible for working with the Wordsmith API and the organisation's website.

As with all kinds of data projects, cleaning and preparing the data is an immensely important activity, but once organised, it is the selection and use of templates that allows throughput, the transformation of those data into some form of narrative. The primary elements of such through-put via templates are the use of branches – as indicated previously with a simple example dealing with increasing or decreasing share prices – and synonyms, allowing variations on similar structures when converting data into stories. After a data structure has been defined, templates are constructed using Boolean true/false formulas (which, if commonly employed, can be further converted into templates nestled into other branching templates).

Between 2007 and 2013, automated or robot journalism had made huge developments, but the parameters of such work were extremely limited: while services such as Automated Insights and Narrative Science were clearly capable of producing a greater number of pieces of content than the combined workforce of media organisations, many of these were very simple presentations of data such as charts or league tables and even when there were narrative stories, these were confined to extremely clearly defined, highly structured categories such as sport and finance where data could be presented in a non-messy format. More surprising, however, was an announcement in late 2017 that automated journalism could be used to write local news. In December 2017, AP announced that it was setting up a trial of a publishing service in the UK and Ireland called RADAR (Reporters and Data and Robots) in conjunction with Urbs Media and 14 local publishing groups (including Johnston Press, Newsquest, and Trinity Mirror), having made its first editorial hires and launched a pilot in November.[59] The service, launched with investment from the €150 million Google's Digital News Initiative and tested out hyperlocal variants of stories focussing on trends in birth registrations, cancelled operations, a breakdown of social mobility and life chances for disadvantaged children, and localised traffic data. These stories, published by 20 titles, were the first automated local news stories to be published by established brands in the world, and all drew heavily on data drawn from the Office of National Statistics, the NHS, the Social Mobility Commission, and Department of Transport. One such story, by Tom Matthews and Ralph Blackburn, identified as a "Radar Data Reporter", was published as follows in the *Croydon Advertiser* on 4 December, 2017:

Seven potentially life-saving operations were cancelled in Croydon in October

Latest health data have revealed that the body which runs Croydon's hospitals was one of 40 trusts in England to cancel at least one important procedure.

Croydon Health Services NHS Trust cancelled seven urgent and potentially life-saving operations in October, the latest health data have
revealed.

It was one of only 40 hospital trusts in England to cancel at least one important procedure in October, according to statistics from the NHS.
More than two-thirds of the country's trusts did not rearrange a
single urgent operation over the same time period.

Such operations can include swift action needed to save patients' lives,
limbs, and organs.

In the last 12 months, the trust, which runs Croydon University Hospital, has stopped 69 key surgeries.

And one patient has had an operation cancelled twice in the space of just
four weeks, over the past year. Cancellations can be due to shortages
of beds or staff as well as surgeries running over time, or adminis-
trative errors.

The trust cancelled less surgeries this year than in the same month in
2016, when 13 were stopped.

The figures may spark concern given the winter months are fast approaching, when more pressure is expected to be placed on NHS
services.

Between last December, January, and February 14, urgent operations
were cancelled.

The chief executive of NHS England Simon Stevens recently warned min-
isters that waiting times would continue to rise unless more money
was put into the health service, after the chancellor Philip Hammond promised £350 million in the Budget to help this winter.[60]

The story is quoted in full to show how, in many respects, it looks extremely similar to many other types of article carried by hundreds of
publications around the country each day. The absence of direct quotation is probably the only telling feature that this story is mostly automatically generated, drawing attention to the fact that this is one area
where such journalism will struggle for some time to come. Compare
this copy to the following extract published only a few days earlier in
the *Shropshire Star*:

Shropshire's hospitals "full": Appointments cancelled under growing pressure

Shropshire's two main hospitals have been forced to cancel elective day
cases and are using extra capacity to cope with high demand, health
bosses have revealed.

Shrewsbury and Telford Hospital NHS Trust (SaTH), which runs Royal
Shrewsbury Hospital and Telford's Princess Royal Hospital, said it
had been very busy this week but bosses were taking steps to ensure
patients received the best possible care.

Monday was the second busiest day of 2017 for its emergency departmentments, with 426 people coming through the doors.

On Tuesday, that figure rose to almost 800 people in two days.

A total of 18 elective day cases have also been cancelled since Monday.

Debbie Kadum, chief operating officer at the trust, said: "This has meant that we have had to implement our 'hospital full' protocol, using extra capacity where available to ensure our emergency departments can continue to function."

"We have also, unfortunately, had to cancel some elective day cases since the beginning of the week, to accommodate medical patients and we would like to apologise to anybody who has been affected while we deal with this period of extraordinary demand on our services."

"This is just one example of why we would like to separate our planned and emergency care, to ensure that we can best treat as many people as possible at times of high demand."

"During this busy time, we would again ask people to please think carefully about whether alternative local services, which can avoid what can be a lengthy and stressful visit to hospital, might be more appropriate."

"I would again like to thank our incredible staff for all of their hard work this week."[61]

This story, published on November 23, begins in a very similar format to the *Croydon Advertiser* piece, with an emphasis on facts and figures related in the standard, impersonal style common to much reporting, but half of the story is given over to direct quotations from the CEO of the hospital trust, providing an emphasis on a more personalised response. In the immediate future, it is precisely the inability of software to interview respondents that marks the primary difference between local reporting via robot journalism and that conducted by people, but in terms of reportage style, it is clear that the algorithm of news can be repeated very effectively by software.

Following news of the RADAR experiment, stories appeared with headlines such as "Robots can save local journalism", and "Would you care if this feature had been written by a robot?"[62] Yet, it remains the case that algorithmic journalism, while capable of prodigious output, remains extremely limited in terms of its capabilities. At present, the number of stories bearing tag lines such as "Radar data reporter" remains extremely small as publishers experiment with formats that can build upon widely available – and reliable – data but also require templates that go beyond sports statistics or quarterly financial reports. What is more, the limited stories that appear also tend to be mediated strongly by editorial staff working with RADAR. As Alison Kanski pointed out in a story for *PR Week* as the trial was being launched, the stories were typically being edited by journalists before being syndicated and were very much limited to open government data sets. Nonetheless, as she also observed, "for those communities that have lost these local reports on crime or unemployment when their local paper shut down, services such as RADAR can help fill the gap."[63] Algorithmic journalism as yet lacks the flexibility to work across a vast range of topics that cannot automatically be structured to clearly defined templates, but in many places as news is gutted by a rapidly changing and often hostile commercial environment, the choice is increasingly not between robot journalists and human journalists, but between robot journalists and no journalists at all.

Augmented Journalism

As has previously been noted, in 2013, automated software produced 300 million pieces of content, more than all legacy media companies combined according to Ulanoff. More recent specific figures outside of clients such as Associated Press, who are very public about both which articles are produced by software and how many are published at any time, are more difficult to ascertain; many other organisations that use Wordsmith are less forthcoming about the fact that their content is produced by an algorithm. Assuming that clients include realtors and sports sites as well as Amazon, Ai's more recent claim that it has "written billions of articles" may be true. With such a vast quantity of content being produced algorithmically and set to move into the field of local reporting, it would seem that algorithmic journalism is not the future but has already arrived. Yet before rushing to consider a future dominated by robot reporters, a few other factors should be borne in mind before we consign people to the dustbin of journalism. One of those factors is another piece of electronic communication in which, in terms of quantity alone, machines appear to reign supreme: email.

According to the research group Radicati, global email traffic at the beginning of 2018 was estimated at 281.1 billion emails per day being sent between over 3.8 billion accounts, and predicted to rise to more than 333 billion messages per day by 2022.[64] There are no reliable statistics for the quantity of daily messages which are spam but, according to Statista, in March 2018, more than 48 per cent of emails were spam.[65] As a great deal of spam is automatically generated by spambots – a very crude version of the algorithmic content generation employed by Wordsmith – it would not be unreasonable to presume that software is producing billions of messages daily, the vast majority of which is never read by its intended audience because it is filtered out. Automatically generated content is a significant portion of daily messages transmitted across the globe, but that does not mean that it is automatically read. The work done by Associated Press and Automated Insights is very, very far from the crudely produced content seeking to promote adult goods or fake merchandise; it is closer in part to the process patented by Philip Parker for ICON Group in 2007, which set to produce hundreds of thousands of books and reports from databases of material available in the public domain. Although not exactly the same NLG process used by Wordsmith, ICON's software-driven formatting technique is capable of writing books with titles such as *The World Market for Frozen Edible Offal of Sheep and Horses: A 2016 Global Trade Perspective* and *The 2016–2021 World Outlook for 1 MW Solar Photovoltaic Government Projects* far more quickly than any individual with a word processor.[66] Such books are unlikely to win any major prizes soon, just as algorithmic journalism – despite the bravado of Kris Hammond – is unlikely to win its robot author a Pulitzer. To consider some of the hurdles that remain, it is worth turning to a piece of data-driven journalism that *did* win that prize.

In 2017, Eric Eyre, a journalist at the *Charleston Gazette-Mail* based in Western Virginia, accepted a Pulitzer for Investigative Reporting for a series of articles written by him in 2016 that sought to expose the flood of opioids into depressed counties in the region, resulting in the highest rate of deaths by overdose in the USA.[67] His three winning stories – "Drug firms fueled 'pill mills' in rural W.Va." (May 22, 2016), "Pill rules not enforced" (December 19 2016), and "780M pills, 1,728 deaths" (December 18 2016) – drew heavily on public health statistics, as is clear from the opening paragraphs to the December 18 story:

780M pills, 1,728 deaths

Follow the pills and you'll find the overdose deaths.

The trail of painkillers leads to West Virginia's southern coalfields, to places like Kermit, population 392. There, out-of-state drug companies shipped nearly 9 million highly addictive — and potentially lethal — hydrocodone pills over two years to a single pharmacy in the Mingo County town.

Rural and poor, Mingo County has the fourth-highest prescription opioid death rate of any county in the United States.

The trail also weaves through Wyoming County, where shipments of OxyContin have doubled, and the county's overdose death rate leads the nation. One mom-and-pop pharmacy in Oceana received 600 times as many oxycodone pills as the Rite Aid drugstore just eight blocks away.

In six years, drug wholesalers showered the state with 780 million hydrocodone and oxycodone pills, while 1,728 West Virginians fatally overdosed on those two painkillers, a Sunday Gazette-Mail investigation found.

The unfettered shipments amount to 433 pain pills for every man, woman, and child in West Virginia.[68]

Stephen Hawking once famously observed in *A Brief History of Time* that "each equation I included in the book would halve the sales", and on the surface of it Eyre's news story would seem daunting to most readers. While the equation (780 million pills equal 1,728 deaths) is implicit rather than explicit, the use of statistics and pharmaceutical terminology offers no concessions. Yet far from alienating readers, these stories were part of a transformative narrative within Americans that influenced the government and began a far-reaching debate into an epidemic responsible for a rising number of deaths. As with stories produced by Ai, Eyre was reliant on data for his articles, but at that point, the similarities between the two methods of journalism cease.

Joseph Burns in a piece for the Association of Health Care Journalists noted that the power of Eyre's work came, at least in part, from "hard data" and "big numbers", providing strong evidence as to the scale of the flood of opiates into depressed West Virginia counties.[69] Such information was important: while facts themselves do not automatically constitute truth, as we have noted in the previous chapter, any interpretation of events that ignores or refutes such facts can never aspire to be a truthful interpretation. Much of the authoritative nature of Eyre's journalism came from his careful use of a range of hard data. Yet, as he made clear in an interview with Arka Gupta, simply collecting that information reveals a problem for any form of investigative journalism that many reporters will recognise immediately: the unwillingness of those who hold data to make it public. The investigation actually began with a tip off in 2013 that the state Attorney General was involved in a lawsuit against drug wholesalers, the details of which (along with another case in 2016) were sealed at the request of both the companies and the Attorney General. Intervening in the latter case, Eyre and the *Charleston Gazette-Mail* argued that the information should be made publicly available, which, in turn, led him to file a number of freedom of information access requests to the office of the Attorney General in order to release information from the Drug Enforcement Agency.[70] To make matters more complicated, as Eyre told Linda Wertheimer, the *Gazette-Mail* was a small newspaper with a circulation of some 40,000 copies, meaning that he had to put the story aside from time to time to work on the rest of his day job.[71] While robot journalists can churn out millions of articles that will effortlessly convert statistics into quarterly reports, there are none in operation yet that can go to a court of law to ensure that data are made publicly available in the first place.

Algorithmic journalism can only deal with information that is made available (and then only if it has been structured in a machine-readable format, rather than countless letters, notes, and recordings), which remains a fundamental problem for software when it comes to finding stories. In terms of the raw numbers game, robots win every time – within a very limited field of operations. Yet, what is also outstanding about

Eyre's story is his prose style: as was made clear earlier in this chapter, there is a brand of Anglo-American reporting that has effectively created a "news algorithm", and indeed even in the comparison of hospital cancellations produced by an algorithm and a person in the previous section, there is frequently little difference in the style of writing. However, a virtue of a series of rules – which Eyre frequently abides by to provide his story with greater authority – is that these can then be broken for the greatest effect. This, indeed, is what Eyre does in the first sentence of his story: rather than providing the who, why, what, where, when, and how of his data, he employs a narrative hook used by a great many writers – though more brutally and more effectively than most, emphasising the moral consequences and judgements of the story he will tell. In lesser hands, this would be editorialising, but Eyre's strength is then to hold those judgements in reserve, to allow his data to inform the reader.

As the entire article unfolds, Eyre interweaves other elements that are currently impossible for software to provide: interviews with authorities and those on the receiving end of prescription opioids. There is no algorithm at present that has demonstrated itself remotely capable of sourcing quotations and stories from interviewees, but there are also fundamental problems with language processing that create extremely high barriers for the extension of algorithmic journalism beyond certain limited fields. In 2002, Robert Cameron described the four concepts of natural and computer languages as syntax, semantics, pragmatics, and metalanguage, and while many developments have forged ahead in the past 15 years with regard to semantics and syntax (what words mean and how they are arranged together into meaningful sentences), dealing with pragmatics (the context of messages) has often proved more difficult. While textbooks such as *Programming Language Pragmatics* address in great detail the issues surrounding the interpretation of syntax trees as a basis for understanding the contexts of language, such things as creating variables for environmental references assume that these can be easily quantified.[72] When it comes to programming Alexa or Siri to understand that "play next" refers to a song on your Spotify list, or that "turn off the lights" can be set to a particular circuit of bulbs in the living room, algorithms are improving all the time. Creating the emotional and intellectual variables that will understand the anger, pain, humiliation, and fear of dealing with opioid addiction – or the recalcitrance, evasion, and lies of those who wish to cover their tracks – like many things appears to be currently beyond the capabilities of NLP.

This is not to make a glibly pro-humanist and anti-software statement, nor is it to assert that emotional intelligence (or at least aspects of it) can never be programmed. After all, in many respects, it is precisely his education at Loyal University of New Orleans and his experience on the *Gazette-Mail* that "programmed" Eric Eyre to be able to spot a story and craft it into such a compelling series of articles. Yet as was noted in the first chapter of this book, general artificial intelligence remains a grail that is often the stuff of legend rather than reality. As such, the issue of algorithmic journalism, of robots versus humans, is again much more accurately considered a topic of *automation* rather than real AI. In the field of journalism and reporting, there are many types of cognitive work that are repetitive and iterative, that need to be presented in a consistent way according to clear criteria and source of data, the processes of which can be routinely and effectively described by algorithms. In the fields of sports and financial reporting, particularly for minor sports or companies where there simply are not enough – and have never been enough – human journalists to cover those activities, and where information is clearly structured and readily available, people will not be able to compete against software in domains where people are looking for information, for data, provided in a clear narrative form. And yet, as with the example of Eric Eyre but also the countless journalists reporting on Donald Trump, fundamentals such as determining what the data actually are and then collating them from multiple, often unreliable, sources into something that is coherent appear to be a task that, for the foreseeable future, is beyond the capacity of machines.

Not that Eyre's strengths as a reporter have been an unmixed blessing to the *Charleston Gazette-Mail*: in 2015, two years before receiving his Pulitzer, he along with other journalists had to reapply for his job when the *Gazette* and the *Daily Mail* merged, while in 2018 the company that owned the newspaper filed for bankruptcy, eventually selling the title to HD Media in March. As with so many other areas, the *Gazette-Mail* was struggling to compete in an environment where both sales and advertising revenues were declining rapidly. The role of technology, then, is very often not a question of capabilities of human versus algorithmic journalists, but rather one of costs and finances. Technical innovation is frequently driven by such constraints, and the impetus for algorithmic journalism is frequently to drive down costs by replacing peoples' salaries with software subscriptions. In the analytics-driven world of contemporary journalism, traffic is all and some of the wiser producers such as AP have begun to invest in the "long tail" of audiences, a mass production of hundreds of thousands of stories that will only capture a small number of readers each but which aggregate into significant numbers overall. Within such a difficult environment, however, there are significant challenges for extending automated journalism. Associated Press and other organisations will certainly begin to use algorithmically generated content for health, crime, some social reporting, and other elements where clear data are publicly available, but any form of investigative journalism appears beyond the abilities of even the best software for the foreseeable future. Yet, to repeat, this is not some simplistic rendition of human versus machine: in those areas where algorithms are not capable of generating content, what we more often see is *augmented* journalism.

In using this phrase, I am not particularly referring to augmented reality journalism, a potentially interesting medium but one which, frankly, still remains in a very embryonic stage at the time of writing. This is instead the use of things such as big data and technologies to make journalism more effective and more efficient – a practice which is as old as the deployment of the printing press for seventeenth-century news-sheets. For Eric Eyre, the ability to analyse and track data is what helped him write his story, organising the information that he gathered via very human perseverance. In his 2012 analysis of machine-written news, van Dalen observed that journalists did not simply reject automated assistance, but instead – with regard to algorithmic sports stories – began to re-evaluate their own core skills and consider ways in which they could make their content "more human", with a greater emphasis on interviews, commentary, and context than pure data.[73] Similarly, Thurman, Dörr, and Kunert observe that while journalists are sceptical (rightly in my opinion) about the ability of robot journalists to source news stories, the rise of algorithmic journalism will also expand the depth, breadth, and immediacy of information for them to work with on their own stories.[74]

In less than a decade, algorithmic journalism has become a fixed element of news cycles particularly in the USA and the UK. Viewed from the perspective of sheer volume, it would not be unreasonable to assume that automatically produced content is *the* future of journalism, and yet during that time, the advances made by software have largely been quantitative (more stories) than qualitative (moving into completely different forms and genres of storytelling). This is by no means a blithe assumption that such software is incapable of these developments, although the distinction referred to in Chapter 1, between what Dreyfus calls "knowing-what" (which can be codified) versus "knowing-how" (which cannot), posits a potential hard limit to what AI will be able to achieve. For the foreseeable future, algorithmic journalism will work best with information that is highly structured and in the public domain – and the effect of such information on creating narratives from the huge amounts of data which satisfy such conditions should not be underestimated. For more complex alternatives, however, the immediate changes that are taking place are a greater use of algorithms and software to help human journalists collate and understand data, what is called here augmented journalism: the reporter today must be a cyborg, perhaps, but the role of people in crafting stories remains as important as ever.

Notes

1 Jason Hall, *Nineteenth Century Verse and Technology: Machines of Meter*, London: Palgrave, 2017, p. 113.
2 Automated Insights, "Rite Aid Posts 3Q Profits", *Yahoo! Finance*, 3 January 2018, https://finance.yahoo.com/news/rite-aid-posts-3q-profit-212946446.html?guccounter=1.

3 Josh Boak, "Buffett's Berkshire Hathaway Reports a \$12B 2Q Profit", *Associated Press*, 4 August 2018, www.apnews.com/f35ca8cc056f4219 8e6d1bda2b94ab41/Buffett's-Berkshire-Hathaway-reports-a-\$12B-2Q-profit.
4 Lia-Paschalia Spyridou, Maria Matsiola, Andreas Veglis, George Kalliris, and Charalambos Dimoulas,"Journalism in a State of Flux Journalists As Agents of Technology Innovation and Emerging News Practices", *The International Communication Gazette,* 75.1(2013), pp. 76–98.
5 Mary Lynn Young, and Alfred Hermida, "From Mr. and Mrs. Outlier to Central Tendencies Computational Journalism and Crime Reporting at the Los Angeles Times", *Digital Journalism*, 3.3(2015), pp. 381–397.
6 Henrik Örnebring, and Raul Ferrer Conill, "Outsourcing Newswork" in Tamara Witschge, C. W. Anderson, and David Domingo (eds.), *The SAGE Handbook of Digital Journalism*, London: Sage, 2016, pp. 207–221.
7 Örnebring and Conill, p. 215.
8 Terry Flew, Christina Spurgeon, Anna Daniel, and Adam Swift, "The Promise of Computational Journalism", *Journalism Practice*, 6.2(2012), pp. 157–171.
9 Christopher W. Anderson, "Towards a Sociology of Computational and Algorithmic Journalism", *New Media and Society*, 15.7(2012), pp. 1005–1021.
10 Tal Montal, and Ziv Reich, "I, Robot. You, Journalist. Who Is the Author?" *Digital Journalism*, 5.7(2017), pp. 829–849, p. 831.
11 Jean K. Chelaby, *The Invention of Journalism*, London: Palgrave, 1998; John Downing, *Internationalizing Media Theory: Transitions, Power, Culture*, London: Sage, 1996; Kevin Williams, "Competing Models of Journalism? Anglo-American and European Reporting in the Information Age", *Journalistica*, 2(2006), pp. 43–65.
12 Chelaby, p. 69.
13 Williams, p. 44.
14 Chelaby, p. 132.
15 John Maxwell Hamilton, and Heidi J. S. Tworek, "The Natural History of the News: An Epigenetic Study", *Journalism*, 18.4(2017), pp. 391–407, p. 392.
16 Matt Carlson, "The Robotic Reporter", *Digital Journalism*, 3.3(2015), pp. 416–431.
17 Carlson, p. 422.
18 Carlson, p. 426.
19 Nicole Cohen, "From Pink Slips to Pink Slime: Transforming Media Labor in a Digital Age", *The Communication Review*, 18.2(2015), pp. 98–122, p. 98.
20 Cohen, p. 99.
21 Bill Ryan, *Making Capital from Culture: Corporate Form of Capitalist Cultural Production*, Berlin: Walter de Gruyter, 1992, p. 140.
22 See Andrew Ross, "In Search of the Lost Paycheck", in Trebor Scholz (ed.), *Digital Labor: The Internet as Playground and Factory*, London: Routledge, 2012, p. 14.
23 Montal and Reich, p. 831.
24 Andreas Graefe, *Guide to Automated Journalism*, New York: Tow Center for Digital Journalism, 2016, p. 10.
25 Graefe, pp. 36–37.
26 Konstantin Nicholas Dörr, "Mapping the Field of Algorithmic Journalism", *Digital Journalism*, 4.6(2016), pp. 700–722.
27 Francine Prose, "Nothing about the Trump Presidency Is Normal. Keep Remembering That", *The Guardian*, 20 July, 2017, www.theguardian.

com/commentisfree/2017/jul/20/nothing-normal-trump-presidency-remember-that.

28 Walter Shapiro, "Never Normal Is the New Normal at the White House", *Roll Call*, 7 February 2017, www.rollcall.com/news/opinion/donald-trump-walter-shapiro-never-normal.

29 Gaye Tuchman, "Making News by Doing Work: Routinizing the Unexpected", *American Journal of Sociology*, 79.1(1973), pp. 110–132.

30 Tuchman, pp. 111–112.

31 Johan Galtung, and Mari Ruge, "The Structure of Foreign News: The Presentation of the Congo, Cuba and Cyprus Crises in Four Norwegian Newspapers", *Journal of Peace Research*, 2.1(1965), pp. 64–90.

32 Tony Harcup, and Deirdre O'Neill, "What Is News? News Values Revisited (Again)", *Journalism Studies*, 18.12(2016), pp. 1470–1489.

33 Stijn Joye, Ansgard Heinrich, and Romy Woehlert, "50 Years of Galtung and Ruge: Reflections on Their Model of News Values and Its Relevance for the Study of Journalism and Communication Today", *CM: Communication and Media*, 11.36(2016), pp. 5–29.

34 Soo Jung Moon, and Patrick Hadley, "Routinizing a New Technology in the Newsroom: Twitter as a News Source", *Mainstream Media, Journal of Broadcasting & Electronic Media*, 58.2(2014), pp. 289–305.

35 Jannie Møller Hartley, "Routinizing Breaking News: Categories and Hierarchies in Danish Online Newsrooms", in David Domingo, and Chris Paterson (eds.), *Making Online News: Newsroom Ethnography in the Second Decade of Internet Journalism*, New York: Peter Lang, 2011, pp. 73–86.

36 Michael Latzer, Katharina Hollnbuchner, Natascha Just, and Florian Saurwein, "The Economics of Algorithmic Selection on the Internet", in Johannes Bauer, and Michael Latzer (eds.), *Handbook on the Economics of the Internet*, Cheltenham: Edward Elgar Publishing, 2016, pp. 395–426, p. 397.

37 W. John Hutchins, "The Georgetown-IBM Experiment Demonstrated in January 1954", www.hutchinsweb.me.uk/AMTA-2004.pdf.

38 Eli Goldberg, Norbert Dreidger, and Richard I. Kittredge, "Using Natural-Language Processing to Produce Weather Forecasts", *IEEE Expert*, 9.2(1994), pp. 45–53.

39 Jacques Robin, and Kathleen McKeown, "Empirically Designing and Evaluating a New Revision-Based Model for Summary Generation", *Artificial Intelligence*, 85.1–2(1996), pp. 135–179.

40 François Portet, Ehud Reiter, Albert Gatt, Jim Hunter, Somayajulu Sripada, Yvonne Freer, and Cindy Syjes, "Automatic Generation of Textual Summaries from Neonatal Intensive Care Data", *Artificial Intelligence*, 173.7–8(2009), pp. 789–816.

41 Charles Callaway, and James Lester, "Narrative Prose Generation," *Artificial Intelligence*, 2.139(2002), pp. 213–252.

42 Reiter and Dale, 2000, cited in Dörr, p. 700.

43 Dörr, p. 702.

44 "Google DeepMind Teaches Artificial Intelligence Machines to Read", *MIT Technology Review*, 17 June, 2015, www.technologyreview.com/s/538616/google-deepmind-teaches-artificial-intelligence-machines-to-read/.

45 Alison Linn, "Microsoft Creates AI That Can Read a Document and Answer Questions about It as Well as a Person", *Microsoft: The AI Blog*, 15 January 2018, https://blogs.microsoft.com/ai/microsoft-creates-ai-can-read-document-answer-questions-well-person/.

46 Anthony Cuthbertson, "Robots Can Now Read Better Than Humans, Putting Millions of Jobs at Risk", *Newsweek*, 15 January 2018, www.newsweek.com/robots-can-now-read-better-humans-putting-millions-jobs-risk-781393.

47 Tom Simonite, "AI Beats Humans at Reading! Maybe Not", *Wired*, 18 January 2018, www.wired.com/story/ai-beat-humans-at-reading-maybe-not/.

48 James Vincent, "No, Machines Can't Read Better Than Humans", *The Verge*, 17 January 2018, www.theverge.com/2018/1/17/16900292/ai-reading-comprehension-machines-humans.

49 Dörr, p. 710.

50 "From CEO to Student", *Automated Insights*, no date, https://automatedinsights.com/blog/from-ceo-to-student-from-the-desk-of-robbie-allen/.

51 B. Jay Coleman, "Identifying the 'players' in Sports Analytics Research", *Interfaces*, 42.2(2012), pp. 109–118; Matthew S. Bothner, Young-Kyu Kim, and Edward Bishop Smith, "How Does Status Affect Performance? Status as An Asset vs. Status as a Liability in the PGA and NASCAR", *Organization Science*, 23.2(2012), pp. 416–433; David M Waguespack, and Robert Salomon, "Quality, Subjectivity, and Sustained Superior Performance at the Olympic Games", *Management Science*, 62.1(2015), pp. 274–290.

52 "StatSheet Changes Name to Automated Insights, Scores $4 Million", *TechCrunch*, 12 September, 2011, https://techcrunch.com/2011/09/12/statsheet-changes-name-to-automated-insights-lands-4-million/.

53 Lance Ulanoff, "Need to Write 5 Million Stories a Week? Robot Reporters to the Rescue", *Mashable*, 2 July 2014, https://mashable.com/2014/07/01/robot-reporters-add-data-to-the-five-ws/?europe=true#DCo04xCPugqU.

54 Bernard Marr, "Can Big Data Algorithms Tell Better Stories Than Humans?", *Forbes*, 22 July 2015, www.forbes.com/sites/bernardmarr/2015/07/22/can-big-data-algorithms-tell-better-stories-than-humans/#716d62714b59.

55 Christer Clerwall, "Enter the Robot Journalist Users' Perceptions of Automated Content", *Journalism Practice*, 8.5(2014), pp. 519–531.

56 Elizabeth Blankespoor, Ed deHaan, and Christina Zhu, "Capital Market Effects of Media Synthesis and Dissemination: Evidence from Robo-Journalism", *Review of Accounting Studies*, 23.1(2017), pp. 1–36.

57 Joseph Lichterman, "Want to Bring Automation to Your Newsroom? A New AP Report Details Best Practices", *NiemenLab*, 5 April 2017, www.niemanlab.org/2017/04/want-to-bring-automation-to-your-newsroom-a-new-ap-report-details-best-practices/.

58 Daniel Faggella, "News Organization Leverages AI to Generate Automated Narratives from Big Data", *TechEmergence*, 19 January 2018, www.techemergence.com/case-studies/Automated-Insights/news-organization-leverages-ai-generate-automated-narratives-big-data/.

59 "Trial of Automated News Service Underway as RADAR Makes Its First Editorial Hires", *Press Association*, 12 December 2017, www.pressassociation.com/2017/12/12/trial-automated-news-service-underway-radar-makes-first-editorial-hires/.

60 Ralph Blackburn, and Tom Matthews, "Seven Potentially Life-Saving Operations Were Cancelled in Croydon in October", *Croydon Advertiser*, 4 December 2017, www.croydonadvertiser.co.uk/news/health/seven-potentially-life-saving-operations-875281.

61 Lisa O'Brien, "Shropshire's Hospitals 'Full': Appointments Cancelled under Growing Pressure", *Shropshire Star*, 23 November 2017, www.shropshirestar.com/news/health/2017/11/23/elective-ops-cancelled-as-growing-pressure-mounts-on-shrewsbury-and-telford-hospitals/.

62 Alexander Fanta, "Robots Can Save Local Journalism. But Will They Make It More Biased?" *Data Driven Journalism*, 16 March 2018, http://datadrivenjournalism.net/news_and_analysis/robots_can_save_local_journalism._but_will_they_make_it_more_biased; Chris Baraniuk, "Would You Care If This Feature Had Been Written by a Robot?", BBC *News*, 30 January 2018, www.bbc.co.uk/news/business-42858174.

63 Alison Kanski, "AI Revolutionizes Journalism", *PR Week*, 2 October 2017, www.prweek.com/article/1445839/ai-revolutionizes-journalism.

64 The Radicati Group, *Email Market, 2018–2022*, www.radicati.com/wp/wp-content/uploads/2018/01/Email_Market,_2018-2022_Executive_Summary.pdf.

65 "Global Spam Volume as Percentage of Total E-Mail Traffic from January 2014 to March 2018, by month", *Statista*, www.statista.com/statistics/420391/spam-email-traffic-share/.

66 David J. Hill, "Patented Book Writing System Creates, Sells Hundreds of Thousands of Books on Amazon", *SingularityHub*, 13 December 2012, https://singularityhub.com/2012/12/13/patented-book-writing-system-lets-one-professor-create-hundreds-of-thousands-of-amazon-books-and-counting/.

67 "The 2017 Pulitzer Prize Winner in Investigative Reporting: Eric Eyre of *Charleston Gazette-Mail*, Charleston, WV", *The Pulitzer Prizes*, www.pulitzer.org/winners/eric-eyre.

68 Eric Eyre, "Drug Firms Poured 780M Painkillers into WV Amid Rise of Overdoses", *Charleston Gazette-Mail*, 17 December 2016, www.wvgazettemail.com/news/cops_and_courts/drug-firms-poured-m-painkillers-into-wv-amid-rise-of/article_99026dad-8ed5-5075-90fa-adb906a36214.html.

69 Joseph Burns, "Eyre's Pulitzer-Winning Work Shows Power of Hard Data, Big Numbers", *Association of Health Care Journalists*, 11 April 2017, https://healthjournalism.org/blog/2017/04/eyres-pulitzer-winning-work-shows-power-of-hard-data-big-numbers/.

70 Arka Gupta, "On the Opioid Epidemic, Part 1: An Interview with Pulitzer Prize-Winner Eric Eyre", *The Politic*, 12 June 2017, http://thepolitic.org/investigative-journalism-to-combat-the-opioid-epidemic-an-interview-with-pulitzer-prize-winner-eric-eyre/.

71 Linda Wertheimer, "A Pulitzer-Winning Journalist's Advice and Why He Does a Monthly Night Shift", *NPR*, 15 April 2017, www.npr.org/2017/04/15/524076490/a-pulitzer-winning-journalists-advice-and-why-he-does-a-monthly-night-shift?t=1536413363003.

72 Michael L. Scott, *Programming Language Pragmatics*, 4th edition, Burlington, MA: Morgan Kaufmann, 2015.

73 Arjen van Dalen, "The Algorithms behind the Headlines", *Journalism Practice*, 6.5–6(2012), pp. 648–658.

74 Neil Thurman, Konstantin Dörr, and Jessica Kunert, "When Reporters Get Hands-On with Robo-Writing", *Digital Journalism*, 5.10(2017), pp. 1240–1259.

5 Citizens
The Voice of the People in the Age of Machines

On Russell Street, close to Covent Garden, sits a Starbucks that is popular with many of the tourists who visit the nearby markets and shops that were first laid out by the Welsh architect, Inigo Jones, in the sixteenth century. For anyone at all familiar with the thousands of such branches around the world, this particular Starbucks is immediately recognisable and thus perfectly unremarkable. It does, however, preserve a remarkable secret, because this particular location shares a wall with an older building that once was part of a much more famous coffee house: Button's.

The original shop was established in 1712 by Daniel Button, who was set up in business by Joseph Addison. John Timbs, in his nineteenth-century history of the life of clubs in London, wrote that Button had been a servant of the Countess of Warwick and that, with Addison's patronage, Button's became the great rival to Will's, which had dominated the life of London wits during Dryden's time, citing the poet Alexander Pope's observations on activities at the coffee house:

> Addison usually studied all the morning, then met his party at Button's, dined there, and stayed five or six hours; and sometimes far into the night. I was of the company for about a year, but found it too much for me: it hurt my health, and so I quitted it.[1]

It was during his time at Button's that Addison set up his *The Guardian* newspaper, a short-lived successor to *The Tatler* and *The Spectator*, which received contributions via its famous lion's head letterbox. Various writers such as Pope were included in *The Guardian*, but the cosy atmosphere of Button's was not to last: Pope himself suffered a breach with Addison in 1715, caused by political rivalries between Whigs and Tories, and also by the perceived autocracy of Addison who presided over his coffee house court as, in Pope's words, a "Grand Turk":

> We have, it seems, a great Turk in Poetry, who can never bear a Brother on the throne; and has his Mutes too, a sett of Nodders,

Winkers, and Whisperers, whose business is to strangle all other offsprings of wit in their birth. [...] I appeal to the People, as my rightful judges and masters; and if they are not inclin'd to condemn me, I fear no arbitrary high-flying proceedings from the small Court faction at Button's.[2]

Since the appearance of Habermas's *The Structural Transformation of the Public Sphere* in English translation in the 1980s, coffee houses across London have assumed an almost mythical status in the history of the development of the public sphere, a place where the wits of the seventeenth and eighteenth centuries could gather to debate any subject without reference to class seniority or the status of inheritance. Markman Ellis offers one of the clearest accounts of their development: modelled on similar businesses found in the Ottoman Empire (which makes Pope's caricature of Addison as "Grand Turk" all the more appropriate, referring as it does to the practice of some sultans to remove all relatives who could be potential threats to the throne), the ideal of the English coffee house was that it also encouraged a much wider range of debates and discussions than were possible under the Ottomans.[3] While Habermas tended to idealise the quality of conversation at coffee houses which, as with the *salons* of France, he envisaged as a place where "a certain parity of the educated" was possible,[4] Ellis points out that their actual scope was in practice highly restricted: what he calls "exclusionary mechanisms" were often in place to regulate debate, unstated expectations that, most notoriously, operated in terms of excluding women from discussion.[5] Even leaving aside such straightforward practices of censorship, the atmosphere of the coffee houses was often much more rambunctious and divisive than later figures would recognise – a place for open fights rather than civil discourses in the service of truth. Rather than "relatively contained and egalitarian spaces of calm rational-critical debate", as Habermas described them, Laurier and Philo describe them perhaps more accurately as spots where scores could be settled and falsehoods set loose.[6]

If there was a golden age of a perfectly rational, liberal public sphere, the seventeenth century was probably not it. Indeed, while commentators today may bemoan the current divided state of public debate in the media, it often has far too much in common with the vicious conflicts of that earlier time. The main difference is that while it was the commerce of the coffee shop that enabled or troubled the flow of information in the seventeenth century, today it is big tech that frequently distorts the debate of ideas. This chapter will concentrate on two particular case studies that claim to speak for wider masses: the first of these, Infowars, is an example of what happens when a particular brand of publication comes to rely entirely on social media for disseminating its peculiar brand of fake news, while the latter,

The Washington Post, is much more important as an example of some of the future directions that mainstream journalism looks set to follow in coming years.

Infowars in the Digital Coffee House

In many respects, Infowars is an example of everything that has gone wrong in relation to the influence of big tech and journalism, being a new breed of publication whose widespread influence was only made possible by the new platforms considered in this book and which was then cut off by tech giants without recourse to third parties. In a strange way, however, it also very much belongs to the early era of the press. During the English Civil War, an intense propaganda war was carried out between Royalists and Parliamentarians, drawing on a tradition that, as Peacey observes, had its roots in Henry VIII's revolution and the break with Rome but resulting in a print explosion that was ostensibly concerned with "educating" the public.[7] Pamphlets were relatively cheap to produce, could be distributed easily to larger sections of the population than books, and often had a profound effect in terms of radicalising readers. Their vast popularity was also often associated with "slander or scurrility" and critics worried that they would turn readers from "good" reading.[8] In terms of our own contemporary media, the pamphlet wars of the early modern period had all the hallmarks of what we now would call a moral panic. Some pamphleteers clearly took advantage of the liminal nature of their format, such as John Taylor's infamous *The Arraignment, Conviction and Imprisoning of Christmas* (1646) which satirised the Puritans' unpopular attacks on Christmas festivities. Others belonged to the truly bizarre world of seventeenth-century conspiracy theories, such as Thomas Totney, who, after a revelation in 1648, changed his name to Thereau John Tany, declaring in works such as *Theous Ori Apokolipkal* (1651) that he was destined to restore the Jews to their homeland: after attacking Parliament single-handedly when Oliver Cromwell was offered the crown in 1654 and having changed his name to Ram Johoram, he left England to gather up European Jews and was eventually drowned at sea.[9]

Tany sometimes reads like a pamphleteering variant of Alex Jones, the founder and bizarrely charismatic presenter of Infowars – although if Tany appears to have genuinely believed that he had been divinely chosen to be king of the Jews, Jones presents a much more ambiguous figure. Jones seems to have been genuinely radicalised during the 1990s and, in a recent paper, Jessica Jones discusses the ways in which Infowars regularly appears as a source for those who, in turn, shift further towards the alt- or far right.[10] In the decades before social media talk radio in particular seems to have served the same role for Alex Jones that his website would provide for younger individuals. Thus, he accused the Clinton administration of organising the Oklahoma City bombing of 1995 in which 168 people died and in 1998 released his first film, *America Destroyed by Design*: it was such activities that led Zaitchik to label him "the most paranoid man in America".[11] And yet Jones himself has offered a refutation of this view of himself, most notably via legal representation in court cases which would end up presenting him with considerable difficulties. In 2017, during a long-running divorce case, his attorney Randall Wilhite described his client as "really a performance artist" who was "playing a character" and nothing like his online persona in real life.[12] Then in 2018, during the defamation lawsuit brought against him by parents from the Sandy Hook shooting (concerning which Jones had promoted various conspiracy theories), the defence argued that his show was really a satire and that at no point did Jones speak factually, and that "no reasonable person would expect that Jones spoke factually on his show".[13] While Jones, then, may come across to viewers as a modern-day Thereau John, his tactic when faced with legal challenges is to assert that, in this modern-day pamphlet war, he is closer to John Taylor. Infowars is satire and entertainment and not, as many of its readers actually seem to believe, news for "infowarriors".

The site itself was established by Jones in 1999, essentially a home page advertisement for various documentaries promoted by him with titles such as *Wake Up or Waco* and *Police State 2000*. At this stage, Jones was also carrying appeals to help rebuild the Branch Davidian church destroyed during the siege of Waco in 1993, and it was this radicalisation against what he saw as the global order that drove much of his transmission of conspiracy theories. According to an early profile by Lee Nichols, Jones appeared to sincerely believe that David Koresh and his followers were peaceful people who had been murdered by the Bureau of Alcohol, Firearms and Tobacco, and he was removed from a rally for George W. Bush that year when he constantly interrupted the Governor's speech.[14] In its early stage, the website was a minor adjunct to *The Alex Jones Show*, which was set up as a public-access TV programme in Austin, Texas, and its influence barely spread across the entire state, let alone outside it.

Throughout the early 2000s, Infowars.com promoted Jones's show and a basic news aggregator for stories that Jones found interesting, largely disseminating a generally libertarian view that opposed increased government and "deep state" intervention, whether in terms of military action, ecological policies, or opposition to personal rights. Most content that was originated by Jones for the website consisted of adverts for documentaries or his book, *9-11 Descent into Tyranny*, in which he attacked the "Bush crime family". Even those generalisations, however, cover the very eclectic range of Jones's tastes: for example, in late 2002, his attention shifted to GM-crops (which were also entangled by him with the anti-vaccination movement), drawing upon organisations such as Friends of the Earth insofar as they helped him in his opposition to big government in all its forms. Likewise, in 2004, Infowars regularly carried articles on the Abu Ghraib atrocities and other events of the war on terror, 9-11 being an inside job forming the ur-conspiracy that lay behind all others, promulgating the central message of his 2002 book, *9-11,* the subtitle of which promised to reveal "The New World Order's dark plans to turn Earth into a prison planet".[15] Indeed, 9/11 provided a useful nursery for the techniques that Jones would deploy later. As Stempel, Harvey, and Stempel discovered in their 2007 analysis of 9-11 conspiracy theories, members of less powerful groups (whether racial minorities, people of younger ages, those of lower social classes, and so on) were more likely to believe at least one of the conspiracies, while consumers of mainstream media were less likely – but also that political affiliation affected which theories respondents believed, with Democrats more likely to believe that the US government did nothing to prevent the attacks, while Republicans tended towards the conspiracies that the Twin Towers were deliberately demolished or the Pentagon was bombed by the military. Significantly, by 2007, the authors suggested that "conspiracy thinking is a normal part of mainstream political conflict in the United States".[16] The Internet had a huge role to play in the dissemination of such theories – with Infowars being a significant player – but Clarke could also observe in 2007 that while online communications helped to disseminate non-mainstream ideas and were quickly taken up by conspiracy theorists, this also contributed to a fragmentation of theories and, in the hypercritical atmosphere of online bulletin boards, may even have led to slowing down of the development of those theories so that advocates were less keen to fix on specific versions that they knew would attract criticism.[17]

9-11, as Cohnitz has observed, provided a clear example of the epistemological frameworks by which conspiracy theories operate, while also taking issue with interpretations of Karl Popper's theory in *The Open Society and its Enemies* that such theorists believe every event is due to successful planning. Cohnitz argues instead that Popper was really interested in the emerging field of sociology's engagement with such theories rather than conspiracy *per se*, and that a more sophisticated view of them that is twofold: first, that agents secretly conspire to achieve a common end (which, he suggests, allows such theories to be rationally believed), but that such conspiracies are maliciously motivated which is where paranoia starts to enter into the equation; such paranoia, however, is driven by *scepticism*, a refusal to believe readily available explanations, which makes such belief appear hyper-rational.[18] An additional factor which comes into play with the dissemination of such theories concerns their delivery: Cohnitz argues (perhaps a touch naively) that mainstream media in open societies does a relatively effective job of presenting alternative ideas, but that the scepticism of conspiracy theorists drives them to seek out alternative sources of information. Indeed, the notion of these seekers as lazy and gullible does not at all accord with their sceptical application of criteria to understand underlying causes: that they often make mistakes in applying those criteria is where such theories often fail. In 2007, 9-11 represented the height of conspiracy theorising, with strange echo chambers operating across the Internet aslant to mainstream media and largely operating under its radar: these micro-public spheres were relatively easily dismissed as cranks, and while a significant percentage of the population were susceptible to different forms of such conspiracies, none seemed likely to affect wider political activities.

The changes that took place from 2008 onwards, particularly with regard to Infowars, were twofold. First, the election of Barack Obama as the President would eventually shift the attention of Jones and fellow contributors away from the Bush administration; secondly, transformations in engagement with digital media changed completely the audience for conspiracy theories. Cohnitz is critical of the value of social media sites such as Facebook with regard to true conspiracy theorists, arguing that the echo-chamber conditions of such spaces do not fit well with the sceptical nature of those seekers.[19] That may very well be true, but in enabling such echo chambers to speak to thousands, then hundreds of thousands, and then millions of less sceptical citizens, social media had a crucial role to play in modifying audiences' behaviour in the public sphere. Prior to this, Infowars had largely operated on the fringes of general media discourse, providing the kind of "citizen journalism" that a smaller number of radicalised – but not necessarily uncritical – readers desired and actively sought out.

The response by Infowars to Obama's election in 2008 did not initially allocate any special status to the Senator from Illinois: critical remarks regarding the bailout after his election but prior to his inauguration, such as those written by Infowars' editor at large, Paul Joseph Watson, tended to be more concerned with the wider role of the deep state and the role of the Federal Reserve,[20] and even in the first year of the new administration, the effects of the global financial crisis drove many of the stories on the site, with occasional doses of 9-11 conspiracy theory thrown in. Before long, however, stories surrounding Obama's citizenship (and thus his legitimacy to be the president) were being widely circulated, building on previous claims about his real identity as a Muslim that had surfaced following his election to the Senate in 2004.[21] Beginning with a call in the *National Review* by Jim Geraghty to release his birth certificate, the movement disparagingly known as "birtherism" grew into an attempt to discredit Obama. By 2010, the *TexasMonthly* noted that *The Alex Jones Show* was becoming increasingly popular among conservatives who hated Obama, "capturing the national zeitgeist" with his discussions of the birth certificate and "death panels" as part of pro-posals for Obamacare.[22] With stories such as "Obama Signs Executive Order Barring Release of His Birth Certificate" and "New Obama Birth Certificate is a Forgery", according to Infowars, Obama was now com-pletely implicated in the deep state plot to subvert American freedoms by any means necessary. Prior to his second term as the President, another US citizen was beginning to share similar concerns: as Donald Trump told *Good Morning America*, he was himself "sceptical" about Obama's citizenship.[23]

The combination of birtherism and greater hostility to Islam with the rise of Islamic State seems to have resulted in a shift towards rheto-ric that was increasingly sympathetic to sectors of the white supremacy movement in the United States, but it was with his broadcasts on the Sandy Hook shooting that Jones demonstrated the true toxicity of his brand of conspiracy theory. The murder of 20 children between the ages of six and seven years, and six adults at the elementary school in Newton, Connecticut, by Adam Lanza on December 14, 2012, was the largest mass school shooting at the time. The event led to renewed calls for gun control, and Jones and Infowars entered the debate with what would prove to be a particularly potent conspiracy theory: that there was no shooting at the school, but that instead the whole event had been performed by "crisis actors" to push through gun control legislation. From early 2013 onwards, the site began publishing sto-ries with titles such as "Sandy Hook AR-15 hoax? Still no school sur-veillance footage released"[24] and "FBI says no one killed at Sandy Hook".[25] In 2015, the site included a bizarre and grotesque conver-sation between contributor Rob Drew and his uncle, "a former FBI agent famous for investigating the Mafia", who demonstrated the al-leged inconsistencies in the story that were pored over by conspiracy theorists.[26] A decade earlier, Jones had regularly hosted stories that argued 9-11 was an inside job; yet, the reaction to Sandy Hook was much more extreme, including harassment of the parents of children killed at Sandy Hook who were forced to move repeatedly because of threats against them, which they alleged were caused by stories carried on Infowars. Certainly, the site had gained a considerable following in the intervening years: by 2015, Donald Trump appeared on *The Alex Jones Show* in which the presidential candidate told his host that he had an "amazing reputation".[27] That Infowars stories also seemed to inspire the audience to direct action seemed confirmed in the case of Edgar Maddison Welch, a regular watcher of Jones's show who, in December 2016, entered the Comet Ping Pong pizza restaurant in Washington, D.C. with an AR-15, determined to release victims of the so-called "Pizzagate" conspiracy theory, in which it was claimed that the pizzeria was the site of a child-sex trafficking ring run by se-nior Democrats. "Pizzagate" was discredited easily, but the fact that it gained traction so quickly and spread so widely demonstrated some important differences between the role of conspiracy theories in 2002 and those in 2012–2016.

Stempel, Harvey, and Stempel have argued that it was those most likely to be suffering some degree of social disaffection who were more likely to believe in conspiracy theories; yet, Clarke and Cohnitz have suggested that the hypercritical nature of conspiracy sites leads to scepticism on the part of seekers. More likely, Stempel et al. and Clarke and Cohnitz are discussing separate (if interrelated) groups of readers likely to read conspiracy theorists: those who actively seek out such information, and those who discover it serendipitously via social media. It is probable that, prior to 2008, there was a substantive difference in those who were more likely to read conspiracy theories in that the relative effort required to find out information on such theories would filter out the more easily gullible. A consistent stereotype for the conspiracy theorist during the latter part of the twentieth century had been of the young, lone male, typically living in his parents' bedroom and consuming non-mainstream media to feed a hunger for outrageous alternative facts. It is also telling that Cohnitz explicitly excludes social media sites such as Facebook from the preferred sources for true seekers, in that these echo chambers are too easy to access. And yet, this precisely is what happened from 2008 onwards: as social media sites such as Facebook and YouTube flourished, material that for years had lain entirely outside the sphere of mainstream media became instantly accessible to readers who were not sceptical at all of videos and posts shared with them by friends and family. When it had been restricted to Austin, Texas, *The Alex Jones Show* was necessarily limited in its audience: by contrast, in 2018, the Alex Jones channel on YouTube had nearly 2.5 million subscribers with more than 35,000 videos that had been shared a staggering 1.6 billion times. Facebook and YouTube in particular had made Jones a star, and he regularly took credit for having been one of those figures who had woken American audiences to vote for Donald Trump.

And yet, as Jones was about to discover, with great power comes great responsibility – a responsibility that he did everything he could to evade. In April and May 2018, some of the families of children at Sandy Hook filed a defamation lawsuit against him in Connecticut and Texas, in which they stated: "Jones is the chief amplifier for a group that has worked in concert to create and propagate loathsome, false narratives about the Sandy Hook shooting and its victims, and promote their harassment and abuse."[28] In response in late July, Jones's lawyer responded with the assertion that no reasonable person would assume that he was speaking factually on his show, but instead provided entertainment. Writing in *The New York Times* on July 31, Elizabeth Williamson observed that he faced a "legal crossroads",[29] while Megan Garber, in

The Atlantic, invoked Michiko Kakutani's *The Death of Truth* to discuss the upside-down world of "post-truth" that the world appeared to have fallen into after Trump's election, of which Jones was a symptom.[30] Both writers – and many more – noted that by Saturday, 4 August, some posts had been removed from social media sites because of accusations of hate speech. At that moment, it appeared that the event would be a slow-burning story over the Summer.

On Sunday evening, everything changed. Apparently following a meeting between CEO Tim Cook and the vice president of software and services, Eddy Cue, the decision was made to begin removing Infowars posts from the Apple podcasts service.[31] At 3 a.m. Pacific Time, Mark Zuckerberg and his team made the decision to begin removing pages from Facebook. By midday GMT, news organisations around the world were reporting on the decision by Apple, Facebook, YouTube, and Spotify to effectively remove Infowars from their services, with Facebook issuing a statement that the pages had been removed "for glorifying violence, which violates our graphic violence policy, and using dehumanizing language to describe people who are transgender, Muslims and immigrants, which violates our hate speech policies".[32] The speed with which the ban took place and its extent astonished many commentators, with social media observers generally (and wrongly) attributing it to an assault on the First Amendment and failing to realise that while even hate speech is protected from being abridged by the government, private companies are not necessarily bound by its regulation.[33] Within days, the majority of platforms had followed suit – with the notable exception of Twitter, which attracted considerable attention for its attention not to ban both Jones and Infowars as they had with other figures such as Milo Yiannopoulis and Paul Golding. Jack Dorsey issued a statement noting that Jones had not violated Twitter's terms of service, and it later transpired that the same conditions applied at Apple, where hate speech was prohibited in the terms of service for podcasts but not for apps, leading the Infowars app to trend in the news charts in the days following the ban.[34]

In many respects, Infowars was simply one of the most visible of a number of American organisations or outlets that tested the limits of free speech. In terms of hate speech, however, a much more important test had come in the preceding five years when terrorist groups, notably Al Qaeda and Islamic State, had spent a great deal of time weaponising social media in their pursuit of "electronic *Jihad*".[35] While Al Qaeda had led the way, ISIS had extended cyberterrorist activities in order to attract recruits, publicise propaganda, and even wage war in places such as Syria.[36] It was precisely this effectiveness, however, that had led to a range of practices being implemented by social media networks from 2016 onwards, following the United Nations Security Council's request that the Counter-Terrorism Committee propose an "international framework" to curb Islamic State's activities online.[37] From 2016, the censorship of groups associated with Islamic extremism proceeded with little other than praise across the media when it was reported at all; in 2018, conservatives had begun to complain that their voices were being censored more generally on the major platforms, but that process of filtering content was well underway with a concerted effort to take down Jihadist accounts on social media. In 1997, the Supreme Court had afforded online speech the highest level of protection (although it was not an absolute right, as in *Brandenburg v. Ohio*, where it was determined that speech was not protected when it expressly advocated violation of a law). Following the *Holder v. Humanitarian Law Project* (2010), however, it had been determined that providing "material support" to a foreign terrorist organisation constituted a federal crime, thus limiting the broad protection of free speech.[38] This online offensive against terrorist organisations was so effective that in 2017, Islamic State militants sought to create their own social media platforms, and Facebook reported that it alone had removed some 1.9 million pieces of extremist content in the first three months of 2018.[39] In practice then, if not in overt principle, social media platforms had already begun to shift away from the early, more libertarian rhetoric of being guarantors of free speech: while critics complained about Infowars as a source of hate speech, it did not operate in any form as a terrorist organisation (and indeed, although Jones was a fierce advocate of second amendment gun ownership rights, he consistently opposed military violence). Nonetheless, when the decision came to question content insofar as it would harm the perception of the major content platforms, Apple, Facebook, Google, and others were already used to analysing the material they carried. Facebook's own volte-face was particularly sudden. In an interview with Kara Swisher for *Recode* magazine in mid-July, Zuckerberg indicated that he would not ban a site such as Infowars and that, despite being Jewish, he would not even remove Holocaust deniers from the site, remarking "I don't believe that our platform should take that down because I think there are things that different people get wrong."[40] Twitter did lock down the account briefly in mid-August in response to a tweet that it alleged was an example of harassment, but in somewhat different circumstances, Jack Dorsey continued to defend a decision not to remove Infowars from the site once it had been banned by Apple and others, arguing that it had not broken Twitter's terms of service.[41] While many commentators disagreed with that stance, it became evident that – as the Infowars app rocketed up Android and iOS download charts in subsequent days – while Apple had a written policy with regard to hate speech (which it had used to justify removing Infowars from its podcasts), it did not have a similar policy with regard to apps themselves.[42]

The impact of the platform ban for Infowars was likely to have been immediate. In 2013, Seitz-Wald estimated that Jones was making

$10 million a year from his media empire, largely through sales of body building and health supplements, having grown from a reported $1.5 million turnover in 2009.[43] By 2017, Seth Brown believed that Jones had moved beyond the typical sources of revenue for a talk-show host – advertising and syndication fees – in order to transform Infowars into a constant infomercial for his range of dietary supplements.[44] Again, figures (such as Brown's $25 million) are entirely hypothetical, but it is clear that the 1.6 billion views on YouTube alone would be worth a great deal to Jones in terms of driving an audience to his own products on InfowarsStore.com. Indeed, the small scale of Jones's production efforts enabled him to take advantage of the new conditions that had disrupted a century or more of traditional media financing and which were explored in Chapter 2: while a large number of views certainly provided him with advertising revenue, he had found a way to leverage a huge social media presence for e-commerce. This boon for Jones, however, also proved its Achilles' heel: for previous generations, the distribution of Infowars via cable or print would have both been more limited to begin, but at the same time such a channel would also have been less vulnerable to a takedown by the major tech giants The reaction by Jones was, unsurprisingly, vociferous if also (equally unsurprisingly to anyone who had followed the site for any length of time) tangential: as well as immediately accusing the tech companies of engaging in censorship to promote their liberal interests, Jones repeatedly claimed that the real reason for the ban was due to "Chinese communist infiltration of Silicon Valley" and of the Democratic party.[45] When Twitter issued a temporary ban ten days later, the President weighed in, accusing social media platforms of "totally discriminating" against conservatives and engaging in "very dangerous" censorship.[46] The sense of aggrievement over this sense of innate bias only increased when sites such as Breitbart began to report that executives at Alphabet, Google's parent company, had expressed dismay over Trump's election.[47] Over the ensuing weeks, Jones appeared to unravel further: after confronting Dorsey in September about alleged shadow banning of conservatives (the practice of downgrading or removing such accounts from searches) after the Twitter CEO had attended a meeting of the Senate Intelligence Committee, Jones was banned from the site permanently (he had also confronted Senator Marco Rubio and CNN's Oliver Darcy). By the end of the month, PayPal banned Infowars from its services and with apps finally removed from Apple the site was effectively locked out of the majority of distribution channels for reaching a huge audience. As Higgins observed, as with so many other aspects of conservative politics, elements such as Infowars which had existed on the fringes of opinion and which had appeared to be ready to enter the mainstream following the election of President Trump were placed in jeopardy precisely because of that election[48]: exposed to a level of scrutiny within a wider public sphere which he was not used to, Jones' particular brand of fake news "entertainment" attracted increasing levels of hostility.

This extended case study does not in any way reflect on the status of that site as an exemplar of so-called citizen journalism. Rather, it demonstrates how notions of "citizen journalism" were frequently hijacked by an "alt-journalism" brigade with Infowars being perhaps the highest-profile site disseminating fake news across digital channels. As such, it posed a particular problem for social media companies that sought to present themselves as proponents of free speech but which were also being held increasingly responsible for the spread of disinformation. More acutely, the banning of Infowars threw into sharp relief the power of big tech companies to direct and even dominate the flow of information within various public spheres. After a half-decade of attempting to evade being labelled as media companies (with the threat of regulation that would attend such a classification), the reconfiguration of media power from production to distribution that was the subject of Chapter 2 came into full force with the effective censoring of Alex Jones and related accounts.

One of the most pertinent analyses was provided by David Greene, the civil liberties director for the Electronic Frontier Foundation (EFF): writing in *The Washington Post* shortly after action was taken against Infowars, he commented on the millions of posts removed and thousands of accounts closed by the digital duopoly in particular but also other big tech players. Such closures took place in a wide variety of countries and across very different types of accounts – black and Muslim activists, atheists in religious countries, and women posting images of breast feeding as well as right-wing conspiracy theorists. Remarking that

> we should be extremely careful before rushing to embrace an Internet that is moderated by a few private companies by default, one where the platforms that control so much public discourse routinely remove posts and deactivate accounts because of objections to the content.

Greene observed that content moderation placed too much power in the hand of a few tech giants to determine what would and would not be available in the public sphere.[49] Referring back to the EFF's Santa Clara Principles that had been proposed in February 2018,[50] Greene argued that signing up to such a voluntary framework would offer at least transparency with regard to moderation; companies would report on the numbers of posts and accounts they moderated, by providing notice to those determined to be violating community rules, and to allow a meaningful appeal system against such closures. In some respects, the big tech companies were experiencing a greater degree of scrutiny in the public sphere than even Infowars: becoming in effect media companies in all but name, they were finding it increasingly difficult to treat their decisions as trade secrets. By pursuing their moderation processes secretively, digital companies were effectively censoring individual expression: in their rush to disrupt media in pursuit of profit, big tech has found itself in the increasingly exposed and unenviable position of being the arbiter of public taste and thus the unelected police force of the public sphere.

The Eternal Start-up

The example of Infowars is less an indication of how citizen journalism can thrive in the new digital environment of news publishing, more how the frontier of social media journalism allows charlatans to flourish. The reason why so many people heard of Alex Jones and his fake news was because of big tech and the digital duopoly in particular. While becoming the most powerful media companies in the world (and resisting as much as possible being defined as such because of the attendant regulation), there is one example of a CEO of a major technology company who has become much more overtly involved in the journalism industry: Jeff Bezos.

Bezos, the richest man in the world at the time of writing, is best known, of course, for founding the company that shares the title of world's largest retailer alongside the Chinese online seller, Alibaba. Started in 1994 as Cadabra Inc., Bezos famously set up an online bookstore because, out of the list of items he considered selling – including computer software, office supplies, apparel, and music – books were pure commodities (an item in one store was exactly the same as in another), involved only two distributors at the time in the USA (Ingram and Baker and Taylor), and there were 3 million titles in print, which could never be housed in a bricks-and-mortar store.[51] As Stone points out, the name Amazon was chosen both for its exotic quality and because it would appear near the top of alphabetical lists, while setting up headquarters in Seattle gave access to considerable technological expertise (it was the home of Microsoft) but, with a smaller population than California, Bezos would pay lower sales taxes in Washington State.[52] Within a year of its start-up, the company was selling books across all 50 states of the USA as well as in 45 other countries, and by 1997 had gone public with an initial public offering of stock which raised $54 million – a far cry from the billion-dollar tech IPOs in the twenty-first century.

Indeed, for the first decade of its existence, Amazon was far from being a sure-fire success. Repeatedly, commentators questioned its ability to make a profit, and the company only posted its first net profit of $5 million (or 1 cent per share) in the fourth quarter of 2002, a story which *The New York Times* ran with the headline: "A Surprise from Amazon: Its First Profit".[53] As has been recognised since then, however, and which Michael Porter first drew attention to back in 2001, Amazon was pursuing a very different strategy: observing that the technology of the Internet provided "better opportunities for companies to establish distinctive strategic positionings" that previous generations of IT, and that, in any case, "creative accounting" techniques had distorted revenue, cost, and share price data throughout the 1990s, Amazon was taking advantage of online distribution to spread itself as widely as possible rather than simply generate profit.[54] The extent of this strategy was not entirely clear to Porter, who believed at the time that the integration of Internet and traditional bricks-and-mortar consumption would provide the winning strategy (and which Amazon does indeed seem to be dabbling with via its physical stores); moreover, his observation that "as all companies come to embrace Internet technology ... the Internet itself will be neutralized as a source of advantage"[55] failed to see how this would come into effect a mere decade and a half later. The advantages of many hundreds, or even dozens, of retailers were increasingly nullified not by the dispersal of technology across those companies but by their domination by one. Outside of China, at least, Amazon was the king, memorably described by Joshua Mou as a company "built for greatness, not ... profitability".[56]

The company's low profit margins became part of a deliberate strategy: while using technology to pare costs back wherever possible, Amazon could deliver greater savings to consumers – driving up its popularity and, in turn, generating huge operating revenues which were not redistributed to shareholders but instead ploughed back into further purchases in its attempt to become the "store of everything". This process began with Telebook.de and Bookpages.co.uk in 1998, which became Amazon.de and Amazon.co.uk, and further acquisitions included: IMDB (1998), the big data company Alexa.com (1999), Audible (2008), the footwear and apparel site Zappos (2009), Goodreads (2013), and Whole Foods Market (2013). Some of these purchases ran into the billions ($13.7 billion for Whole Foods Market, for example) and clearly extended Amazon's activities into new markets, while others removed competitors or consolidated its operations (Goodreads, for example, founded in 2006 had become the largest online reviewing and recommendation site by the time it was bought by Amazon for an undisclosed amount[57]). Alongside these expansions into retail, Amazon also established itself as an incredibly important disruptor in another area: web services. In the late nineties, Bezos realised that much of Internet structure would not be able to provide the level of operations that he required and so the company invested heavily in infrastructure, making this available to third parties as Amazon Web Services in 2002, and by mid-2018, 40 per cent of public sites were run on AWS (compared to 20 per cent for the nearest competitors, Microsoft's Azure and Google[58]). As Foer observes, such clear and overt monopolisation of retail was made possible by the fact that antitrust legislation such as the 1890 Sherman Act and activities by figures such as Thurman Arnold at the Justice Department's Antitrust Division were driven by the reasonable desire to be on the side of the consumer and to prevent cartel's inflating prices rather than to enforce diverse competition for its own sake.[59] By keeping prices low, Amazon has been able to take advantage of lax interventions by US authorities for the past two decades to expand without interruption.

Galloway provides a very neat term to describe another factor which many commentators have realised contributed to Amazon's apparently inexorable rise: "visionary capital". By promising continuous growth, immediate profitability became less important to investors than the continued prospects of future profits from a company that appears almost endless in its ability to extend its market cap. Amazon, like the other Big Tech players, is able "to attract cheap capital by articulating a bold vision that is easy to understand".[60] Indeed, this has led to a paradox noted by large numbers of commentators. Mou, for example, remarked in late 2017 that Amazon would never be able to increase its profits to justify its market capitalisation – and yet that capitalisation continued to grow as Amazon continued to expand. It had already passed Walmart, previously the most valuable retailer in the world, by 2015; yet while revenue grew to $43 billion in the final quarter of 2017, net income was still $0.26 billion.[61] Cash flow was more important than profits, however: in 2016, the company had nearly $16.5 billion which was constantly ploughed back into acquisitions and further growth – and the ever-receding horizon of profits tomorrow. From a stock price of $18 in 1997, Amazon shares were traded at more than $1,800 dollars each in 2018, leading Forbes to predict in August that it would be the next trillion-dollar company after Apple, which indeed happened a month later.[62] After 20 years, Amazon refused to renege on its disruptive origins: to all intents and purposes, the company remains what Rocio Summers called an "eternal start-up" driven by its appetite for growth.[63]

Such factors are well known; yet while explaining Amazon's rise to becoming one of the most powerful monopolies in the world, they do not help us understand the impact of the company on journalism. In one very obvious area – book distribution – Amazon is a monopoly to the digital duopoly of Google and Facebook considered in Chapter 2, and unlike both those companies, it has even become involved in media production via Amazon Prime Video. During the presidency of Trump, however, Amazon has become important in terms of the public sphere for one very simple reason: the decision by Jeff Bezos to purchase *The Washington Post* in 2013.

Media Moguls and Citizen Caine

Throughout this book, we have considered various means by which big tech has been extremely disruptive in terms of reconfiguring both journalism and the public sphere, typically reorganising the distribution of information in order to maximise profits away from the producers of content and towards themselves. Bezos's acquisition of *The Washington Post*, however, seems to follow a more traditional pathway. After the purchase, there were plenty of articles comparing him to Charles Foster Kane as played by Orson Welles, with titles such as "If anyone can save the *Washington Post* it's Jeff Bezos" or "Amazon's Jeff Bezos: A 21st Century Citizen Kane".[64] Less mythical – and generally less flattering although perhaps more accurate – comparisons lie with the media moguls of the 1960s to the 1990s, a period when areas such as journalism were frequently dominated by a number of colourful and powerful personalities. Tunstall and Palmer provided a classic analysis of such figures in their 1991 book, *Media Moguls*, detailing the rise of a range of disparate corporate owners such as Robert Maxwell, Rupert Murdoch, and Silvio Berlusconi, some of whom like Bezos began business outside the media before establishing powerful conglomerates. The transformation that lay ahead in the 1990s, the authors noted, was the prospect of emerging global media markets. This would occur at the time when an apparent American-Japanese media alliance dominated in music and film, by means of which six companies could dominate production. Associated with this was European–US hegemony in news with flows controlled by AP, Reuters, and AFP, with increasing consolidation that, in turn, led to ever more cautious attitudes and a decline of the more flamboyant behaviours of an earlier generation of moguls.[65]

Not necessarily flamboyant, but certainly indicative of an earlier age of businessman-publisher (and it always was a business*man*), while being a more accurate role model for Bezos than figures such as Berlusconi and Maxwell, was Roy Thomson. Born in Toronto in 1894, Thomson had engaged in a number of failed occupations, including being a farmer and selling radios, before buying his first newspaper, the *Timmins Daily Press* in 1934. By the 1950s, his business consortia included various manufacturing industries as well as 19 newspapers; at the end of the decade, he purchased the Kemsley group of newspapers, which included *The Sunday Times,* and to these he added *The Times* in 1966.[66] His Thomson Organisation became a multinational holding company for his interests in publishing, television, and travel, and his final major engagement was to join with J. Paul Getty to explore for oil in the North Sea. The comparison with Bezos should not be stretched too far – while his commercial interests were more diverse than those of Murdoch, who bought *The Times* and *The Sunday Times* in 1979, they remained much more closely tied to core activities in the publishing sector than Bezos (as demonstrated by the eventual formation of Thomson Reuters in 2008). Where the comparison is apt, however, is that both men became responsible for highly prestigious newspapers that were operating at a commercial loss yet provided considerable political influence.

Closer to home in terms of both geographically and in terms of the technology sector is the example of Microsoft in the 1990s, dominated as it was at that time by Bill Gates. Microsoft is instructive as an earlier example of how the decision by a major technology company to invest in media played out nearly two decades prior to Bezos's decision to acquire the *Post*. When Microsoft decided to launch a joint venture with NBC in 1996, it was at that time by far the biggest of the tech giants, having overtaken IBM in terms of market capitalisation and on its way to its peak value of more than $613 billion in 1999. So successful had the company's launch of Windows 95 been the previous year that Gates was investing more in MSN than on integrating web services into the company's operating system (indeed, in his book *Business at the Speed of Thought* he revealed that in 1993, Microsoft was connected to the net by just three machines sitting on an eight-foot folding table with the cords held in place by duct tape[67]). By 1996, the company had made considerable investments into MSN as its main portal although already Gates had turned his company around with regard to the Internet, playing catch up with Netscape in particular to catch up with the oncoming "tidal wave" and redirecting staff efforts in a famous memo sent out in May 1995.[68] It was quite clear, however, that the world of dial-up was not ready for immersive consumer entertainment, a factor noted by Gates when he observed that "many technical issues need to be resolved to ensure a simple and totally digital television experience for viewers",[69] the emphasis being on *television* rather than the web.

As such, Microsoft's attempts to move into the news and entertainment market (which already included some successful gaming ventures, soon to be joined by the launch of the Xbox) focussed on television rather than online. On July 15, 1996, MSNBC was launched, delivering news and commentary, Microsoft having invested $221 million for a 50 per cent share of the cable channel and sharing the $200 million cost of a newsroom in Secaucus, New Jersey: as John Calhoun observed in 1997, the style of the new channel was intended to create a "homey" feeling that would encourage viewers to tune in,[70] and indeed the venture was an early extension of Microsoft's determination to dominate the home as its software dominated the business world at the time. The channel's reputation was boosted following the 9/11 attacks when its rolling-news format, like that of CNN, proved immensely popular and it began calling itself "America's News Channel": significantly, considering its later liberal reputation, this makeover was accompanied by the hiring of opinionated right-wing hosts such as Tucker Carlson and Pat Buchanan, a period that also began to coincide with a slide in its ratings against the newly resurgent Fox News.[71] Indeed, by 2002, rumours were circulating that Microsoft was unhappy with the arrangement (primarily because it had to subsidise the channel for $30 million each year regardless of performance[72]). In 2005, the company effectively removed itself from the television side, allowing NBC to purchase another 32 per cent share of the company while it retained some involvement in the website msnbc. com, although even this was then bought out in 2012.[73]

In many ways, the 16-year experiment by Microsoft was the one that had begun at the wrong time. As Chris Preimesberger remarked at the time of the split in 2012, the idea of "two major powers in complementary businesses joining to create a sum larger than its parts" was probably a good one, but at root the failure to attract enough viewers – and profits – doomed it to failure.[74] Preimesberger, like several other commentators, remarked that the increasingly liberal shift of MSNBC during the Obama administration did not sit particularly well with Microsoft, a big tech company that had come of age before the era of social media and which, as with IBM, was not afraid to project a business-like conservative and Republican image. Yet more important than this, Microsoft had decided to invest in cable at the time when, with hindsight, it was about to become a medium in decline. Although the full effects of "cord-cutting" would not become clearly visible for another six years, as when *Fortune* magazine reported in 2018 that viewers were ditching cable for online streaming services faster than anyone had expected,[75] developments in broadband technology, mobile platforms, and online systems made television much less central than it had been. In 1996, Gates had rightly considered the web unable to provide the kind of immersive news and entertainment that viewers demanded but, unlike CNN which had been launched in 1980, MSNBC no longer had the luxury of developing in a format that many Americans considered essential.

In retrospect, a contributing factor to the successes of the current Big Four tech companies was that they were not Microsoft in the 1990s. Facebook did not exist, Google only gained a toehold at the end of the decade, Amazon was a moderately successful start-up, and Apple faced annihilation prior to Steve Jobs' return. None of them had the luxury to consider investing in wider media environments and so never had to face up to the paucity of experience in online communications at the time versus the more established media of the twentieth century. Furthermore, as Microsoft faced its own difficulties following the threatened antitrust investigation by the Department of Justice, leading to what would be referred to as its "lost decade" by Kurt Eichenwald,[76] each of these companies was able to take advantage of massive developments in digital technologies without being shackled to older infrastructure and organisational structures. For Apple, the breakthrough came with iTunes and its entry into music followed by apps; YouTube and Facebook, while resisting being labelled as media companies as we have seen repeatedly throughout this book, benefited most from the movement of media from television and print to online environments. All three learned an important lesson from Microsoft: don't become responsible for creating content. It was left to Amazon to both ignore this message in terms of its own video production (to lure in Amazon Prime customers), and to invest in one of the oldest media formats around: a newspaper.

Founded in 1877, *The Washington Post* was the first newspaper to be published seven days a week in Washington, D.C. (when a Sunday edition was added in 1880), and in its early decades, it promoted the agenda of the Democratic Party before becoming more sympathetic to the Republicans after it was bought by financier Eugene Meyer in 1933.[77] It was Meyer who re-established the *Post's* reputation and financial health; he was succeeded by his son-in-law, Philip Graham, and then, after his death in 1963, his wife Katherine Graham. During her tenure, the paper published its most famous series of stories chronicling the investigation of Watergate, leading President Nixon to tell Admiral Thomas Moorer, "The press is your enemy".[78] Woodward's and Bernstein's editor, Ben Bradlee, was described by his biographer as "the living avatar of old-school journalistic integrity and rough-hewn charm",[79] although many others working in the industry saw the introduction of a Style section (which was consequently repeated across all national newspapers) as his "clearest personal monument".[80] Certainly, Graham was more ambivalent about the achievements of Watergate: in an article for *New York Magazine* published three months after Nixon left office, she made clear what the fight with the former president had cost her: millions in fees for legal defence and to protect TV licences, and the low value of *The Post* on Wall Street. She considered the temptation of journalists to consider themselves "heroes" to be a dangerous one, but also that to ensure freedom of the press – an expensive activity – the newspaper had to be profitable.[81] For a period, she achieved this, raising the *Post* to first place in income growth during the 1980s and increasing her own personal fortune to $1.1 billion although, in a harbinger of future woes, the paper stopped contributing to the reporters' pension fund during that decade and journalists' salaries fell from first place to fourteenth.

Graham was very much a twentieth-century media mogul, but in the subsequent decades, the newspaper began to suffer a considerable decline. Dave Kindred's 2010 book, *Morning Miracle*, detailed how the title struggled to maintain profitability and journalistic standards in the face of alternative digital sources, and thought that the *Post* was "a great newspaper dying with dignity".[82] The paper had struggled with profitability during its entire existence: although Meyer had increased circulation to 162,000 and pushed advertising from 4 million lines to 12 million in the 1930s, it struggled to make money at many times throughout its history. US daily newspaper circulation peaked between 62 and

63.5 million in the 1970s and 1980s, while that for Sunday editions hit a high of just over 62.5 million in 1993; by 2017, the estimate for daily titles was less than 31 million, lower than at any period since the outbreak of the Second World War. The impact on revenue was even more dramatic – a fall from just over $49 billion in 2004 and 2005 to less than $16.5 billion in 2017. Significantly, the drop in advertising rates did not coincide entirely with the decline in print circulations: for a decade or so after titles such as the *Post* set up online, they managed to capitalise on advertising in print but also, to a lesser degree, across digital formats: with the shift of advertising revenue online and the rise of the digital duopoly, that line of profit would begin to dry up. The website, washingtonpost.com, had been launched in 1996, but it was not until 2009 that print and online operations were integrated: like many titles, the *Post* almost certainly held off such integration because print was its only real hope of making money from journalism, but by the end of the first decade of the twenty-first century, print circulation was falling off a cliff. So dire were the circumstances in 2010 that the *Post* sold *Newsweek* to Harman Media for a rumoured $1 following a 38 per cent drop in revenue between 2007 and 2009,[83] but little seemed to be able to stem the losses that the newspaper was haemorrhaging. If Graham's observation was true, that freedom of the press was an expensive business that required profits to survive, it appeared as though the *Post* would soon be consigned to media history books. From 2003 to 2013, 400 editorial jobs were cut, with final staffing figures of 600 far below the 1,000 plus team that had run the title in its Watergate heyday.[84]

The *Post* was clearly in decline when, in August, 2013, a potential new owner emerged: Jeff Bezos. After announcing his intention to acquire the paper, the transaction was completed on October 1 of that year, ending four generations of ownership by the Graham family. Paul Farhi, writing in the *Post*, described it as "a sudden and stunning turn of events" for the newspaper, an opinion shared by many as news of the negotiations had not been widely shared.[85] As a "legacy" media organisation, the newspaper had failed to escape the turmoil affecting newspapers more generally, but in the immediate years following the sale, it was not entirely clear why Bezos was interested in purchasing the title. In 2016, he revealed that he had paid $250 million for the *Post* without doing any due diligence,[86] and there was considerable speculation that the purchase had been a billionaire's whim. In an interview with *The New York Times*, he even indicated his initial scepticism: "I don't know anything about the newspaper business."[87] Yet, an early challenge seemed to have presented itself as an entrepreneurial one. Bezos had, via Amazon, entirely disrupted retail and bookselling: would his ownership of *The Washington Post* allow him to do the same with the news industry? At the very least, returning the *Post* to profitability seemed to be worthwhile as a hobby.

For the next two years, beyond the surprise of one of the most venerable news titles in the United States now belonging to a big tech mogul,
much of Bezos's influence on the newspaper appeared largely benevolent
and not especially surprising. In a 2014 interview with Henry Blodget for
Business Insider, he expanded on his claim that he knew little about the
newspaper business with an observation that he did know a great deal
about the Internet.[88] On the whole, it appeared that he had no intention
of becoming involved in the paper's editorial direction but instead would
concentrate on making it "a media and technology company".[89] By the
end of 2015, commentators such as Lukas Alpert and Jack Marshall at
The Wall Street Journal were observing that Bezos involvement in the
newspaper was having a direct influence in the operations of the *Post*,
although not necessarily in the manner that most would necessarily have
expected or feared: without particularly interfering in the editorial direction of his staff, Bezos brought with him a focus on customer experience that became "a near mandate within the news operation". [90]
Hülsen likewise noted that Bezos injected considerable enthusiasm for
a digital future at the title, but also transformed the core mission from
fulfilling the expectations of readers to engaging customers, evident in
47 per cent growth of online visitors to the website within the space of
a year.[91] By January 2016, he was investing in physical infrastructure,
having moved journalists from "drab offices" atop a former printing
press to sleek spaces on K Street.[92]

In an interview to promote his book *The Last of the President's Men*
in 2016, when asked by Dan Kennedy what effect the founder of Amazon had made on the *Post*, Bob Woodward replied simply: "I think he's
helping us as a business."[93] With Bezos's focus on digital rather than
print, the *Post* finally invested itself fully in online technologies so that it
performed much better on the web and on mobile, although after three
years, it was not entirely clear either how much of its growing success
was due to such improvements in performance or Bezos's deep pock-
ets. Furthermore, alongside such vast financial resources, the location of
the *Post* in Washington and its proprietor's ability to channel the news
site through various Amazon resources made it difficult to see whether
the changes being made at one such newspaper could be replicated elsewhere. Nonetheless, as Kennedy observed, not all such changes were
due entirely to Bezos's almost unique status as one of the richest men in
the world: first of all, by taking the company private, Bezos was able to
ignore the demands that had been made on the title as a publicly traded
paper under the Grahams, allowing him to invest (slowly, it should be
noted) in new staff without worrying about demands for short-term
profitability. In addition, the focus of the new title was now fixed on
implementing technological changes that would allow the site to benefit
from digital as opposed to print distribution, and as part of this, the *Post*
grew massively in terms of its online footprint, moving ahead of *The*

New York Times in terms of traffic in October 2015. While this was not converting into massive advertising revenue at the time (as Nicco Mele of the *Los Angeles Times* observed, a print ad reaching half a million people could earn $50,000, while a Google-served ad would only make $20 for a similar readership[94]), the *Post* was clearly setting itself up as a brand that would have a wider base for conversions to subscriptions and ad sales should the market change in future.

Where Bezos had, probably not entirely intentionally, transformed editorial directly was by opening up the *Post* to a much wider range of reporting. As discussed in Dave Kindred's *Morning Miracle*, in May 2004, the managing editor Steve Coll suggested to then publisher, Don Graham, an aggressive Internet strategy that he called "Beyond Washington": although it was the top print newspaper in the country, a resolute focus on Washington news was denying it an even wider readership. Although not opposed to the Internet, Graham wanted to maintain the monopoly on reporting Washington news that had made the print paper so profitable in the past and so restricted such growth.[95] As such, while much of Bezos's liberating effect on the *Post* was undoubtedly due to the financing he brought with him, it was also because he gave the title a second chance to be "truly national and international" according to Executive Editor Marty Baron.[96] Alongside this, however, another development took place which indicated the way in which big tech would influence the *Post* much more effectively than by simply opening it up to an international audience: Arc.

While Bezos may not have been hands-on in terms of directing editorial policy, almost certainly recognising that to draw direct attention to himself as a new Citizen Kane would allow him to become a target for critics. Even silence was not a perfect protection, as became evident during the disappearance of *Washington Post* journalist, Jamal Khashoggi, at the Saudi consulate in Istanbul on 2 October, 2018. As gruesome details began to emerge linking that disappearance to murder on the part of the Saudis, stories began to circulate that Bezos's own lack of response was due to conflicts between the *Post*'s reporting and the Amazon's commercial interests in the region.[97] This was a particularly sharp version of such conflicts, but for his part, Bezos's own preference more generally seemed to be to reorganise the *Post* behind the scenes. Gerry Smith reported for *Bloomberg* in December 2015 that, according to the *Post*'s CIO, he had "his fingerprints in a lot of things".[98] One of those things was Arc: built as a content management system for the paper, it was designed to be an easy-to-use WYSIWYG editor for contributors but also the one that employed powerful analytics tools to allow senior editors to see which stories were attracting most attention. Just as Amazon had learned a great deal about consumer's shopping habits, the *Post* would be able to gather data on what readers were viewing, allowing a constant tweaking of content: by the end of 2015, the news site was publishing 1,200 items a day, including some 500 news stories, more than twice the number of its nearest competitor, *The New York Times*, and allowing it to create as wide a funnel as possible to attract readers.[99] As with Amazon Web Services, Bezos also saw an opportunity to licence this new system to other publishers (the Canadian *The Globe and Mail* media group was one of the first to do so in 2016).[100] Within two years, Bezos had laid the foundations to transform his news title into a high-end, mass-market newspaper, employing many of the successful techniques that had driven Amazon forward. A few people paid polite interest, but his ownership attracted relatively little attention overall. That would begin to change when Donald Trump, famously descending an elevator in Trump Tower on June 16, 2015, announced his intention to enter the race to become the President of the United States and won a highly contentious election in November 2016.

When Billionaires Collide

The ways in which Donald Trump has dominated the news cycle since the announcement of his bid for the presidency is by no means restricted to *The Washington Post*, and indeed it is also worth considering briefly the consequences of Trump securing the Republican nomination and eventually being elected the President for two other news organisations: *The New York Times* and CNN. While it was the CEO of CBS, Les Moonves, who said of Trump's nomination, "It may not be good news for America, but it's damn good for CBS",[101] that nomination raised considerable revenues for television networks in particular. Journalists such as the late Rupert Cornwell reported that coverage of Trump had provided him with some $1.9 billion of free publicity compared to $1.2 billion for the other 16 candidates combined,[102] but spending on political ads increased to $9.8 billion and it was political channels such as Fox News and CNN that benefited greatly; indeed, according to media trackers Borrell Associates, ad campaign spending decreased for broadcast television, while it shot up on cable channels.[103] For Cornwell, such spending militated against democracy, but just as CBS profited from the carnival show surrounding Trump so did CNN, even as he sought to criticise it. In his notorious attacks against the media as an "enemy of the people", the President particularly singled out CNN, *The New York Times*, and NBC News,[104] but in 2016, Cable Network News had its most profitable year ever, earning $1 billion in profit as its parent company, Time Warner, saw share prices rise by 21 per cent.[105] Similarly, the more Trump attacked *The New York Times* as "fake news" and "failing", so an ever-greater number of readers took out subscriptions, driving its revenue from that source to over $1.7 billion in 2017.[106] In both cases, legacy media companies had managed to pivot from their old platforms to the web and mobile and thus provide instant, widespread coverage of the new President. In such an environment, the *Post* was just as prepared – if not more – to offer rolling news on Trump's ascendancy, using Arc to saturate digital media with stories that it knew would strike home with a huge number of online customers. For decades, Washington stories had often appeared stale to outsiders: now for the first time in a generation, the *Post*'s old monopoly on stories on the capital would provide it with a major advantage.

Not everyone applauded. In the early days of Trump's election victory, Patrick Maines wrote for *The Hill* that under Bezos's guardianship, the *Post* had "grossly abandoned the practice of separating news from opinion in its news pages".[107] With headlines such as "It's beyond debate that Donald Trump is unfit to be president" and "Donald Trump is a unique threat to American democracy", it seemed hard to disagree with Maines's general point. That only two of the top 100 newspapers actually endorsed circulation during the 2016 election[108] did not detract from the fact that, as one of the premier titles in the country, *The Washington Post* was leading the transformation of editorial standards away from objective reporting and into editorialising. The emergence of Trump merely accelerated this transformation: as Seargeant and Tagg noted in their survey of Facebook users, in an attempt to avoid conflict with the diverse members of their social networks, one unfortunate side effect was to polarise debate into filter bubbles, in which only stories backing up particular perspectives tended to be shared.[109] Bezos, the Internet businessman, may have realised implicitly that the way for the *Post* to successfully engage with such bubbles would be to create provocative points of view that could break through to be shared by more readers. It is highly likely, in the drive to increase customers, that he would have considered editorialising a price worth paying for increased audience share.

The changes that had taken place within the first years of Bezos's acquisition of *The Washington Post* were almost inevitably going to bring both him and his newspaper into conflict with candidate, and then President, Trump. Having fully embraced digital platforms, with a new content management system that emphasised widespread consumption of news stories, and with finances easily able to support expansion of this media empire, the *Post* became one of the most widely read sources for stories on Trump. If Bezos does not interfere with the editorial policy of his staff – and every editor and senior participant have been adamant in this case – then his enthusiasm for the *Post* has at the very least created an environment in which antagonistic copy could be disseminated more quickly than ever before into the public domain in the quest for more readers. During the early stages of the campaign, candidate Trump largely ignored Bezos, but on 7 December, 2015, clearly stung by some of the negative press he was beginning to receive from the *Post*, he posted on Twitter:

> The @washingtonpost, which loses a fortune, is owned by @Jeff-Bezos for purposes of keeping taxes down at his no profit company, @amazon.

Bezos, new himself to Twitter, responded that he could send the candidate into space,[110] but such bravado began to slip as Trump's hold on the Republican nomination solidified. In May 2016, Trump began to attack Amazon's slippery tax practices, claiming in an interview with Sean Hannity that Bezos was not only using the *Post* to attack his candidacy but also to shore up tax benefits: while this was more than a little hypocritical from a candidate who had refused to release his tax returns, it was also, as columnists such as Emily Jane Fox observed, an easy strike in an election in which the aggressive financial gains by big companies since the crash of 2008 were deeply unpopular.[111] The *Post* itself played the conflict – one which would only intensify after Trump became the President – as a personal grievance on Donald Trump's part, stemming from his "lifelong rivalry with billionaires who surpass him on lists of the planet's richest men".[112] As an *ad hominem* attack, it may have been fairly effective with its intended, elite audience, but it did little to deter Trump supporters' distaste for what they saw as a deceitful mainstream media.

In February 2017, for the first time in its 140-year history, the *Post* adopted a motto: "Democracy dies in darkness". Response was, to say the least, mixed, although probably the best rejoinder was *Slate*'s "15 Metal Albums Whose Titles Are Less Dark Than *The Washington Post's* New Motto".[113] According to the *Post* itself, Jeff Bezos had used the phrase the previous May, apparently having heard it from Bob Woodward during a presentation for *The Last of the President's Men*. Woodward, in turn, appeared to have adapted it from Judge Damon J. Keith, who ruled in a pre-Watergate case that the government could not wiretap individuals without a warrant, remarking that, "democracy dies in the dark".[114] Numerous commentators have, unsurprisingly, viewed the motto as a direct rebuke to President Trump and his repeated attacks on the media as the "enemy of the people", evoking the myth of the fourth estate as a watchdog of the state and the friend, not enemy, of the populace. Yet, a proper public sphere has never been synonymous with monopolies of the media. Democracy may, indeed, die in the dark; however, when the few hold too powerful a lamp against which all other lights fade, democracy may also be too easily blinded.

Far from the Madding Media

A recurring theme throughout this book has been how truly fake news, of the kind peddled by Infowars and many alt-"journalists", has subverted the early promises of citizen journalism that were presented in a rather rose-tinted fashion by commentators such as Dan Gillmor at the start of the millennium. While it has been propagated all too easily across those social media networks that, in the space of a decade, have become the conduits of news consumption (with algorithmic gatekeepers often unable to discern truth from obvious lies), the mainstream media itself has undergone incredible transformations when it seeks to gain traction in this noisy and combative digital marketplace. The golden age of the Anglo-American model of objective news is long departed – if it ever existed. Yet while Donald Trump creates a reality distortion field around the American presidency that is, for the moment at least, far more effective than that which Steve Jobs notoriously threw about Apple, away from his effects on news media the impact of social media can be very different.

On 10 August, 2018, Capital FM Malawi reported that the national police service had been caught in another corruption scandal. According to its Facebook page,

This latest scandal is on the procurement and distribution of police uni-forms during the 2001/2002 and 2004/2005 fiscal years.
According to a legal document from Ritz Attorney's, Karim Abdul of Africa Commercial Agency fraudulently received over K585 million from the Police in the contract.
The company is accused of inflating figures and failing to supply the goods as per the contract.[115]

The story had been picked up by a number of news sites in the country, such as the *Nyasa Times* and *Malawi24* (the latter under the rather salacious title "Malawi blood sucking title"), but of western publications, only the *Financial Times* reported on the incident as part of a wider story by Joseph Cotterill on graft allegations against Peter Mutharika. While it is possible to listen to Capital FM online (at www.capitalradiomalawi. com), much of the output is in Chichewa, which is spoken by over half of the country's population, despite the official language of Malawi being English. As such, it is easier to follow stories on the company's Facebook page, which highlights radio shows such as "Power to the People" (which, despite the black power fist, is largely dedicated to listeners contacting the radio so that their favourite vintage hits will be played) as well as a large number of local stories in English and Chichewa. The station was launched in Malawi by journalist Alaudin Osman in 1999, providing music and news and "aims to give the people of Malawi a voice, by providing quality broadcast news, information and entertainment programming that will assist them to speak out for better services and good governance".[116] Its partners include the BBC World Service and Voice of America, and Moyo has explored the role played by the Internet and social networking sites in "democratizing participation for radio publics" in Malawi.[117] As such, this particular instance offers a very different perspective on social media in general – and Facebook in particular – than has been the case for this chapter, or, indeed, the majority of this book. Throughout the preceding chapters, I have regularly criticised Facebook as part of the digital duopoly that is restructuring the public sphere in the early years of the twenty-first century, and have frequently been sceptical of the company's objective to "bring the world closer together". Nonetheless, while the social media company has clearly – and very much to its surprise – emerged as a divisive factor in recent years, there are times when, quietly and without much attention from major media outlets, it achieves precisely this task. With its 70,000 followers on Facebook (a tiny fraction of the 18 million population living in Malawi, admittedly), it has managed to overtake the larger radio station Zodiak Broadcasting Station (ZBS) online by engaging in a conversation with its audience that better understands the promise – if not always the practice – of social media as a move away from simple broadcasting.[118]

The relationship between journalistic media and its audience has thus far been a somewhat ironic, even cynical one. If Alex Jones is the charlatan who exploits the unregulated boundaries of social media to sell snake oil (or dietary supplements) to its citizens, Jeff Bezos is the Citizen Kane who is far removed from the ordinary concerns of an audience even as he transforms them from readers into customers for a particular vision of democracy that he wishes them to receive gratefully. Jones is essentially a blip, a passing case study demonstrating the stranglehold that big tech has over communication at present, but Bezos is likely to be a lasting influence on media in the USA and, to a lesser degree, the world. When dealing with mass effects of the media, it is Bezos and his ilk who form the new monopolies of the information age and a familiar theme of this book has been how Amazon, along with Facebook, Google, Apple, and a handful of others, have replaced Time Warner, Bertelsmann, and Sony as the titans of the new media age.

Yet, the temptation is to view the influence of such monopolists as actually greater than it is – which is always the case with all monopolies. In the 1990s, the great fear was that American corporations were leading to the "coca-colonization" of world culture;[119] yet by the end of the decade, it was clear to figures such as Bagdikian that the cartel was more complex, taking in Europe, Australia, and even Japan as part of its formation.[120] Much of the content of this book has been very focussed on US examples because, for the best part of a decade, the shift of media monopolies has been to the large American tech companies, but this is not inevitably an enduring state of affairs: in ten years' time, it is very likely that at least one Chinese company will be challenging the Big Four for media domination, and while Facebook and Google may remain the largest disseminators of information across the globe, the ways in which individuals in very different countries make use of them can vary enormously.

Before considering a single example of this participation between citizens and journalists in a manner that is not dictated by cynical consumerist demands, it is worth returning briefly returning to some of the themes and issues regarding the relations between digital media, the public sphere, and citizen journalists that were explored in the introduction. In particular, the gap between the optimism that was often on display from commentators in the 1990s and what is more frequently witnessed today is worth considering. Figures such as Sclove, Dahlberg, and Moore, even if they were sometimes critical of the role that the Internet had to play in the transmission of public goods, seemed to have been affected by the opening of new communication channels outside of mainstream media that coincided with the view, in the words of Held, that "democracy has become the fundamental standard of political legitimacy in the current era".[121] A mere 20 years later and the end of history as a triumph of liberal democracy as envisaged by Fukuyama seem much less certain. Criticism of the democratic potential of digital technologies – which increasingly begins to appear as a deficit – is commonplace and, in her recent study of the public sphere in China, Ya-Wen Lei describes a much more contentious space that is often (although not always) controlled by the authorities, a state of affairs that will only become more significant as the power of China extends across the international stage.[122] As Balnaves and Willson observe, one reason for a sense of dissatisfaction may ultimately stem from extremely positive demographic changes in online usage: early Internet users were more homogeneous – overwhelmingly white males, usually younger – and part of the challenging discourse online today stems from the fact that digital media is much more diverse.[123] Nonetheless, if the form of the public sphere celebrated by Habermas was liberal, that encountered online today is more frequently described by critics as a neoliberal space.

Such views, however, should be tempered by the recollection that, aside perhaps from a brief interlude in its initial form, the public sphere was always subject to interference by powerful organisations, typically governments in the earlier stages then commercial entities later. While people focus on the coffee shops and salons, Habermas himself is more concerned in his book with the *structural transformation* of that early space into something more suitable for the commercial and political requirements of organised elites, something that could better display the "Janus face of enlightenment and control".[124] My argument throughout this book has often been that control and neoliberal greed for profits has gained the upper hand in the public sphere, creating new, even more powerful tech monopolies: yet, the face of technology is always double-sided, providing potential *enlightenment* as well as control.

The example of Capital FM is just one tiny example of an attempt to provide a participatory element to mainstream media in the public sphere. On a macro level, the shifting patterns of the past decade seem clearly to form as increasingly powerful monopolies and oligarchies that, as in the case of Infowars, can quickly (although not unproblematically) stifle flows of information that do not serve their economic and social agendas. Yet, this is not often the experience of users who participate in those platforms: it is only rarely that people find themselves actively blocked or challenged by the platforms they use. Instead, most of the time they share stories, request for videos or music to be played, and contribute information. Looking at another African country, Zimbabwe, Hayes Mabweazara points out just how important social media sites such as Facebook have become in recent years as a primary starting point to gather information from the public,[125] an experience shared across every country with the Internet and a mainstream media. Returning to Capital FM, it is very much a product of a regulatory system formed by the Communications Act (1998) and Malawi ICT Policy (2003) that both modernised Malawi's broadcasting and telecommunications industry and subjected it to the Malawi Communications Regulatory Authority (MACRA).[126] Such controls, as was common across much of Europe (and had long existed in the USA), was largely *de*regulatory, liberalising radio broadcasting after the collapse of the one-party state system that had maintained a strict control over all broadcasting in the country. Capital FM was launched into this new environment not simply because it was possible to communicate with an audience that could participate in a multiparty-political system, but because it was also possible to make money from things such as advertising. The advantages available to Capital were made very clear by Moyo when comparing that station to another, more rural one – Dzimwe Community Radio – which simply did not have Internet in its newsroom and whose audience experienced all the technological, economic, and social effects of a digital divide.[127] The experience afforded by Capital, then, is far from utopian access to all: the mobility of digital capitalism is limited to the middle- and high-income classes who can "afford consistent and meaningful use of the Internet and mobile phones".[128] And yet, in the three years even since Moyo wrote, African communications, like those across much of the world, continue to be revolutionised by mobile technologies, with mobile subscriptions hitting 960 million (out of a population of 1.2 billion) by April 2017.[129]

The effects of such participation in communications should not be overstated: in the aftermath of the so-called Arab Spring, social media was often hailed as a radical new platform for engagement with a new breed of citizen journalists.[130] In only a brief period of time, such participation has led to much greater scepticism as a contributory factor in the spread of fake news. Likewise, for many of the users of the

Facebook page for Capital FM, most listeners prefer to use it as a medium to request music or to congratulate the team on their work. There are, however, also comments on political stories that indicate a steady stream of engagement with the information provided, and generally of a much politer level than is often found on western media sites. The toxic effects of things such as loud and partisan reporting on Donald Trump or American politics more generally have frequently polluted our engagement with the public sphere, and big tech must take its share of the blame in such matters. For smaller, daily encounters, however, the future of journalism is not necessarily so dark.

Notes

1 Cited in John Timbs, *Club Life of London*, vol. II, London: Richard Bentley, 1866, p. 56.
2 Cited in Pat Rogers, "'The Monster of Ragusa': Pope, Addison, and Button's Wits", *The Review of English Studies*, 67.280(2016), pp. 496–522, p. 503.
3 Markman Ellis, "An Introduction to the Coffee-House: A Discursive Model", *Language & Communication*, 28.2(2008), pp. 156–164.
4 Jürgen Habermas, *The Structural Transformation of the Public Sphere: An Inquiry into a Category of Bourgeois Society*, transl. by Thomas Burger, London: Polity, 1989, p. 32.
5 Ellis, pp. 162–163.
6 Eric Laurier, and Chris Philo, "'A parcel of muddling muckworms': Revisiting Habermas and the English Coffee-Houses", *Social & Cultural Geography*, 8.2(2007), pp. 259–281, p. 275.
7 Jason Peacey, *Politicians and Pamphleteers: Propaganda During the English Civil Wars and Interregnum*, London: Routledge, 2017, pp. 33–39.
8 Joad Raymond, *Pamphlets and Pamphleteering in Early Modern England*, Cambridge: Cambridge University Press, 2007, pp. 9–10.
9 Christopher Hill, *The World Turned Upside Down: Radical Ideas during the English Revolution*, revised edition, London: Penguin, 1991, pp. 225–226.
10 Jessica Jones "The Self-Radicalization of White Men: 'Fake News' and the Affective Networking of Paranoia", *Communication, Culture & Critique*, 11.1(2018), pp. 100–115.
11 Alexander Zaitchek, "Meet Alex Jones", *Rolling Stone*, 2 March 2011, www.rollingstone.com/culture/culture-news/meet-alex-jones-175845/.
12 Corky Siezmako, "Infowars' Alex Jones Is a 'Performance Artist,' His Lawyer Says in Divorce Hearing", *NBC News*, 17 April 2017, www.nbcnews.com/news/us-news/not-fake-news-Infowars-alex-jones-performance-artist-n747491.
13 Dan Solomon, "Alex Jones's Attorneys Argue That No Reasonable Person Would Believe What He Says", *TexasMonthly*, 31 July 2018, www.texasmonthly.com/politics/alex-joness-attorneys-defamation-suit-argue-no-reasonable-person-believe-says/.
14 Lee Nichols, "Psst, It's a Conspiracy: KJFK Gives Alex Jones the Boot", *The Austin Chronicle*, 10 December 1999, www.austinchronicle.com/news/1999-12-10/75039/.
15 Alex Jones, *9-11 Descent into Tyranny: The New World Order's Dark Plans to Turn Earth into a Prison Planet*, Austin, TX: AEJ Pub, 2002.

16 Carl Stempel, Thomas Hargrove, and Guido H. Stempel, "Media Use, Social Structure, and Belief in 9/11 Conspiracy Theories", *Journalism and Mass Communication Quarterly*, 84.2(2007), pp. 353–372, p. 353.

17 Steve Clarke, "Conspiracy Theories and the Internet: Controlled Demolition and Arrested Development", *Episteme: A Journal of Social Epistemology*, 4.2(2007), pp. 167–180.

18 Daniel Cohnitz, *Critical Citizens or Paranoid Nutcases: On the Epistemology of Conspiracy Theories*, Utrecht: University of Utrecht, 2017, pp. 16–18.

19 Cohnitz, p. 18.

20 Paul Joseph Watson, "Cost of Bailout Hits $8.5 Trillion", *Info"ars*, 26 November 2008 https://web.archive.org/web/20081202232726/http://www.Infowars.com:80/?p=6194.

21 Martin Parlett, *Demonizing a President: The "Foreignization" of Barack Obama*, Santa Barbara, CA: Praeger, 2014, p. 126.

22 Nate Blakeslee, "Alex Jones Is About to Explode", *TexasMonthly*, 8 March 2010, www.texasmonthly.com/politics/alex-jones-is-about-to-explode/.

23 Ashley Parker, and Steve Eder, "Inside the Six Weeks Donald Trump Was a Nonstop Birther", *The New York Times*, 2 July 2016, www.nytimes.com/2016/07/03/us/politics/donald-trump-birther-obama.html.

24 Mike Adams, "Sandy Hook AR-15 Hoax? Still No School Surveillance Footage Released", *Natural News/Infowars*, 14 January 2013, www.Infowars.com/sandy-hook-ar-15-hoax-still-no-school-surveillance-footage-released/.

25 Adan Salazar, "FBI Says No One Killed at Sandy Hook", *Infowars*, 24 September 2014, www.Infowars.com/fbi-says-no-one-killed-at-sandy-hook/.

26 Rob Drew, "Mega Massive Cover Up: Retired FBI Agent Investigates Sandy Hook", *Infowars*, 7 July 2015, www.Infowars.com/mega-massive-cover-up-retired-fbi-agent-investigates-sandy-hook/.

27 Eric Bradner, "Trump Praises 9/11 Truther's 'amazing' Reputation", *CNN*, 2 December 2015, https://edition.cnn.com/2015/12/02/politics/donald-trump-praises-9-11-truther-alex-jones/index.html.

28 Emily Shugerman, "US Shock Jock Alex Jones Sued by Six More Families of Sandy Hook Victims", *The Independent*, 25 May 2018, www.independent.co.uk/news/world/americas/alex-jones-sued-sandy-hook-victims-families-defamation-Infowars-a8368346.html.

29 Elizabeth Williamson, "Alex Jones, Pursued over Infowars Falsehoods, Faces a Legal Crossroads", *The New York Times*, 31 July 2018, www.nytimes.com/2018/07/31/us/politics/alex-jones-defamation-suit-sandy-hook.html.

30 Megan Garber, "The Lasting Trauma of Alex Jones's Lies", *The Atlantic*, 4 August 2018, www.theatlantic.com/entertainment/archive/2018/08/the-lasting-trauma-of-alex-joness-lies/566573/.

31 Dylan Byers, *Pacific with Dylan Jones*, 7 August 2018, https://mailchi.mp/cnn/pacific-august-7-2018?e=4e0d6f7d41.

32 Facebook, "Enforcing Our Community Standards", *Facebook Newsroom*, 6 August 2018, https://newsroom.fb.com/news/2018/08/enforcing-our-community-standards/.

33 Mike Snider, "Why Facebook Can Stop Infowars and Not Break the First Amendment", *USA Today*, 9 August 2018, https://eu.usatoday.com/story/tech/news/2018/08/09/why-facebook-can-censor-Infowars-and-not-break-first-amendment/922636002/.

34 Jack Nicas, "Tech Companies Banned Infowars. Now, Its App Is Trending", *New York Times*, 8 August 2018, www.nytimes.com/2018/08/08/technology/Infowars-app-trending.html.

35 Martin Rudner, "Electronic *Jihad*: The Internet as Al Qaeda's Catalyst for Global Terror", *Studies in Conflict and Terrorism*, 40.1(2016), pp. 10–23.

36 Imran Awan, "Cyber-Extremism: Isis and the Power of Social Media", *Social Science and Public Policy*, 54.2(2017), pp. 138–149, p. 140.

37 Janice Yu, "Regulation of Social Media Platforms to Curb ISIS Incitement and Recruitment: The Need for an 'international framework' and Its Free Speech Implications", *Journal of Global Justice and Public Policy*, 4.30(2018), pp. 1–29, p. 1.

38 Yu, pp. 11–12.

39 David Ingram, "Facebook Says It Is Taking Down More Material about ISIS, al-Qaeda", *Reuters*, 23 April 2018, https://uk.reuters.com/article/facebook-extremism-int/facebook-says-it-is-taking-down-more-material-about-isis-al-qaeda-idUKKBN1HU2PY.

40 Cited in Kurt Wagner, "Here's Why Mark Zuckerberg Doesn't Think Infowars Should be Banned", *Recode*, 18 July 2018, www.recode.net/2018/7/18/17584488/mark-zuckerberg-facebook-Infowars-censorship-conspiracy-theory-news-feed.

41 Mark Serrels, "Twitter CEO Jack Dorsey Explains Why Alex Jones and Infowars Can Still Tweet", *CNet*, 7 August 2018, www.cnet.com/news/twitters-ceo-jack-dorsey-explains-why-alex-jones-and-Infowars-is-still-on-twitter/.

42 Shoshana Wodinsky, "Apple and Google Haven't Banned Infowars Apps, and Their Downloads are Booming", *The Verge*, 7 August 2018, www.theverge.com/2018/8/7/17660564/apple-google-Infowars-app-ban-downloads.

43 Alex Seitz-Wald, "Alex Jones: Conspiracy Inc.", *Salon*, 3 May 2013, www.salon.com/2013/05/02/alex_jones_conspiracy_inc/.

44 Seth Brown, "Alex Jones's Media Empire Is a Machine Built to Sell Snake-Oil Diet Supplements", *New York Magazine*, 4 May 2017, http://nymag.com/selectall/2017/05/how-does-alex-jones-make-money.html.

45 Tom Hains, "Alex Jones to Donald Trump: You Need to Blow the Whistle on Chinese Communist Infiltration of Silicon Valley, Democratic Party", *Real-Clear Politics*, 7 August 2018, www.realclearpolitics.com/video/2018/08/07/alex_jones_to_donald_trump_you_need_to_blow_whistle_on_chinese_communist_infiltration_of_silicon_valley_democratic_party.html.

46 Emily Stewart, "Trump Buys into the Conspiracy That Social Media Censors Conservatives", *Vox*, 18 August 2018, www.vox.com/policy-and-politics/2018/8/18/17749450/trump-twitter-bias-alex-jones-infowars.

47 Allum Bokhari, "Leaked Video: Google Leadership's Dismayed Reaction to Trump Election", *Breitbart*, 12 September 2018, www.breitbart.com/tech/2018/09/12/leaked-video-google-leaderships-dismayed-reaction-to-trump-election/.

48 Tucker Higgins, "The Bizarre Political Rise and Fall of Infowars' Alex Jones", *CNBC*, 14 September 2018, www.cnbc.com/2018/09/14/alex-jones-rise-and-fall-of-infowars-conspiracy-pusher.html.

49 David Greene, "Alex Jones Is Far from the Only Person Tech Companies Are Silencing", *The Washington Post*, 12 August 2018, www.washingtonpost.com/opinions/beware-the-digital-censor/2018/08/12/997e28ea-9cd0-11e8-843b-36e177f3081c_story.html?noredirect=on&utm_term=.30a2841ce509.

50 "The Santa Clara Principles on Transparency and Accountability in Content Moderation", Scale Conference, 2 February 2018, https://newamericadotorg.s3.amazonaws.com/documents/Santa_Clara_Principles.pdf.

51 Brad Stone, *The Everything Store: Jeff Bezos and the Age of Amazon*, London: Corgi, 2013, pp. 25–26.

52 Stone, pp. 31–32.
53 Saul Hansell, "A Surprise from Amazon: Its First Profit", *The New York Times*, 23 January 2002, www.nytimes.com/2002/01/23/business/technology-a-surprise-from-amazon-its-first-profit.html.
54 Michael Porter, "Strategy and the Internet", *Harvard Business Review*, March 2001, pp. 63–78, pp. 64–65.
55 Porter, p. 78.
56 Joshua Mou, "Amazon: Built for Greatness, Not Built for Profitability", *Seeking Alpha*, 29 September 2017, https://seekingalpha.com/article/4107984-amazon-built-greatness-built-profitability.
57 Alison Flood, "Amazon Purchase of Goodreads Stuns Book Industry", *The Guardian*, 2 April, 2013, www.theguardian.com/books/2013/apr/02/amazon-purchase-goodreads-stuns-book-industry.
58 Tanwen Dawn-Hiscox, "Synergy: AWS Dominates the Public Cloud Market across the World", *DCD*, 26 June 2018, www.datacenterdynamics.com/news/synergy-aws-dominates-the-public-cloud-market-across-the-world/.
59 Franklin Foer, *World without Mind: The Existential Threat of Big Tech*, London: Jonathan Cape, 2017, pp. 188–191.
60 Scott Galloway, *The Four: The Hidden DNA of Amazon, Apple, Google and Facebook*, London: Corgi, 2018, p. 186.
61 Rani Molla, and Jason Del Ray, "Amazon's Epic 20-Year Run as a Public Company, Explained in Five Charts", *Recode*, 15 May 2017, www.recode.net/2017/5/15/15610786/amazon-jeff-bezos-public-company-profit-revenue-explained-five-charts.
62 Gene Marcial, "Why Amazon Will Be The Next $1 Trillion Company", *Forbes*, 18 August 2018, www.forbes.com/sites/genemarcial/2018/08/18/why-amazon-will-be-the-next-1-trillion-stock/#7ba25a4164a5.
63 Rocio Summers, "The Appetite for Growth", *RSIBC*, 23 October 2017, www.rsibc.com/blog/the-appetite-for-growth.
64 Farhad Manjoo, "If Anyone Can Save the Washington Post, It's Jeff Bezos", *Slate*, 6 August 2013, www.slate.com/articles/technology/technology/2013/08/jeff_bezos_can_save_the_washington_post_why_amazon_s_great_innovator_could.html?via=gdpr-consent&via=gdpr-consent; Jon Friedman, "Amazon's Jeff Bezos: A 21st Century Citizen Kane", *MarketWatch*, 6 August 2014, www.marketwatch.com/story/amazons-jeff-bezos-a-21st-century-citizen-kane-2014-08-06.
65 Jeremy Tunstall, and Michael Palmer, *Media Moguls*, London: Routledge, 1991, pp. 206–208.
66 *The New York Times*, "Lord Thomson Dies: Built Press Empire", 5 August 1976, p. 65.
67 Bill Gates, *Business at the Speed of Thought: Using a Digital Nervous System*, London: Penguin, 1999, p. 164.
68 *Wired*, "May 26, 1995: Gates, Microsoft Jump on 'Internet tidal wave'", 26 May 2010, www.wired.com/2010/05/0526bill-gates-internet-memo/.
69 Gates, p. 124.
70 John Calhoun, "High-Tech Homey: Production Design Group's Work on MSNBC Newsroom", *TCI: Theatre Crafts International*, October 97, vol. 31, pp. 36–39.
71 Rebecca Dana, "Slyer than Fox", *The New Republic*, 25 March, 2013, https://newrepublic.com/article/112733/roger-ailes-msnbc-how-phil-griffin-created-lefts-fox-news.
72 Jon Lafayette, "What Does Microsoft Really Think of the MSNBC Venture?", *Cable World*, 14.37(2002), p. 13.

73 Erin Kim, "Microsoft and NBC End 16-Year MSNBC Partnership", *CNN Money*, 16 July 2012, https://money.cnn.com/2012/07/16/technology/microsoft-nbc-split/index.htm.

74 Chris Preimesberger, "Why Microsoft's 16-Year Experiment with MSNBC.com Ended", *eWeek*, 16 July 2012, www.eweek.com/cloud/why-microsoft-s-16-year-experiment-with-msnbc.com-ended.

75 David Z. Morris, "Viewers Are Ditching Cable for Streaming Faster Than Anyone Expected", 29 April 2018, http://fortune.com/2018/04/29/viewers-cable-streaming/.

76 Kurt Eichenwald, "Microsoft's Lost Decade", *Vanity Fair*, August 2012, www.vanityfair.com/news/business/2012/08/microsoft-lost-mojo-steve-ballmer.

77 Katharine Graham, *Personal History*, New York: Vintage, 1998, p. 61.

78 Bob Woodward, and Carl Bernstein, *The Original Watergate Stories*, New York: Diversion Books, np.

79 Jeff Himmelman, *Yours in Truth: A Personal Portrait of Ben Bradlee, Legendary Editor of the Washington Post*, New York: Random House, 2017, p. 4.

80 Himmelman, p. 121.

81 Deborah Davies, *Katharine the Great: Katharine Graham and Her Washington Post Empire*, New York: Institute for Media Analysis, 1991, p. 259.

82 Dave Kindred, *Morning Miracle: Inside the Washington Post a Great Newspaper Fights for Its Life*, New York: Knopf Publishing Group, 2010.

83 Frank Ahrens, "Harman Media Buys Newsweek from Washington Post Co. for Undisclosed Amount", *The Washington Post*, 3 August 2010, www.washingtonpost.com/wp-dyn/content/article/2010/08/02/AR2010080203970.html.

84 Isabell Hülsen, "Jeff Bezos Takes Washington Post into Digital Future", *Spiegel Online*, 20 February 2015, www.spiegel.de/international/business/jeff-bezos-takes-washington-post-into-digital-future-a-1015425.html.

85 Paul Farhi, "Washington Post to Be Sold to Jeff Bezos, the Founder of Amazon", *The Washington Post*, 5 August 2013, www.washingtonpost.com/national/washington-post-to-be-sold-to-jeff-bezos/2013/08/05/ca537c9e-fe0c-11e2-9711-3708310f6f4d_story.html?utm_term=.cbbf66e201d2.

86 Eugene Kim, "Amazon CEO Jeff Bezos Signed the $250 Million Washington Post Deal with No Due Diligence", *Business Insider*, 24 March 2016, http://uk.businessinsider.com/amazon-ceo-jeff-bezos-bought-washington-post-with-no-due-diligence-2016-3.

87 Mike Isaac, "Amazon's Jeff Bezos Explains Why He Bought The Washington Post", *The New York Times*, 2 December 2014, https://bits.blogs.nytimes.com/2014/12/02/amazons-bezos-explains-why-he-bought-the-washington-post/.

88 Henry Blodget, "I Asked Jeff Bezos The Tough Questions — No Profits, The Book Controversies, The Phone Flop — And He Showed Why Amazon Is Such A Huge Success", *Business Insider*, 13 December 2014, http://uk.businessinsider.com/amazons-jeff-bezos-on-profits-failure-succession-big-bets-2014-12?r=US&IR=T.

89 Rob Lever, "Bezos Takes Page from Amazon to Push WaPost to Future", *Business Insider*, 30 January 2016, www.businessinsider.com/afp-bezos-takes-page-from-amazon-to-push-wapost-to-future-2016-1?IR=T.

90 Lukas I. Alpert, and Jack Marshall, "Bezos Takes Hands-On Role at Washington Post", *The Wall Street Journal*, 20 December 2015, www.wsj.com/articles/bezos-takes-hands-on-role-at-washington-post-1450658089.

91 Hülsen, "Jeff Bezos Takes Washington Post into Digital Future".

92 Gabriel Sherman, "Good News at the *Washington Post*", *New York Magazine*, 28 June 2016, http://nymag.com/daily/intelligencer/2016/06/washington-post-jeff-bezos-donald-trump.html.

93 Dan Kennedy, "5 Things Publishers Can Learn from How Jeff Bezos Is Running The Washington Post", *NiemenLab*, 8 June 2016, www.niemanlab.org/2016/06/5-things-publishers-can-learn-from-how-jeff-bezos-is-running-the-washington-post/.

94 Cited in Kennedy, "5 Things Publishers Can Learn from How Jeff Bezos Is Running The Washington Post".

95 Kindred, p. 288.

96 Cited in Hülsen, "Jeff Bezos Takes Washington Post into Digital Future".

97 Ari Levy, "Jeff Bezos Has Been Quiet on the Disappearance of Washington Post Journalist Jamal Khashoggi", *CNBC*, 17 October 2018, www.cnbc.com/2018/10/17/jeff-bezos-has-been-quiet-on-wapos-jamal-khashoggi.html.

98 Gerry Smith, "Bezos's Behind-the-Scenes Role in the Washington Post's Web Growth", *Bloomberg*, 20 December 2015, www.bloomberg.com/news/articles/2015-12-20/bezos-s-behind-the-scenes-role-in-washington-post-s-web-growth.

99 Robinson Meyer, "How Many Stories Do Newspapers Publish Per Day?", *The Atlantic*, 26 May 2016, www.theatlantic.com/technology/archive/2016/05/how-many-stories-do-newspapers-publish-per-day/483845/.

100 Dean Carter, "The Globe Adopts The Washington Post's Arc Publishing Technology", *The Globe and Mail Media Group*, 2 June 2016, http://globelink.ca/the-globe-adopts-the-washington-posts-arc-publishing-technology/.

101 Alex Weprin, "CBS CEO Les Moonves Clarifies Donald Trump 'Good for CBS' Comment", 19 October 2016, www.politico.com/blogs/on-media/2016/10/cbs-ceo-les-moonves-clarifies-donald-trump-good-for-cbs-comment-229996.

102 Rupert Cornwell, "Donald Trump Might Not Be Good News for America, but He's Great News for the TV Networks", *The Independent*, 19 March 2016, www.independent.co.uk/voices/donald-trump-might-not-be-good-news-for-america-but-hes-great-news-for-the-tv-networks-a6941441.html.

103 Kate Kaye, "Data-Driven Targeting Creates Huge 2016 Political Ad Shift: Broadcast TV Down 20%, Cable and Digital Way Up", *AdAge*, 3 January 2017, https://adage.com/article/media/2016-political-broadcast-tv-spend-20-cable-52/307346/.

104 Kevin Lamarque, "Trump: Media Is 'Enemy of the American People'", *Daily Beast*, 14 February 2017, www.thedailybeast.com/trump-media-is-enemy-of-the-american-people.

105 Brett Edkins, "CNN Thriving Despite Trump's 'Fake News' Attacks, Says Network President", *Forbes*, 17 February 2017, www.forbes.com/sites/brettedkins/2017/02/17/cnn-thriving-despite-trumps-fake-news-attacks-says-network-president/#20d0a394208e.

106 Sydney Ember, "New York Times Co. Subscription Revenue Surpassed $1 Billion in 2017", *The New York Times*, 8 February 2018, www.nytimes.com/2018/02/08/business/new-york-times-company-earnings.html.

107 Patrick Maines, "Jeff Bezos Owns The Washington Post — and the Journalism It's Practicing", *The Hill*, 29 November 2016, https://thehill.com/blogs/pundits-blog/media/307886-jeff-bezos-owns-the-washington-post-and-the-journalism-its.

108 Reid Wilson, "Gary Johnson Getting More Paper Endorsements Than Trump", *The Hill*, 5 October 2016, https://thehill.com/homenews/campaign/299309-gary-johnson-getting-more-paper-endorsements-than-trump.

Citizens 161

109 Philip Seargeant, and Caroline Tagg, "Social Media and the Future of Open Debate: A User-Oriented Approach to Facebook's Filter Bubble Conundrum", *Discourse, Context & Media*, 25(2018), pp. 1–8, p. 2.
110 Chris Cillizza, "Donald Trump Called Out Jeff Bezos on Twitter. Then Bezos Called His Bluff", *The Washington Post*, 7 December 2015, www.washingtonpost.com/news/the-fix/wp/2015/12/07/donald-trump-called-out-jeff-bezos-on-twitter-then-bezos-called-his-bluff/?utm_term=.f64488c9601b.
111 Emily Jane Fox, "Donald Trump Slams Jeff Bezos over Taxes: 'Amazon is getting away with murder'", *Vanity Fair*, 13 May 2016, www.vanityfair.com/news/2016/05/donald-trump-jeff-bezos-amazon-taxes.
112 Marc Fisher, "Why Trump Went after Bezos: Two Billionaires across a Cultural Divide", *The Washington Post*, 5 April 2018, www.washingtonpost.com/politics/why-trump-went-after-bezos-two-billionaires-across-a-cultural-divide/2018/04/05/22bb94c2-3763-11e8-acd5-35eac230e514_story.html.
113 Will Oremus, "15 Metal Albums Whose Titles Are Less Dark Than the Washington Post's New Motto", *Slate*, 22 February 2017, www.slate.com/blogs/the_slatest/2017/02/22/_15_classic_metal_albums_whose_titles_are_less_dark_than_the_washington.html.
114 Paul Farhi, "The Washington Post's New Slogan Turns Out to Be an Old Saying", *The Washington Post*, 23 February 2017, www.washingtonpost.com/lifestyle/style/the-washington-posts-new-slogan-turns-out-to-be-an-old-saying/2017/02/23/cb199cda-fa02-11e6-be05-1a3817ac21a5_story.html?utm_term=.57e3c035a880.
115 Capital FM Malawi, www.facebook.com/pg/CapitalFMMalawi/posts/?ref=page_internal.
116 Capital FM Malawi, about, www.facebook.com/pg/CapitalFMMalawi/about/?ref=page_internal.
117 Last Moyo, "Converging Technologies, Converging Spaces, Converging Practices: The Shaping of Digital Cultures and Practices on Radio", in Hayes Mawindi Mabweazara, Okoth Fred Mudhai, and Jason Whittaker (eds.), *Online Journalism in Africa: Trends, Practices and Emerging Cultures*, London: Routledge, 2013, p. 48.
118 See, for example, Keith N. Hampton, Inyoung Shin, and Weixu Lu, "Social Media and Political Discussion: When Online Presence Silences Offline Conversation", *Communication & Society*, 20.7(2017), pp. 1090–1108; Angela J. Aguayo, "Paradise Lost and Found: Popular Documentary, Collective Identification and Participatory Media Culture", *Studies in Documentary Film*, 7.3(2013), pp. 233–249.
119 Reinhold Wagnleitner, *Coca-Colonization and the Cold War*, Chapel Hill: University of North Carolina Press, 1994.
120 Ben Bagdakian, *The New Media Monopoly*, Boston, MA: Beacon Press, 2004, p. 5.
121 David Held, *Models of Democracy*, 3rd edition, Stanford, CA: Stanford University Press, 1996, p. 1.
122 Ya-wen Lei, *The Contentious Public Sphere: Law, Media, and Authoritarian Rule in China*, Princeton, NJ: Princeton University Press, 2017, p. 71.
123 Mark Balnaves, and Michele A. Willson (eds.), *A New Theory of Information & the Internet: Public Sphere meets Protocol*, Frankfurt: Peter Lang Publishing, 2011, p. 3.
124 Jürgen Habermas, *The Structural Transformation of the Public Sphere: An Inquiry into a Category of Bourgeois Society*, transl. by Thomas Burger, London: Polity, 1989, p. 203.

125 Hayes Mabweazara, "Zimbabwe's Mainstream Press in the 'Social Media Age'", in Hayes Mawindi Mabweazara, Okoth Fred Mudhai, and Jason Whittaker (eds.), *Online Journalism in Africa: Trends, Practices and Emerging Cultures*, London: Routledge, 2013, pp. 72–76.
126 Moyo, pp. 53–54.
127 Moyo, p. 58.
128 Moyo, p. 59.
129 *AllAfrica.com*, "Mobile Penetration of Africa Hits 80pc", 25 April 2017, https://allafrica.com/stories/201704251054.html.
130 Heather Brown, Emily Guskin, and Amy Mitchell, "The Role of Social Media in the Arab Uprisings", *Pew Research Center*, 28 November 2012, www.journalism.org/2012/11/28/role-social-media-arab-uprisings/; see also Saba Bebawi, and Diana Bossio (eds.), *Social Media and the Politics of Reportage: The 'Arab Spring'*, London: Palgrave, 2014.

Conclusion
The Future of Journalism

As with many of the previous chapters in this book, predictions about the future of journalism begin in the past – in this case, 1 June, 1980, when Ted Turner presented an inaugural address on his new channel, Cable News Network, that included lines adapted from a poem written by the Director of the Woolf Institute, Ed Kessler:

> To act upon one's convictions while others wait,
> To create a positive force in a world where cynics abound,
> To provide information to people when it wasn't available before,
> To offer those who want it choice,
> For the American people, whose thirst for understanding and a better life has made this venture possible,
> For the cable industry, whose pioneering spirit caused this great step forward in communication,
> And for those employees of Turner Broadcasting, whose total commitment to their company has brought us together today,
> I dedicate the News Channel for America,
> The Cable News Company.[1]

CNN, as it is better known, grew out of Turner's independent station in Georgia, WTBS, and displayed a grandiloquent sense of its own self-importance from the start but, as Küng-Shankleman has observed, there was something quite visionary in CNN's original mission to reinvent the news. Until the mid-1990s, the intensely competitive broadcast news industry in the United States did not consider cable to be a major challenge, and so for 15 years, CNN had "the field of 24-hour international news coverage to itself".[2] By the end of the nineties, however, a number of competitors had entered the field, including the Fox News Channel, MSNBC, and BBC World, all of which offered 24-hour services. In 2000, the number of Internet users had grown to just over 350 million from 16 million in 1995 – a remarkable increase but still less than 6 per cent of the global population, with approximately 40 per cent of Americans able to access the net, mostly via slower dial-up connections. As such, the news revolution at the turn of the century relied on cable and satellite television. Cushion identifies three phases of 24-hour news television, a "coming of age" phase following the launch of CNN, a race for transnational reach and influence, and finally increased competition *within* nations as satellite and cable channels proliferated.[3] A major concern of this proliferation, discussed by Cushion as well as other commentators such as Rosenberg, was how CNN pushed the speed of communications, with a demand for a truncated news cycle that greatly reduced the amount of time devoted to checking and verifying stories, a "speed mentality" that continues to reverberate across journalism.[4]

One particular consequence of this speeded-up news cycle was noted in 2008 by Jeffrey Cohen, in his book *The Presidency in the Era of 24-Hour News*. Beginning from the counter-intuitive proposition that news media in the early twenty-first century influenced public opinion less than it had a generation previously, despite the fact that there was more news, Cohen suggested that there was a growing disconnect between things such as reports in the media and public opinion over the Clinton–Lewinsky scandal than there had been for Watergate. In the "new media" era that began in the late 1970s, television audiences began to fragment and, among other factors, those audiences began to rely more and more on channels that conformed to pre-existing political leanings.[5] Cohen's analysis is important for the following reason: it draws attention to an underlying structural shift in mass audiences that predate digital technologies (but which are greatly reinforced by online news habits), and as such that the filter bubble has now been in effect for nearly 40 years.

The introduction of cable and satellite news, then, represented an important shift in media ecologies in the late twentieth and early twenty-first centuries. Initially a poor companion to the established networks, it was via CNN and its competitors that audiences first became used to the compressed cycles of always-available news and the transformations via gatekeeping, production, and distribution that would lead to substantial changes in audience behaviour. Two decades after most of these competitors were launched, however, Sambrook and McGuire could ask whether such news channels were finished as broadcasters sought to close gaps in their finances caused by the shift to online and mobile platforms in particular. As they point out, 24-hour news is expensive and fails in its original proposal, which was to break news first: instead, the Internet provides even greater speed and potentially depth of coverage, with social media having taken up the role of primary influencer over news channels, which themselves "are a symptom of the age of satellite which... is now all but over".[6] As channels were a symptom of satellite, a development from the distribution of terrestrial broadcast, even web pages and sites are beginning to look long in the tooth in an age when readers are more likely to encounter their news via social media accounts such as Facebook, Twitter, and Instagram.

The evolution of satellite news demonstrated an appetite for constant news but, as Cohen demonstrates, this showed up a disconnect between the quantity of information available and public reactions during previous decades. One very notable effect of this vast quantity of news has been what Postman has called the transformation of the "liberating stream" of information into a "deluge of chaos".[7] Postman, originally writing in 1990, despaired that he would ever be able to keep up with the 260,000 billboards, 11,520 newspapers, 11,556 periodicals, 40,000 new book titles, and 362 million TV sets (let alone the 60 billion pieces of junk mail produced each year). The number of newspapers has dropped by up to a third since then, but in their place are 3 million blog posts, 500 million tweets, and 3.5 billion Google searches – made every *day*.[8] In the face of an explosion of data that was unimaginable when Gutenberg first invented his printing press, it is not surprising at all that automation has risen to take the place once occupied by human editors and gatekeepers. Throughout this book, I have been sceptical of the role of general artificial intelligence, but when faced with the huge amount of posts and content produced each day, gaining any sense of order is only possible via algorithms capable of processing information (however restricted) much faster than human minds. The myth of a singularity, that moment when computers become more intelligent than their creators, seems no more than fantasy at present, but potential developments in another area, that of self-driving automobiles, can demonstrate just how profoundly even mindless automation could change our world.

While the actual technology of creating autonomous transport is only slowly developing at the time of writing, and legal considerations of how to implement such vehicles are even slower, one aspect of a future revolution is already in place. When Uber introduced its taxi-hailing app in 2009, it began the process of implementing a scalable network to connect drivers to riders – one that, technically at least, could be easily rolled out even if the company's often-notorious business practices generated resistance in city after city. In a scenario depicted by Justin Rowland, Uber's ability to cut the price of rides will be further reduced once driverless cars are in place, powered by renewable energy that will render such transport so cheap that most current owners will not care to own a vehicle. At present, the various social, economic, and technological factors appear too difficult to overcome easily, but as Rowland observes, once the Model T Ford rolled off production lines in 1908, the equestrian age barely lasted another decade in the USA.[9] In photos of New York's 5th Avenue from 1900, there is not a car to be seen among all the horse-drawn carriages: by 1913, the situation is reversed. Should such a transition occur, it will, of course, have immense consequences for social and economic activities: in a 2017 report, Goldman Sachs estimated that once driverless automation was fully underway, job losses would peak at 25,000 per month.[10]

In the field of editorial gatekeeping, this has already occurred: strictly speaking, rather than simply replacing human jobs, the role of algorithmic editors has been to monitor and channel much of the vast amount of new information that has been produced and shared since Postman wrote in 1990 or CNN was launched a decade earlier. It is worth remembering that when Yahoo! began in January 1994, it remained for a long time in a list of websites compiled by Jerry Yang, David Filo, and their employees; that was possible in an environment where the number of estimated websites was little more than 2,500. When Google was launched in 1998, this number had increased to some 2.5 million and the new search engine was based on automated bots that could crawl and index many more of those sites than any human editorial team could manage. With an estimated 4.75 *billion* pieces of content shared across Facebook each day, the information loaded into a user's page is determined by software rather than human intervention.[11] With many of the cognitive tasks used to sort information – including features such as face recognition – algorithmic gatekeepers are a fact of everyday life, though ones that may be easily gamed. With regard to writing, the future of algorithmic journalism is more uncertain: it is quite clear that ever increasing amounts of content will be produced automatically, but it is not certain that such robo-journalism will ever be able to break out of restrictions around the need for structured data to make sense of the world and produce readable narratives. Instead, what appears to be increasingly likely in coming years is what I have referred to as *augmented* journalism, not the use of augmented reality (AR) but instead supplementing human activities via an increasing reliance upon algorithms, apps, and software to collate information and present it in suitable forms to be worked up by journalists. In a world where more and more news is produced by fewer and fewer people, we are already seeing a number of cognitive tasks being farmed out to machines to free up workers for more complex operations that defy being converted into an algorithm.

Technology clearly changes behaviour: the various rituals around consumption of news and how we relate to stories which appear to be selected for us by close acquaintances (even if they really originate with code provided by Google or Facebook) lead us to respond in different ways to stories than if they had clearly derived from legacy or mainstream media. As has been made aware in recent years, that trust may be given to news that is patently false and, while writing this book, it has become evident to me just how volatile the nature of news is in the era of a President who appears remarkably adept at using Twitter to manipulate his message to a relatively narrow band of followers. What has also been somewhat surprising is how rapidly attitudes to the Big

Five have changed since I began writing. In 2011, when Eric Schmidt defined the "gang of four" (excluding Microsoft) as the major shapers of technology, he caught the cusp of a new definition of the digital age in which Amazon, Apple, Facebook, and Google were the coolest companies to work for in the world. Some of their lustre – with the exception of Apple – had already begun to tarnish by the time of Donald Trump's announcement for the presidency in 2015, but over the next three years, all of them would be affected by accusations of tax avoidance, poor employment practices, and, in the case of the digital duopoly of Google and Facebook, of putting democracy itself in danger. Jonathan Taplin, citing Robert Reich, outlines the dangers of the monopolisation of particular areas of the economy clearest, drawing attention to how libertarian attempts to gut anti-monopoly regulation since the Reagan era have allowed them to thrive: "Big Tech has been almost immune to serious antitrust scrutiny, even though the largest tech companies have more market power than ever. Maybe that's because they've accumulated so much political power."[12] To be most effective, however, such power benefits most where it is almost invisible, and in the age of Trump, Facebook, Google, and Amazon (the latter especially through Jeff Bezos's ownership of *The Washington Post*) are coming under ever greater scrutiny, assaulted by the political left and right for their activities. The half-trillion-dollar club that Schmidt alluded to in 2011 now have a combined market worth that is only superseded by the very largest nations, but they also find themselves subject to potential trade wars and legislation by governments outside the USA that are less amenable to turning a blind eye to various light-touch fiscal agreements after a decade of austerity. The Big Five are likely to dominate lists such as the Fortune 500 for the next few years, and after a century even Standard Oil, the monolith of the early twentieth century, is still a force to be reckoned with as Exxon. Nonetheless, the easy trajectory upwards they have enjoyed in recent years appears to be generating more antagonism and demands for oversight. At various times throughout this book, the spectre of China has also appeared as the site of the next major tech company which has manipulated markets to limit the power of companies such as Facebook and Google in particular. The inevitability of a Chinese technology breakthrough is made more uncertain by the trade wars initiated by Donald Trump, but all the big tech companies realise the importance of entering the largest growing market in the world to secure their own futures.

In his recent book on the rise and decline of the United States as a global power, Alfred McCoy argues that President Trump is dismantling the pillars that had sustained American hegemony in the post-war period, but that this fall from grace had begun long before his tenure in office. In 1945, the USA accounted for approximately half of manufacturing power in the world and, at the end of the Cold War, half of its military forces; nonetheless diplomatic alliances, had already begun to fail and its economic position was under increasing threat from China which was transforming itself into a "world island" reaching from Beijing to western Europe and South America.[13] The end of the "American century" is by no means certain, with some observers noting that it is China that seems increasingly vulnerable in the trade wars initiated by Trump.[14] Yet it also remains the case that engagement with China remains key to successful growth for the Big Five. China became the world's second largest economy in 2010 and, by 2015, was already three times the size of the third largest, Japan. Such a shift (with other countries, most notably India, emerging from their status as developing nations) will also inevitably transform the world's media from a focus on the USA and, to a lesser extent, Europe towards Asia in particular. Already companies such as CCTV (China Central Television) and the search engine Baidu rank among the largest media conglomerations in the world, rising through the ranks with each year as their audiences grow by the millions. A resurgent Google, willing to compromise the supposedly sacred objectives of western liberalism in pursuit of profit in such markets, seems likely to provide a censored search engine to gain access to China once more, and in such circumstances, the model for a public sphere may be closer to that described by Lei which presents the media as controlled by authoritarian prescriptions regarding what can or cannot be said. That process is by no means complete, and the proliferation of digital technologies provides opportunities for the exercise of civil power as well as control.[15] More and more governments, however, seem willing to engage with Chinese models of media regulation than the previous standards espoused by the West – a process made easier as the supposed liberal European and American public spheres have demonstrated themselves fragmented and easily infiltrated by fake news. What is almost certain is that automation will increasingly provide much of the common information that we produce, and that many organisations – at least in the West – will also seek to control some of the excesses of disinformation that have come to light in recent years due to the relentless pursuit of profit by the largest technology companies. Nonetheless, the longer-term future of the media will certainly look upon American hegemony of world flows of news as quaint as executives of Time Warner at the turn of the millennium must have considered the fifteenth-century press devised by Johannes Gutenberg.

Part of that transformation of our understanding of the media will be the role that automation has to play. In a round table for the scientific publisher, Elsevier, five experts discussed the limitations of popular conceptions of artificial intelligence, in particular the idea of some kind of singularity whereby AI would achieve – and then exceed – human capabilities. According to Gary Marcus, Professor of Psychology and Neural Science at NYU and the former CEO of Geometric Intelligence, a machine learning start-up that was later acquired by Uber, the "biggest misconception around AI is that people think we're close to it", a statement that was more or less in agreement with other contributors such as Joanna Bryson, from the University of Bath and Princeton's Center for Information Technology Policy, for whom the very notion of a singularity is logically impossible.[16] While the notion of general AI remains something of a pipe dream, as Bryson observes we already operate at a level of *super*-human activity, in which machines and algorithms operate much faster than human capabilities, although not yet demonstrating anything like human consciousness or the transferability of skills to multiple tasks. Software can, for example, play rule-restricted games better than any person but fail in cognitive tasks that humans take for granted. As the authors of the Elsevier round table observe, the company itself makes use of automation via natural language processing to determine categories for submissions, allowing them to be distributed more quickly to human peer reviewers, just as Facebook's algorithms sift millions of pieces of content, or Ai's Wordsmith software can produce thousands of pieces of content much faster than human editors or writers. Such activities, however, still have to operate within carefully delimited parameters, which is why more complex, non-repetitive cognitive tasks will still require human agency for many years to come.

Economic pressures, particularly those caused by the fallout from a collapsing financial model based on advertising that has been disrupted by big tech in the domain of digital distribution, will mean that publishers will turn more and more to automation to plug gaps that were once filled by journalists. As with the shift towards automation in factories this will result in massive economic shifts with important consequences for those who are failed by the new order. A McKinsey Global Institute report in 2018 placed skills into five categories: physical and manual; basic cognitive; higher cognitive; social and emotional; and technological. McKinsey estimates that by 2030, the amount of time required by human workers for manual and physical tasks such as working on production lines or driving will fall by 11 per cent from approximately 90 billion hours per year in the USA, and by 16 per cent in western Europe, from 113 billion hours in 2018. For basic cognitive tasks, such as handling cash or essential literacy for data inputting, the fall will be 14 per cent fewer hours required in the USA (currently 53 billion hours) and 17 per cent in western Europe (62 billion hours).[17] Higher cognitive, social and emotional skills, and technological requirements are likely to increase over the next decade, but how these are categorised is not always so obvious: it is often assumed that writing, like reading, is a higher cognitive skill, but natural language generation as well as processing indicates that creating simple stories can be done much more efficiently by software than by people. For local news providers struggling to provide the staff to cover essential information regarding healthcare, crime, and government services, algorithmic journalism will play an important role: such information is often freely available but, until it is provided in a narrative format, audiences struggle to understand it. More and more, software will provide the role of an agent in transforming those data into something more usable by us, and the current level of automated assistants such as that seen by Apple's Siri, Amazon's Alexa, and Microsoft's Cortana is very much an early iteration of how an increasing number of us will engage with and organise our environments.

In many cases, the transformations that have taken place in the delivery of journalism since the turn of the millennium have their roots in activities and processes that were begun before the end of the twentieth century, such as the roll-out of 24-hour news or the consolidation of media delivery via multinational monopolies. The two major changes, which were impossible to predict 20 years – or even a decade – ago, are just how much the profitability of the media (and thus, in many although not all cases, its sustainability) has shifted the tech giants who are the main subject of this book, as well as the increasingly important role of automation. I do not have an automatically bleak view of the future of journalism, however. There will, indeed, be a shakeup of many news providers, and conditions for local and regional publishers is pitiful, so much so that even governmental organisations are increasingly concerned about maintaining the links between journalism and local democracy. Yet just as the election of Donald Trump and the vote for Brexit, among other elements, has made politics more relevant for many in the west, so the realisation of just how easily digital platforms can be infiltrated with fake news has also stimulated renewed interest in the sources of journalism, with more people turning to outlets such as *The New York Times* and *The Guardian* than ever before. Each time President Trump declares the *NYT* to be "failing", he appears to drive a few hundred more readers to its pages. Elsewhere in the world, the advantages offered by social media in terms of easily connecting to diverse and disparate audiences have also been taken up with enthusiasm by small media providers who lack the infrastructure to broadcast or distribute news to a wide range of people, and while this book has been extremely critical of the influence of tech giants on journalism, it is also the case that they have frequently improved the lot of small providers. With regard to automation, outside of a very small number of categories, such as financial journalism and some aspects of sport reporting, we are still at the very early stages of algorithmic journalism although robo-gatekeepers already have a crucial role to play in categorising the huge streams of information that flow around the world each day. As has been demonstrated again and again in this book, the implementation of such gatekeeping – often driven by the desire for profit rather than quality – has sometimes been disastrous, but the alternative of legions of human editors is almost certainly impossible nor even necessarily desirable: without appropriate training and profession-alisation, people are even more susceptible to bias. As such, algorithmic editors are here to stay. The situation is much less clear, however, for algorithmic *writers*: for the task of creating stories about the true complexity of our world, particularly in an environment that is evermore chaotic in terms of climate change or political events, the role of big tech and automation must be to aid human intelligence in understanding, challenging, and ultimately transforming that world.

Notes

1 Cited in Lucy Küng-Shankleman, *Inside the BBC and CNN: Managing Media Organisations*, London: Routledge, 2000, p. 152.
2 Küng-Shankleman, p. 110.
3 Stephen Cushion, "Three Phases of 24-Hour News Television", in Stephen Cushion, and Justin Lewis (eds.), *The Rise of 24-Hour News Television: Global Perspectives*, Frankfurt am Main: Peter Lang, 2010, pp. 15–16.
4 Howard Rosenberg, *No Time to Think: The Menace of Media Speed and the 24-Hour News Cycle*, London: Continuum, 2008, p. 43.
5 Jeffrey E. Cohen, *The Presidency in the Era of 24-Hour News*, Princeton, NJ: Princeton University Press, 2008, pp. 15–16.
6 Richard Sambrooke, and Sean McGuire, "Have 24-Hour TV News Channels Had Their Day?" in Stephen Cushion, and Richard Sambrook (eds.), *The Future of 24-Hour News: New Directions, New Challenges*, Frankfurt am Main: Peter Lang, 2016, p. 16.
7 Neil Postman, "Informing Ourselves to Death", in Michael Clough, Joanne Olson, and Dale Niederhuaser (eds.), *The Nature of Technology: Implications for Learning and Teaching*, Rotterdam: Sense Publishers, 2013, p. 12.
8 John Stevens, "Internet Stats & Facts for 2018", *Hosting Facts*, 10 July 2018, https://hostingfacts.com/internet-facts-stats/.
9 Justin Rowland, "Why You Have (Probably) Already Bought Your Last Car", *BBC News*, 10 October 2018, www.bbc.co.uk/news/business-45786690.
10 Goldman Sachs, *Cars 2025*, 20 May 2017, www.goldmansachs.com/insights/technology-driving-innovation/cars-2025/.
11 Facebook, "Did You Know That... 4.75 Billion Pieces of Content Are Shared Daily?", 21 June 2018, www.facebook.com/FacebookSingapore/posts/did-you-know-that-475-billion-pieces-of-content-are-shared-daily/563468333703369/.
12 Cited in Jonathan Taplin, *Move Fast and Break Things: How Facebook, Google and Amazon Have Cornered Culture and Undermined Democracy*, London: Pan, 2018, p. 22.
13 Alfred McCoy, *In the Shadows of the American Century: The Rise and Decline of US Global Power*, London: Oneworld, 2018.
14 See, for example: Patti Dom, "Trade Wars Could Be Worse for China's Economy Than the Pain They Inflict on US", *Market Insider*, 19 September 2018, www.cnbc.com/2018/09/19/chinas-economy-could-feel-far-more-pain-than-us-in-trade-wars.html; *The Economist*, "Is China Losing the Trade War against America?", 11 August 2018, www.economist.com/finance-and-economics/2018/08/11/is-china-losing-the-trade-war-against-america; Brian Brenberg, "Trump's Trade War Has Revealed China's Surprising Vulnerability", *Newsweek*, 22 August 2018, www.newsweek.com/trumps-trade-war-has-revealed-chinas-surprising-vulnerability-opinion-1085132.

15 Ya-wen Lei, *The Contentious Public Sphere: Law, Media, and Author-itarian Rule in China*, Princeton, NJ: Princeton University Press, 2017, pp. 9–10.
16 Sweitze Roffel, and Ian Evans, "The Biggest Misconceptions about AI: The Experts' View", *Elsevier Connect*, 16 July 2018, www.elsevier.com/connect/the-biggest-misconceptions-about-ai-the-experts-view.
17 Jacques Bughin, Eric Hazan, Susan Lund, Peter Dahlström, Anna Wiesinger, and Amresh Subramaniam, *Skill Shift: Automation and the Future of the Workforce*, New York: McKinsey & Company, 2018.

Bibliography

Aguayo, Angela J., "Paradise Lost and Found: Popular Documentary, Collective Identification and Participatory Media Culture", *Studies in Documentary Film*, 7.3(2013), 233–249.

Alderman, John, *Sonic Boom: Napster, P2P and the Battle for the Future of Music*, London: Fourth Estate, 2001.

Al-Marashi, Ibrahim, "The "Dodgy Dossier": The Academic Implications of the British Government's Plagiarism Incident", *Middle East Studies Association Bulletin*, 40.1(2006), 33–43.

Anderson, Chris, "The End of Theory: The Data Deluge Makes the Scientific Method Obsolete", *Wired*, 16.7(2008), www.wired.com/2008/06/pb-theory/.

Anderson, Christopher W., "Towards a Sociology of Computational and Algorithmic Journalism", *New Media and Society*, 15.7(2012), 1005–1021.

Anderson, Sheila, and Blanke, Tobias, "Taking the Long View: From e-Science Humanities to Humanities Digital Ecosystems", *Historical Social Research / Historische Sozialforschung*, 37.3(2012), 147–164.

Atton, Chris, *Alternative Media*, London: Sage, 2002.

Awan, Imran, "Cyber-Extremism: Isis and the Power of Social Media", *Social Science and Public Policy*, 54.2(2017), 138–149.

Bagdikian, Ben, *The New Media Monopoly*, Boston, MA: Beacon Press, 2004.

Balnaves, Mark, and Willson, Michele A. (eds.), *A New Theory of Information & the Internet: Public Sphere Meets Protocol*, Frankfurt: Peter Lang Publishing, 2011.

Banks, Michael, *On the Way to the Web: The Secret History of the Internet and Its Founders*, New York: Apress, 2008.

Barker, Hannah, *Newspapers and English Society, 1695–1855*, Abingdon: Routledge, 1999.

Bartlett, Jamie, *The People Vs Tech: How the Internet is Killing Democracy (and How We Save It)*, London: Ebury Press, 2018.

Bauer, Martin W., *Atoms, Bytes and Genes: Public Resistance and Techno-Scientific Responses*, London: Routledge, 2015.

Beard, Fred K., "The Ancient History of Advertising: Insights and Implications for Practitioners", *Journal of Advertising Research*, 57.3(2017), 239–244.

Bebawi, Saba, and Bossio, Diana (eds.), *Social Media and the Politics of Reportage: The 'Arab Spring'*, London: Palgrave, 2014.

Bell, Emily, "Facebook is Being Taken Somewhere It Never Wanted to Go", *Columbia Journalism Review*, 26 September 2016, www.cjr.org/tow_center/facebook_zuckerberg_napalm_video_palestine.php.

Bughin, Jacques, Hazan, Eric, Lund, Susan, Dahlström, Peter, Wiesinger, Anna, and Subramaniam, Amresh, *Skill Shift: Automation and the Future of the Workforce*, New York: McKinsey & Company, 2018.

Blankespoor, Elizabeth, deHaan, Ed, and Zhu, Christina, "Capital Market Effects of Media Synthesis and Dissemination: Evidence from Robo-Journalism", *Review of Accounting Studies*, 23.1(2017), 1–36.

Boeder, Pieter, "Habermas' Heritage: The Future of the Public Sphere in the Network Society", *First Monday*, 10.9(2005), http://firstmonday.org/article/view/1280/1200.

Boczkowski, Pablo J., *Digitising the News: Innovation in Online Newspapers*, London and Cambridge, MA: MIT Press, 2005.

Bromley, Michael, and O'Malley, Tom (eds.), *A Journalism Reader*, London: Routledge, 1997.

Brown, Heather, Guskin, Emily, and Mitchell, Amy, "The Role of Social Media in the Arab Uprisings", *Pew Research Center*, 28 November 2012, www.journalism.org/2012/11/28/role-social-media-arab-uprisings/.

Buchwitz, Lilly Anne, "A Model of Periodization of Radio and Internet Advertising History", *Journal of Historical Research in Marketing*, 10.2(2018), 130–150.

Burrell, Gibson, and Morgan, Gareth, *Sociological Paradigms and Organizational Analysis*, London and New York: Heinemann, 1979.

Calhoun, Craig, *The Roots of Radicalism: Tradition, the Public Sphere, and Early Nineteenth-Century Social Movements*, Chicago, IL: University of Chicago Press, 2013.

Cali, Dennis D., *Mapping Media Ecology: Introduction to the Field*, Frankfurt am Main: Peter Lang, 2017.

Callaway, Charles, and Lester, James, "Narrative Prose Generation", *Artificial Intelligence*, 2.139(2002), 213–252.

Campbell-Smith, Duncan, *Masters of the Post: The Authorized History of the Royal Mail*, London: Penguin, 2011.

Carlson, Matt, "The Robotic Reporter", *Digital Journalism*, 3.3(2015), 416–431.

Carnoy, David, "Amazon: We Have 70–80 percent of e-Book Market", *CNet*, 2 August 2010, www.cnet.com/news/amazon-we-have-70-80-percent-of-e-book-market/.

Carr, Nicholas, "Zuckerberg's World", *Rough Type*, 18 February, 2017, www.roughtype.com/?p=7651.

Chapman, Jane, *Comparative Media History: An Introduction, 1789 to the Present*, London: Polity, 2005.

Chelaby, Jean K., *The Invention of Journalism*, London: Palgrave, 1998.

Chess, Shira, and Shaw, Adrienne, "A Conspiracy of Fishes, or, How We Learned to Stop Worrying About Gamergate and Embrace Hegemonic Masculinity", *Journal of Broadcasting and Electronic Media*, 59.1(2015), 208–220.

Cho, Deagon, Smith, Michael D., and Zentner, Alejandro, "Internet Adoption and the Survival of Print Newspapers: A Country-Level Examination", *SSRN*, 2015, 1–14.

Chomsky, Noam, "On Cognitive Structures and their Development: A reply to Piaget", in M. Piattelli-Palmarini (ed.), *Language and Learning: The Debate between Jean Piaget and Noam Chomsky*, Cambridge, MA: Harvard University Press, 1980.

Christiansen, Clayton, and Bower, Joseph, "Disruptive Technologies: Catching the Wave", *Harvard Business Review*, 73.1(1995), 43–53.

Clarke, Bob, *From Grub Street to Fleet Street*, London: Revel Barker, 2010.

Clarke, Steve, "Conspiracy Theories and the Internet: Controlled Demolition and Arrested Development", *Episteme: A Journal of Social Epistemology*, 4.2(2007), 167–180.

Clerwall, Christer, "Enter the Robot Journalist Users' Perceptions of Automated Content", *Journalism Practice*, 8.5(2014), 519–531.

Cohen, Nicole, "From Pink Slips to Pink Slime: Transforming Media Labor in a Digital Age", *The Communication Review*, 18.2(2015), 98–122.

Cohnitz, Daniel, *Critical Citizens or Paranoid Nutcases: On the Epistemology of Conspiracy Theories*, Utrecht: University of Utrecht, 2017.

Conboy, Martin, *Journalism: A Critical History*, London: Sage, 2004.

Cox, Jasper, "New Research: Some 198 UK Local Newspapers Have Closed since 2005", *PressGazette*, 16 December, 2016, www.pressgazette.co.uk/new-research-some-198-uk-local-newspapers-have-closed-since-2005/.

Crevier, Daniel, *AI: The Tumultuous Search for Artificial Intelligence*, New York: BasicBooks, 1993, p. 17.

Curran, James, and Seaton, Jean, *Power Without Responsibility: Press, Broadcasting and Internet in Britain*, 7th edition, Abingdon: Routledge, 2009.

Davies, Deborah, *Katharine the Great: Katharine Graham and Her Washington Post Empire*, New York: Institute for Media Analysis, 1991.

Dawes, Simon, "Press Freedom, Privacy and the Public Sphere", *Journalism Studies*, 15.1(2014), 17–32.

de la Cruz Paragas, Fernando, and Lin, Trisha, "Organizing and Reframing Technological Determinism", *New Media & Society*, 18.8(2016), 1528–1546.

Dobbs, Richard, Manyika, James, and Woetzel, Jonathan, *No Ordinary Disruption: The Four Global Fources Breaking all the Trends*, New York: PublicAffairs, 2016.

Dormehl, Luke, *The Apple Revolution: Steve Jobs, the Counterculture and How the Crazy Ones Took over the World*, London: Virgin Books, 2013.

Dörr, Konstantin Nicholas, "Mapping the Field of Algorithmic Journalism", *Digital Journalism*, 4.6(2016), 700–722.

Downing, John, Ford, Tamara, Gil, Genève, and Stein, Laura, *Radical Media: Rebellious Communication and Social Movements*, Thousand Oak, CA: Sage, 2001.

Downing, John, *Internationalizing Media Theory: Transitions, Power, Culture*, London: Sage, 1996.

Dreyfus, Hubert L., *What Computers Can't Do*, New York: MIT Press, 1972.

———. *What Computers Still Can't Do: A Critique of Artificial Reason*, revised edition, New York: MIT Press, 1992.

Ellis, Markman, "An Introduction to the Coffee-House: A Discursive Model", *Language & Communication*, 28.2(2008), 156–164.

Ellul, Jacques, *The Technological Society*, New York and London: Random House, 1967.

Fischer, Claude, *America Calling: A Social History of the Telephone to 1940*, Berkeley: University of California Press, 1994.

Fleishman, Glenn, "How Newsstand Failed the Magazine, and What Apple Should Do", *Macworld*, 30 October 2014, www.macworld.com/article/

2841061/how-newsstand-failed-the-magazine-and-what-apple-should-do.html.

Flew, Terry, Spurgeon, Christina, Daniel, Anna, and Swift, Adam, "The Promise of Computational Journalism", *Journalism Practice*, 6.2(2012), 157–171.

Fodor, Jerry A., *The Language of Thought*, Cambridge, MA: Harvard University Press, 1975.

———. *The Modularity of Mind*, Cambridge, MA: MIT Press, 1983.

Foer, Franklin, *World without Mind*, London: Penguin, 2017.

Fortunati, Leopoldina, and O'Sullivan, John, "Situating the Social Sustainability of Print Media in a World of Digital Alternatives", *Telematics and Informatics*, 10.9(2018), 1–42.

Franklin, Bob (ed.), *The Future of Journalism: In an Age of Digital Media and Economic Uncertainty*, Abingdon: Routledge, 2017.

Galloway, Scott, *The Four: The Hidden DNA of Amazon, Apple, Facebook and Google*, London: Corgi, 2018.

Gans, Joshua, *The Disruption Dilemma*, Cambridge, MA: MIT Press, 2016.

Gates, Bill, *Business at the Speed of Thought: Using a Digital Nervous System*, London: Penguin, 1999.

Gao, Pengjie, Lee, Chang, and Murphy, Dermot, "Financing Dies in Darkness? The Impact of Newspaper Closures on Public Finance", 2018, *SSRN*, https://papers.ssrn.com/sol3/papers.cfm?abstract_id=3175555.

Gentzkow, Matthew, and Shapiro, Jesse, "Media Bias and Reputation", *Journal of Political Economy*, 114.2(2006), 280–316.

Gillmor, Dan, *We the Media: Grassroots Journalism By the People, For the People*, North Sebastopol, CA: O'Reilly Media, 2004.

Glessing, Robert, *Underground Press in America*, Bloomington: Indiana University Press, 1972.

Goldberg, Eli, Dreidger, Norbert, and Kittredge, Richard I., "Using Natural-Language Processing to Produce Weather Forecasts", *IEEE Expert*, 9.2(1994), 45–53.

Gottfried, Jeffrey, and Shearer, Elisa, "New Use Across Social Media Platforms 2016", *Pew Research Centre*, May 26, 2016, www.journalism.org/2016/05/26/news-use-across-social-media-platforms-2016/.

Graefe, Andreas, *Guide to Automated Journalism*, New York: Tow Center for Digital Journalism, 2016.

Graham, Katharine, *Personal History*, New York: Vintage, 1998.

Gurun, Umit G., and Butler, Alexander W., "Don't Believe the Hype: Local Media Slant, Local Advertising and Firm Value", *The Journal of Finance*, 67.2(2012), 561–598.

Habermas, Jürgen, "The Public Sphere: An Encyclopedia Article (1964)", transl. by Sara Lennox and Frank Lennox, *New German Critique*, 3(1974), 49–50.

———. *The Structural Transformation of the Public Sphere: An Inquiry Into a Category of Bourgeois Society*, transl. by Thomas Burger, London: Polity, 1989.

Hall, Jason, *Nineteenth Century Verse and Technology: Machines of Meter*, London: Palgrave, 2017.

Hamilton, John Maxwell, and Tworek, Heidi J. S., "The Natural History of the News: An Epigenetic Study", *Journalism*, 18.4(2017), 391–407.

Hampton, Keith N., Shin, Inyoung, and Lu, Weixu, "Social Media and Political Discussion: When Online Presence Silences Offline Conversation", *Communication & Society*, 20.7(2017), 1090–1108.

Harbor, Catherine, "'At the Desire of Several Persons of Quality and Lovers of Musick': Pervasive and Persuasive Advertising for Public Commercial Concerts in London 1672–1749", *Journal of Marketing Management*, 33.13/14(2017), 1170–1204.

Harcup, Tony, and O'Neill, Deirdre, "What Is News? News Values Revisited (again)" *Journalism Studies*, 18.12(2016), 1470–1489.

Harman, Graham, *The Quadruple Object*, New York: Zero Books, 2011.

Hartley, Jannie Møller, "Routinizing Breaking News: Categories and Hierarchies in Danish Online Newsrooms", in David Domingo, and Chris Paterson (eds.), *Making Online News: Newsroom Ethnography in the Second Decade of Internet Journalism*, New York: Peter Lang, 2011.

Hayes, Kevin J., "Railway Reading", *American Antiquarian Society*, 106(1997), 301–326.

Held, David, *Models of Democracy*, 3rd edition, Stanford, CA: Stanford University Press, 1996.

Hermida, Alfred, "Tweets and Truth: Journalism as a Discipline of Collaborative Verification", *Journalism Practice*, 6.5–6(2011), 659–668.

Himmelman, Jeff, *Yours in Truth: A Personal Portrait of Ben Bradlee, Legendary Editor of the Washington Post*, New York: Random House, 2017.

Hoppensteadt, Frank, "Predator-Prey Model", *Scholarpedia*, 2006, www.scholarpedia.org/article/Predator-prey_model.

Isaacson, Walter, *Steve Jobs: The Exclusive Biography*, London: Abacus, 2015.

Jarvis, Jeff, *Geeks Bearing Gifts: Imagining New Futures for News*, New York: CUNY Journalism Press, 2014.

Jones, Jessica, "The Self-Radicalization of White Men: 'Fake News' and the Affective Networking of Paranoia", *Communication, Culture & Critique*, 11.1(2018), 100–115.

Jordan, Tim, *Hacking: Digital Media and Technological Determinism*, London: Polity, 2008.

Jowett, Garth S., and O'Donnell, Victoria J., *Propaganda and Persuasion*, 6th edition, London: Sage, 2014.

Joye, Stijn, Heinrich, Ansgard, and Woehlert, Romy, "50 years of Galtung and Ruge: Reflections on their Model of News Values and its Relevance for the Study of Journalism and Communication Today", *CM: Communication and Media*, 11.36(2016), 5–29.

Kaplan, Richard L., "Press, Paper and the Public Sphere: The Rise of the Cheap Mass Press in the USA, 1870–1910", *Media History*, 21.1(2015), 42–54.

Keyes, Carl Robert, "History Prints, Newspaper Advertisements, and Cultivating Citizen Consumers: Patriotism and Partisanship in Marketing Campaigns in the Era of the Revolution", *American Periodicals*, 24.2(2014), 145–186.

Kindred, Dave, *Morning Miracle: Inside the Washington Post a Great Newspaper Fights for Its Life*, New York: Knopf Publishing Group, 2010.

Kirkpatrick, David, *The Facebook Effect: The Real Inside Story of Mark Zuckerberg and the World's Fastest Growing Company*, London: Virgin Books, 2011.

Knight, Megan, and Cook, Claire, *Social Media for Journalists: Principles and Practice*, London: Sage, 2013.

Kurzweil, Ray, *The Singularity is Near: When Humans Transcend Biology*, London: Duckworth and Co., 2005.

Latour, Bruno, *Reassembling the Social: An Introduction to Actor-Network-Theory*, Oxford: Oxford University Press, 2005.

Latzer, Michael, Hollnbuchner, Katharina, Just, Natascha, and Saurwein, Florian, "The Economics of Algorithmic Selection on the Internet", in Johannes Bauer, and Michael Latzer (eds.), *Handbook on the Economics of the Internet*, Cheltenham: Edward Elgar Publishing, 2016.

Laurier, Eric, and Philo, Chris, "'A Parcel of Muddling Muckworms': Revisiting Habermas and the English Coffee-Houses", *Social & Cultural Geography*, 8.2(2007), 259–281.

Law, Graham, and Sterenberg, Matthew, "Old v New Journalism and the Public Sphere; or Habermas Encounters Dallas and Stead", *Interdisciplinary Studies in the Long Nineteenth Century*, 2013, www.19.bbk.ac.uk/articles/10.16995/ntn.657/.

Lei, Ya-wen, *The Contentious Public Sphere: Law, Media, and Authoritarian Rule in China*, Princeton, NJ: Princeton University Press, 2017.

Levin, Simon A., and Carpenter, Stephen R., *The Princeton Guide to Ecology*, Princeton, NJ: Princeton University Press, 2012.

Levy, Stephen, *In the Plex: How Google Thinks, Works, and Shapes Our Lives*, New York: Simon and Schuster, 2011.

Lewis, Roger, *Outlaws of America: The Underground Press and its Contexts*, London: Penguin, 1972.

Mabweazara, Hayes Mawindi, Mudhai, Okoth Fred, and Whittaker, Jason (eds.), *Online Journalism in Africa: Trends, Practices and Emerging Cultures*, London: Routledge, 2013.

Manning White, David, "The "Gate-Keeper": A Case Study in the Selection of News", *Journalism Quarterly*, 27(1950), 383–390.

Martin, Bill, and Tian, Xuemei, *Books, Bytes and Business*, London: Routledge, 2010.

Martin, Celeste, and Aitken, Jonathan, "Evolving Definitions of Authorship in Ebook Design", in Ana Alice Baptista, Peter Linde, and Niklas Lavesson (eds.), *Social Shaping of Digital Publishing: Exploring the Interplay Between Culture and Technology*, Amsterdam: IOS Press, 2012.

McCoy, Alfred, *In the Shadows of the American Century: The Rise and Decline of US Global Power*, London: Oneworld, 2018.

McCulloch, Warren, and Pitts, Walter, "A Logical Calculus of the Ideas Immanent in Nervous Activity", *The Bulletin of Mathematical Biophysics*, 5.4(1943), 115–133.

McNair, Brian, *Journalism and Democracy: An Evaluation of the Public Sphere*, London: Routledge, 1999.

Malcolm, Miles, "A Game of Appearances: Public Spaces and Public Spheres", *Art & the Public Sphere*, 1.2(2011), 175–188.

Marquet, Pablo A., Allen, Andrew P., Brown, James H. et al., "On Theory in Ecology", *BioScience*, 64.8(2014), 701–710.

Menn, Joseph, *All the Rave: The Rise and Fall of Shawn Fanning's Napster*, London: Crown Business, 2003.

Merchant, Brian, *The One Device: The Secret History of the iPhone*, New York: Bantam Press, 2017.

Montal, Tal, and Reich, Ziv, "I, Robot. You, Journalist. Who is the Author?" *Digital Journalism*, 5.7(2017), 829–849.

Moon, Soo Jung, and Hadley, Patrick, "Routinizing a New Technology in the Newsroom: Twitter as a News Source", *Mainstream Media, Journal of Broadcasting & Electronic Media*, 58.2(2014), 289–305.

Moore, Martin, and Tambini, Damian (eds.), *Digital Dominance: The Power of Google, Amazon, Facebook, and Apple*, New York: Oxford University Press, 2018.

Myers West, Sarah, "Raging Against the Machine: Network Gatekeeping and Collective Action on Social Media Platforms", *Media and Communication*, 5.3(2017), 28–36.

Nahon, Karine, and Hemsley, Jeff, *Going Viral*, Cambridge: Polity Press, 2013.

Negroponte, Nicholas, *Being Digital*, New York: Alfred A. Knopf, 1995.

Newell, Allen, and Simon, Herbert A., "Computer Science as Empirical Inquiry: Symbols and Search", *Communications of the Association for Computing Machinery*, 19.3(1976), 113–126.

Newman, Nic, "Overview and Key Findings of the 2018 Report", *Digital News Report, 2018*, Reuters, www.digitalnewsreport.org/survey/2018/overview-key-findings-2018/.

Nguyen, Dennis, *Europe, the Crisis, and the Internet: A Web Sphere Analysis*, London: Palgrave, 2017.

Niebisch, Arndt, *Media Parasites in the Early Avant-Garde: On the Abuse of Technology and Communication*, London: Palgrave, 2012.

Örnebring, Henrik, and Conill, Raul Ferrer, "Outsourcing Newswork" in Tamara Witschge, Christopher W. Anderson, and David Domingo (eds.), *The SAGE Handbook of Digital Journalism*, London: Sage, 2016, 207–221.

Parikka, Jussi, *Insect Media: An Archaeology of Animals and Technology*, Minneapolis: University of Minnesota Press, 2010.

Pariser, Eli, *The Filter Bubble: What the Internet is Hiding from You*, London: Penguin, 2012.

Pavlik, John V. "New Media and News: Implications for the Future of Journalism", *New Media & Society*, 1.1(1999), 54–60.

Peacey, Jason, *Print and Public Politics in the English Revolution*, Cambridge: Cambridge University Press, 2013.

Perreault, Gregory, and Vos, Tim, "The Gamergate Controversy and Journalistic Paradigm Maintenance", *Journalism*, September 30 2016, https://doi.org/10.1177/1464884916670932.

Peterson, Theodore, *Magazines in the Twentieth Century*, Chicago, IL: University of Illinois Press, 1956.

Petrović, Vladimir M., "Artificial Intelligence and Virtual Worlds – Toward Human-Level AI Agents" *IEEE Access*, 6(2018), 39976–39988.

Porter, Michael, "Strategy and the Internet", *Harvard Business Review*, March (2001), 63–78.

Postman, Neil, "The Reformed English Curriculum", in Alvin C. Eurich (ed.), *High School 1980: The Shape of the Future in American Secondary Education*, New York: Pitman, 1970, 160–168.

Rodriquez, Clemencia, *Fissures in the Mediascape: An International Study of Citizen's Media*, Cresskill, NJ: Hampton Press, 2001.

Rogers, Simon, *The Hutton Inquiry and its Impact*, London: Politico's publishing Ltd, 2004.

Rudner, Martin, "Electronic *Jihad*: The Internet as Al Qaeda's Catalyst for Global Terror", *Studies in Conflict and Terrorism*, 40.1(2016), 10–23.

Russell, Stuart, and Norvig, Peter, *Artificial Intelligence: A Modern Approach*, revised edition, London: Pearson, 2016.

Ryan, Bill, *Making Capital from Culture: Corporate Form of Capitalist Cultural Production*, Berlin: Walter de Gruyter, 1992.

Schneirov, Matthew, *The Dream of a New Social Order: Popular Magazines in America, 1893–1914*, New York: Columbia University Press, 1994.

Scholz, Trebor (ed.), *Digital Labor: The Internet as Playground and Factory*, London: Routledge, 2012.

Schwanholz, Julia, Graham, Todd, and Stoll, Peter-Tobias (eds.), *Managing Democracy in the Digital Age: Internet Regulation, Social Media Use, and Online Civic Engagement*, New York: Springer, 2017.

Sclove, Richard E., *Democracy and Technology*, New York: Guilford Press, 1995.

Scott, Michael L., *Programming Language Pragmatics*, 4th Edition, Burlington, MA: Morgan Kaufmann, 2015.

Seargeant, Philip, and Tagg, Caroline, "Social Media and the Future of Open Debate: A User-Oriented Approach to Facebook's Filter Bubble Conundrum", *Discourse, Context & Media*, 25(2018), 1–8.

Searle, John, "The Chinese Room", in Robert A. Wilson, and Frank Keil (eds.), *The MIT Encyclopedia of the Cognitive Sciences*, Cambridge, MA: MIT Press, 1999.

Segall, Matthew David, "Cosmos, Anthropos, and Theos in Harman, Teilhard, and Whitehead", *Footnotes to Plato*, 12 July, 2011, https://footnotes2plato.com/2011/07/12/cosmos-anthropos-and-theos-in-harman-teilhard-and-whitehead/.

Shadbolt, Nigel, Van Kleek, Max, Binns, Reuben, "The Rise of Social Machines: The Development of a Human/Digital Ecosystem", *IEEE Consumer Electronics Magazine*, 5.2(2016), 106–112.

Shearer, Elisa, and Gottfried, Jeffrey, "News Use Across Social Media Platforms, 2017", *Pew Research Center: Journalims and Media*, 7 September 2017, www.journalism.org/2017/09/07/news-use-across-social-media-platforms-2017/.

Shoemaker, Pamela J., *Communication Concepts 3: Gatekeeping*, Newbury Park, CA: Sage, 1991.

Shoemaker, Pamela J., and Vos, Tim P., *Gatekeeping Theory*, New York: Routledge, 2009.

Skilton, Mark, *Building Digital Ecosystem Architectures: A Guide to Enterprise Architecting Digital Technologies in the Digital Enterprise*, London: Palgrave Macmillan, 2015.

Smith, Merrit Roe, "Technolgical Determinism in American Culture", in Merrit Roe Smith, and Leo Marx (eds.), *Does Technology Drive Culture? The Dilemma of Technological Determinism*, Cambridge, MA: MIT Press, 1994.

Snyder, Timothy, *The Road to Unfreedom: Russia, Europe, America*, London: Bodley Head, 2018.

Splichal, Slavko (ed.), *The Liquefaction of Publicness: Communication, Democracy and the Public Sphere in the Internet Age*, New York: Routledge, 2018.

Spyridou, Lia-Paschalia, Matsiola, Maria, Veglis, Andreas, Kalliris, George, and Dimoulas, Charalambos, "Journalism in a State of Flux Journalists as Agents of Technology Innovation and Emerging News Practices", *The International Communication Gazette*, 75.1(2013), 76–98.

Stempel, Carl, Hargrove, Thomas, and Stempel, Guido H., "Media Use, Social Structure, and Belief in 9/11 Conspiracy Theories", *Journalism and Mass Communication Quarterly*, 84.2(2007), 353–372.

Stone, Bradm, *The Everything Store: Jeff Bezos and the Age of Amazon*, London: Corgi, 2013.

Strate, Lance, *Media Ecology: An Approach to Understanding the Human Condition*, Frankfurt am Main: Peter Lang, 2017.

Sumner, David, *The Magazine Century: American Magazines Since 1900*, New York: Peter Laing, 2010.

Taplin, Jonathan, *Move Fast and Break Things: How Facebook, Google and Amazon Have Cornered Culture and Undermined Democracy*, London: Pan, 2018.

Tedesco, Richard, "ABC News Tests Net", *Broadcasting & Cable*, 130.1(2000), p. 67.

Tegmark, Max, *Life 3.0: Being Human in the Age of Artificial Intelligence*, London: Penguin, 2018.

Toulouse, Chris, and Luke, Timothy W. (eds.), *The Politics of Cyberspace: A New Political Science Reader*, New York: Routledge, 1998.

Thurman, Neil, Dörr, Konstantin, and Kunert, Jessica, "When Reporters Get Hands-on with Robo-Writing", *Digital Journalism*, 5.10(2017), 1240–1259.

Tunstall, Jeremy, and Palmer, Michael, *Media Moguls*, London: Routledge, 1991.

Turing, Alan, "Computing Machinery and Intelligence", *Mind*, 49(1950), 433–460.

Vaidhyanathan, Siva, *The Googlization of Everything (And Why We Should Worry)*, Berkeley: University of California Press, 2012.

———. *Antisocial Media: How Facebook Disconnects Us and Undermines Democracy*, New York: Open University Press, 2018.

van Dalen, Arjen, "The Algorithms Behind the Headlines", *Journalism Practice*, 6.5–6(2012), 648–658.

Veblen, Thorstein, *The Theory of the Business Enterprise*, New Brunswick, NJ: Transaction Books, 2013[1904].

Vos, Tim P., and Heinderyckx, François (eds.), *Gatekeeping in Transition*, London: Routledge, 2015.

Wagnleitner, Reinhold, *Coca-Colonization and the Cold War*, Chapel Hill: University of North Carolina Press, 1994.

Wallace, Lauren, "19th Century Print Visionaries", *Printweek*, 3 April 2008, p. 21.

Walter, W. Grey, "An Imitation of Life", *Scientific American*, 1 May 1950.

Welbers, Kasper, and Opgenhaffen, Michaël, "Social Media Gatekeeping: An Analysis of the Gatekeeping Influence of Newspapers' Public Facebook Pages", *New Media and Society*, 20.12(2018), 4278–4747.

Williams, Kevin, "Competing Models of Journalism? Anglo-American and European Reporting in the Information Age", *Journalistica*, 2(2006), 43–65.

Wilson, Charles, *First With the News: The History of W.H. Smith, 1792–1972*, London: Jonathan Cape, 1985.

Winner, Langdon, "Upon Opening the Black Box and Finding It Empty: Social Constructivism and the Philosophy of Technology", *Science, Technology, & Human Values*, 18(1993), 362–378.

Winston, Brian, *Media, Technology and Society: A History from the Telegraph to the Internet*, London: Routledge, 1998.

Witt, Stephen, *How Music Got Free: The Inventor, the Music Man, and the Thief*, London: Vintage, 2016.

Yong Jin, Park, Jae Eun, Chung, Dong Hee, Shin, "The Structuration of Digital Ecosystem, Privacy, and Big Data Intelligence", *American Behavioral Scientist*, 62.10(2018), 1319–1338.

Young, Mary Lynn, and Hermida, Alfred, "From Mr. and Mrs. Outlier to Central Tendencies Computational Journalism and Crime Reporting at the Los Angeles Times", *Digital Journalism*, 3.3(2015), 381–397.

Yu, Janice, "Regulation of Social Media Platforms to Curb ISIS Incitement and Recruitment: The Need for an 'International Framework' and its Free Speech Implications", *Journal of Global Justice and Public Policy*, 4.30(2018), 1–29.

Zuckerberg, Mark "Building Global Community", 16 February 2017, www.facebook.com/notes/mark-zuckerberg/building-global-community/ 1010350822115847.

Index

2001, A Space Odyssey 99
4Chan 78, 92

ABC 73, 90
actor-network theory (ANT) 15–16
Addison, Joseph 126, 127
Adobe 56
advertising 49, 50–55, 56–57,
    58–59, 64
AGI *see* artificial general intelligence
AI *see* artificial intelligence
Ai *see* Automated Insights
AirBnB 14
Alderman, John 28, 37n67
Al-Marashi, Ibrahim 76, 95n10
Al Qaeda 134–135
algorithmic gatekeeping 86, 88,
    90–91, 94, 165, 166, 171
algorithmic journalism: and
    automation 8, 101–116, 118–119,
    121, 124–125; and fake bylines
    104; and sports reporting 110;
    future of 166, 169–171
Alibaba 58, 109
Allen, Robbie 110
Alphabet *see* Google
alt-journalism 8, 73–81, 82, 150–151
Amazon: acquisitions 139; Amazon
    Web Services (AWS) 139–140; and
    Alexa, 23, 58, 170; and digital
    ecosystems 17; and disruption
    50; and *The Washington Post* 33;
    market value of 2–3; and Kindle
    31–32, 45; and Prime 65, 140,
    144;and tax practices 150; as one
    of the "big five" 4, 5, 14, 19, 46,
    63, 140; origins of 138–139; sales
    growth of 45, 138–139
Anderson, Chris 17, 35n26

Anderson, Christopher W. 102, 122n9
Anderson, Sheila 13, 34n12
Android *see* Google
Arnold, Thurman 15, 140
AOL 11, 58
AP *see* Associated Press
Apple: and Apple Corp Ltd 28;
    and digital ecosystems 14, 17;
    and disruption 46; and Infowars
    134–135; and the iPad 30–33; and
    the iPhone 12, 14, 30, 56–57, 62;
    and the iPod 28–30, 32; Apple
    Music 65; Apple Pay 14; as one of
    the Big Five 1, 4, 19, 54, 55; iBooks
    31; iMac 27; impact on journalism
    27–33; market value of 1–3;
    iTunes and music 28–29, 31, 143;
    Newsstand 32–33
Aristotle 89, 97
artificial intelligence (AI) 5, 8, 21–27,
    104, 106–110, 116–117 118–119,
    168–169
artificial general intelligence (AGI) 23,
    24, 26–27, 165
Assange, Julian 92
Associated Press (AP) 101, 102,
    110–116, 120, 141
AT&T 3, 4, 11
Atlantic, The 134
Atton, Chris 74, 95n7
augmented journalism 116–121, 166
Australian, The 42
Automated Insights (Ai) 100–101,
    102, 106, 110–116, 121, 124–125
Axel Springer SE 61

Backstrom, Lars 58
Bagdikian, Ben 4, 9n6, 32, 63, 69
Baio, Andy 79, 95n12

Baldwin, Jon 66
Ballard, J. G. 99–100
Balnaves, Mark 6, 10n12
Banks, Michael 66
Bannon, Steve 74, 83, 92
Barker, Hannah 65
Bartlett, Jamie 82, 96n20
Barwise, Patrick 60, 69n79
Bauer, Martin 18, 35n36
BBC 1, 11, 48–49, 50, 63, 76, 102, 151, 163
Beard, Fred K. 67
Bell, Emily 90, 97
Benjamin, Walter 15
Bevan, Kate 29, 37n73
Berlusconi, Silvio 141
Berners-Lee, Tim 11
Bezos, Jeff 8–9, 138, 139, 152; ownership of *The Washington Post* 140, 141–150, 167
big data 13, 16–17, 110–111, 121
"Big Five", the 4–5, 13–14, 15, 33. 62–63, 140, 152, 167–168
Bjerg, Ole 66
Blackberry 57
Blanke, Tobias 13, 34n12
Blankespoor, Elizabeth 111–112, 124n56
Blockbuster 54
blockchain 45, 46
Blodgett, Henry 146
Bloomberg 1, 9, 147
BMG 28, 63
Boak, Josh 100–101, 102, 122
Boczkowski, Pablo J. 34
Boeder, Peter 64, 70n91
Bower, Joseph 52, 54, 68n56
Bradlee, Ben 144
Brady, Matt 13, 34n9
Breitbart 74, 80–81, 92
Brexit 5
Brin, Sergei 19, 55, 56
Bryson, Joanna 169
Buchanan, Pat 142
Buchwitz, Lilly Anne 51–52, 68n53
Bump, Philip 71, 94n2
Burrell, Gibson 19–20, 36n43, 73
Burns, Joseph 118
Bush, George W. 129, 131
Business Insider 146
Butler, Alexander W. 67
Button, Daniel 126
Buzzfeed 93

Cadwalladr, Carole 88–89, 96, 98n52
Cairncross Review 48
Calhoun, Craig 40, 65n5
Calhoun, John 142, 158n70
Cali, Dennis 15, 35n19
Callon, Michel 15
Cambridge Analytica 58, 92–93
Cameron, Robert 119
Campbell, Alistair 76
Campbell-Smith, Duncan 66n121
Canon 52
Capital FM Malawi 151–155
Carlson, Matt 104, 105, 122n16
Carlson, Tucker 142
Carr, Nicholas 18, 35n14
Carruthers, Susan L. 75
CBS 148
CCTV 168
Cernovich, Mike 73, 74, 81
Chapman, Jane 74, 95n5
Charleston Gazette-Mail 117–120
Chelaby, Jean K. 102–103, 122n11
Chicago Tribune, The 12
Cho, Deagon 47, 67n31
Chomsky, Noam 24, 36n55
Chritchlow, Will 62, 65, 69n83
Christiansen, Clayton 52, 54, 68n56
citizen journalism 7, 74–76, 90, 137, 151
Clark, John 99–100
Clarke, Bob 66n13
Clarke, Steve 129, 133, 155n17
Clerwall, Christer 111, 124n55
Clinton, Bill 74, 129, 164
Clinton, Hillary 71, 91, 92
C!Net 29, 37
CNN 12, 73, 90, 136, 142, 148, 163–164, 166
Cohen, Jeffery 164, 171n5
Cohen, Nicole 104–105, 122n19
Cohnitz, Daniel 129–130, 133, 155n18, 155n19
Coll, Steve 147
Comcast 4
Comey, James 94
Compuserve 11, 44
Comscore 50
Conboy, Martin 74, 95n5
Condé Nast 33
Cook, Claire 83, 96n23
Cook, Tim 134
Cornwell, Rupert 148, 160n102

Corsi, Jerome 73
Cosmopolitan 51
Counter Terrorism Committee, the
134–135
Craigslist 49, 50
Cringely, Robert X. 56, 68n65
Croydon Advertiser 113–114, 115
Curran, James 74, 95n5
Cushion, Stephen 164, 171n3

Dahlberg, Peter 153
Daily Express, The 50
Daily Mail, The 50
Dallas, E. S. 40
Davies, Gavyn 76
Dawes, Simon 40
deHaan, Ed 111–112, 124n56
del Rosal, Victor 53, 68n57
DeLanda, Manuel 16
Deep Mind *see* Google
Derousseau, Ryan 2, 9n4
digital duopoly 7, 21, 48, 55–64,
137, 140, 152, 167; *see also*
Facebook, Google
digital ecosystems 13–21
Disney 3–4, 63
disruption 20, 21, 52–55, 85–86
distribution of media 7–8, 39–45,
47–50, 62–65
Dixon, Chris 65, 70n93
Dobbs, Richard 53–54, 68n58
Dormehl, Luke 27, 36, 37n64
Dörr, Konstantin 106, 108, 110, 121,
122, 123n126, 125n74
Dorsey, Jack 135
Downing, John 74, 95n7, 102,
122n11
doxing 79
Dreyfus, Hubert 25, 27, 36n57, 121
Drudge Report, The 74, 77
Dryden, John 126
Dyke, Greg 76

Economist, The 33
Eichenwald, Kurt 143
ELIZA 25
Ellis, Markman 127, 155n3, 155n5
Ellul, Jacques 18, 35
EMI 28
Encarta 54
Encyclopedia Britannica 54
ESPN 110
"Eugene" 26

Evans, Michelle 14, 34n13
Eyre, Eric 117–121, 125

fake news 59, 62, 71–73, 74,
81–83, 86, 91–92, 127, 137; and
conspiracy theories 130–133; and
propaganda 72, 75, 83, 85; and
Russian-sponsored hacking 92–4
Facebook: and Cambridge Analytica
scandal 92–94; and fake news 8, 59,
62, 89–92; and Capital FM Malawi
151–154; and China 63–64; and
filter bubbles 149; and Infowars
131, 133, 134–5; and News Feed
58–60, 62, 63–64, 87, 89–90; and
technological determinism 18, 21;
and the Algorithm 23, 59, 169; as
gatekeeper 90, 135, 166; as one of
the big five 1, 4, 6–7, 143; impact
on journalism 45, 48, 50, 54, 55;
market value 2–3, 58, 60
Fanning, Shawn 28
Feedspot 50
Fenton, Natalie 6, 10n13
filter bubbles 6, 91, 149
Filo, David 166
Financial Times, The 151
Fincher, David 55
Fischer, Claude 18, 35n32
Fleishman, Glenn 33, 37n89
Flew, Terry 101–102, 122n8
Fodor, Jerry 23, 26, 36n51
Foer, Franklin 5, 15, 32, 34n16,
35n39, 37n82, 140
Forbes 3, 14, 45, 46, 50, 54, 111
Fortune 1, 143, 167
Fortunati, Leopaldina 48, 67n32
Fox News 77, 91, 143, 148, 163
Franklin, Bob 82, 96n19
Friendster 58
Fukuyama, Francis 153

Galloway, Scott 5, 19, 32, 35n40,
37n82, 140
Galtung, John 107, 123n31
Gamergate 77–81, 89
Gans, Joshua 54, 68n60
Gao, Pengjie 49, 67n40
Gartner 13, 34
gatekeeping 8, 85–87, 90
Gates, Bill 19, 142, 143
Gentzkow, Matthew 85, 96n26
Gilligan, Andrew 76

Gillmor, Dan 7, 10n16, 75, 77, 95n8, 151
Github 55
Gjoni, Eron 77–78
Glessing, Robert 74
Globe and Mail, The 148
Goldberg, Yoav 109
Goldman Sachs 166
Google: and Android 14, 17, 30, 55–58, 60–62; and China 63–64, 168; and Deep Mind 108–109, 123; and disquiet over Donald Trump 136; and fake news 71, 87–89, 90; and First Click Free (FCF) 60–62: and Google Glass 53; and Google Play 65; and knowledge-based trust 87–88; and Project Dragonfly 64; and search 57; and the Digital News Innovation Fund 62–63, 113; as one of the big five 1, 4, 14, 19, 143; fined by the EU 56, 62; impact on journalism 42–43, 44, 48, 50, 52; origin of 166; market value of 2–3
Graefe, Andreas 104, 105–106, 122n24
Graham, Katherine 144–145
Graham, Philip 144
Grayson, Nathan 77
Greene, David 137
Guardian, The 9, 29, 37, 50, 59, 78, 88, 96, 97, 104, 106, 122, 170
Guardian, The (Addison) 126
Gupta, Arka 118, 125n70
Gurun, Umit G. 67

Habermas, Jürgen 6, 40, 64, 66n8, 70n90, 127, 153, 155n4
Hadley, Patrick 107, 123n34
Hall, Jason 99, 121n1
Hall, Stuart 83
Hamilton, John Maxwell 103, 122n15
Hammond, Kris 111
Harbor, Catherine 50–51, 67n48
Harcup, Tony 107, 123n32
Harman, Graham 16, 35n23
Hawking, Stephen 24, 118
Hayes, Kevin J. 41, 66n16
Heidegger, Martin 27
Heinrich, Ansgard 107, 123n33
Held, David 153, 161n121
Herman, Karl Moritz 109
Hermida, Alfred 84, 96n24, 101, 122

Hewlett Packard 30
Hill, Christopher 155n9
Hill, The 149
HTC 30, 56
Hotwired 58
Huffington Post 77
Hughes, Thomas 13
Hume, David 88
Hutchinson, William 75, 95n9
Hutton Inquiry, the 76

IBM 3, 54, 99, 108, 142, 143
ICON Group 117
Infowars 8, 73, 127, 128–138
Intel 3
Internet Research Agency 93
Isaacson, Walter 29, 37n71, 68
Islamic State 132, 134–135

Jarvis, Jeff 65, 70n95
Jobs, Steve 27–28, 29, 30, 32, 56, 143, 151
Johnson, Lyndon B. 72
Johnston Press 49, 113
Jones, Alex 128–138, 152
Jones, Jessica 128, 155n10
Jordan, Tim 19, 35n37
Journalism: American trust in 84; and the "algorithm of news" 101–106; and the Iraq War "dodgy dossier" 75; and objectivity 83–84; and "post-truth" journalism 80, 81–94; Anglo-American model of 102–103, 119; artificial intelligence and 22; as embedded journalism 75; as mainstream media (MSM) 79–81; bias in 84–85; effects of social media on 8, 12, 58–60, 84, 87, 151–155; gaming journalism 77–78; in Africa 8, 151–155; investigative reporting 116–121, 125; manipulation of 72, 75, 92–93; mobile devices and 30–33; the financing of 8, 47–8
Journatic 104–105
Jowett, Garth J. 83, 96n22
Joye, Stijn 107, 123n33

Kaplan, Richard L. 40, 66n10
Kaur, Rupi 100
Keith, Judge Damon J. 150
Kellner, Douglas 6, 10n11
Kelly, David 76

Kelly, Megyn 91
Kennedy, Dan 146
Kewney, Guy 29, 37n75
Keyes, Carl Robert 51, 68n49
Kessler, Ed 163
Khashoggi, Jamal 147
Kindred, Dave 144, 147, 159n82
Kirkpatrick, David 58, 68n69, 89, 97n39
Kjellberg, Felix see PewDiePie
Kluwe, Chris 79
Knight, Charles 39
Knight, Megan 83, 96n23
Knight Ridder *see* Viewtron
Kodak 54
Koene, Ansgar 90, 91, 97n44
Kotaku 77
Kreuger, Alan 47
Kubrick, Stanley 99
Kuhn, Thomas 15
Kumar, Ranesh 68
Kunert, Jessica 121, 125n74
Küng-Shankleman, Lucy 171n1
Kurzweil, Ray 24, 36n53, 88
Kurtzleben, Danielle 81–82, 95n16

Latour, Bruno 15, 35n20
Latzer, Michael 108, 123n36
Law, Jacky 5, 9n9
Law, John 15
large technology systems – 13–15
Laurier, Eric 127, 155n6
Lee, Chang 49, 67n40
Lei, Ya-Wen 153, 172n15
Lesk, Michael 66
Levy, Stephen 56–57, 68n67
Lewin, Kurt 87
Lewis, Michael 110
Lewis, Roger 74, 95n6
Liberation News Service 74
Lin, Trisha 19–21, 36n42
Livesay, Joseph 39
Loebner,Hugh 25
Local News Partnerships (LNP) 49, 63
Los Angeles Free Press 74
Los Angeles Times 101, 147

Mabweazara, Hayes 154
McCoy, Alfred 167–168, 171n13
McCulloch, Warren 23, 36n50
McGuire, Sean 164, 171n6
McLuhan, Marshall 15
McLure, Samuel 51

McLure's Magazine 51
McNair, Brian 82, 85, 96n18
machine learning 108–110
Mail Online 50
Maines, Patrick 149
Malcolm, Miles 66
Manyika, James 53–54, 68n58
Marcus, Gary 168–169
Markoff, John 45
Marquet, Pablo 16–17
Mashable 104
Maxwell, Robert 141
Mechanical Turk 109
media ecologies 7, 13, 15–21, 27
media monopolies 4–5, 15, 32, 63, 86, 152; and music 28–29, 31–32; and books 31–32
Mediatique 48
Mendoza College of Business 49
Merchant, Brian 30, 37n76
Metro, The 49
Meyer, Eugene 144
Microsoft 1, 4, 19, 27, 30, 54, 55, 56, 57, 63; and artificial intelligence 109, 123; and MSN 58, 142; and MSNBC 142–144, 163; market value of 2–3, 142
Mill, James 39, 43
Mill, John Stuart 43, 66
Minitel 12
Minton, Geoff 24
Mirror, The 49
Montal, Tal 102, 105, 106, 122n10
Moon, Soo Jung 107, 123n34
Moonves, Les 148
Moore, Martin 61, 69n79
Moore, Martin 153
Moore's Law 53
Morgan, Gareth 19–20, 36n43, 73
Morgan, J. P. 52
Mou, Joshua 139, 140, 158n56
Moyo, Last 151–152, 154, 161n117
MSNBC 142–144
Munsey, Frank 51
Munsey's Weekly 51
Murdoch, James 48–49
Murdoch, Rupert 42, 44, 48, 141
Murphy, Dermot 49, 67n40
Musk, Elon 1, 24
MySpace 58

Napster 28–29
Narrative Science 104, 111, 113

National Review, The 131
National Science Foundation 44
Natural Language Processing (NLP) 108–109, 119
Natural Language Generation (NLG) 108, 111, 169
NBC 73, 90, 142–143
Negroponte, Nicholas 44–46, 66n23
Netflix 19, 65
Netscape 19, 142
Newell, Allen 23–24
News Corporation 4, 61, 63
NewsBank 49
NewsWeek 109, 145
newspapers 39–45, 47–50, 51, 86, 144–145
Newsquest 49, 113
News of the World, The 50
New York Times, The 45, 73, 79, 83, 92, 133, 145, 147, 148, 170
Nichols, Lee 129
Niebisch, Arndt 43, 66n20
Nix, Aleksander 92
Nguyen, Dennis 6, 10
Nokia 30
Nystrom, Christine 15, 34

Obama, Barack 91, 93, 131–132, 143
object-oriented ontology 16–17
O'Donnell, Victoria J. 83, 96
O'Malley, Tom 82, 95
Ong, Walter 15
Opgenhaffen, Michaël 87, 95n17
O'Neill, Dierdre 107, 123n32
Osman, Alaudin 151
O'Sullivan, John 48, 67n33

P2P filesharing 28
Page, Larry 19, 55, 56
Paine, Thomas 40
Palmer, Michael 141
Pall Mall Gazette, The 41, 44
Pamphlet wars 128
Paragas, Fernando de la Cruz 19–21, 36n42, 73, 95n4
Parikka, Jussi 42, 66n19
Pariser, Eli 59, 69n74, 97
Parker, Philip 117
Pavlik, John – 12, 34n5
PayPal 45, 136
Peacey, Jason 65, 155n7
Perreault, Gregory 95

Peterson, Theodore 51
PetroChina 1–2
Petrović, Vladimir M. 23, 36n49
PewDiePie 46
Pew Research Center 47–48, 59, 67, 89
Philo, Chris 127, 155n6
Pickard, Victor 64, 70n92
Pitts, Walter 23, 36n50
Pizzagate 73, 131–132
Pfetsch, Barbara 6, 10n13
Politico 77
Polk, James 72
Pope, Alexander 126, 127
Popper, Karl 130
Porter, Michael 139
Postman, Neil 15, 34n17, 165, 166, 171n7
Preimesberger, Chris 143
Pressman, Laura 112
Price, Richard 40
Priestley, Joseph 40
PR Week 115
public sphere, the 5–7, 8, 40, 43, 64, 74, 127–128, 137–138, 153, 155, 168
Putin, Vladimir 93

Quill 111
Quinn, Zoe 77, 78

Radicati 116, 125
Reagan, Ronald 72
Recording Industry Association of America (RIAA) 28
Reddit 78
Reich, Ziv 102, 105, 106, 122n10
Reporters and Data and Robots (RADAR) 113–116
Reuters 12, 34, 102, 141
Ritson, Mark 60, 61, 69n78
robot journalism *see* algorithmic journalism
Rockefeller, J. D. 52, 63
Rodriguez, Clemencia 74
Roe Smith, Merrit 18
Rogers, Pat 155n2
Rogers, Simon 95
Rosenberg, Howard 164, 171n4
Roosevelt, Theodore 4
Rowland, Justin 165
Ruge, Mari 107, 123n31
Ryan, Bill 104–105, 122n21

Salter, Lee 6
Sambrook, Richard 164, 171n6
Samsung 30
Sampson, Anthony 82
Santa Clara Principles 137
Sarkeesian, Anita 78
Saverin, Eduardo 58
Schmidt, Eric 4, 91, 167
Schneirov, Matthew 51, 68n50
Schwarz, H. 75
Sclove, Richard 5–6, 10n11, 153
Scotsman, The 49
Sculley, John 30
Searle, John 23, 25–26, 36n58
Seargeant, Philip 149, 161n109
Sears 52
Seaton, Jean 74, 95n5
Shadbolt, Nigel – 13, 15, 34n11
Shalamov, Varlam 72
Shapiro, Jesse 85, 96n26
Shaw, J. C. 23–24
Sherman Act 31, 140
Shen, Lucinda 1, 9n2
Shoemaker, Pamela 85, 86–87, 96n27
Shropshire Star 114–115
Silverman, Craig 92, 97n50
Simon, Herbert 23–24
SJWs (Social Justice Warriors) 78, 79
Skilton, Mark 13, 34n9
Smith, Gerry 147
Smith, Michael L. 19, 35n38
Smith II, William Henry 39–41, 43, 65
Snyder, Tim 93, 97n57
Social Network, The 55
Solon, Olivia 5, 10n10
Sony 28, 30
South Sea Bubble, the 2
Spectator, The 126
Spiked 76
Spotify 65, 134
Spurgeon, Christina 122
Spyridou, Lia-Paschalia 101, 122n4
Sridhar, Shrihari 48, 67n32
Sriram, Srinivasaraghavan 48, 67n32
Standard Oil 2–3, 52, 63, 167
Standard Question Answering Dataset
    (SQuAD) 109–110
StatSheet *see* Automated Insights
Stead, W. T. 40, 41
Stempel, Carl 133, 156n16
Strate, Lance 15, 35n18
Sumner, David 51, 68n50
Sun, The 49

Sunday Times, The 141
Swisher, Kara 135
Symbian 57

Tagg, Caroline 149, 161n109
Tambini, Damian 61, 70n79
Taplin, Jonathan 52, 62, 63, 68n54,
    167, 171n12
Tatler, The 126
Taylor, John 128, 129
technological determinism 6, 13,
    17–21
Tegmark, Max 21–23, 24, 36n47
Telegraph, The 49, 50, 78
Tesla 1
TexasMonthly 131
Thompson, Robert 61
Thomson, Roy 141–142
Thornhill, John 14
Thurman, Neil 121, 125n74
Time Pathfinder 58
Time Warner 3–4, 12, 63, 148, 168
Time 79, 97
Times, The 44, 141
Tobit, Charlotte 67
Toker, Leona 72, 95n3
Totney, John 128, 129
Tow Center for Digital Journalism
    104, 105–106
Trinity Mirror 49, 113
trolling 7, 79–81
Trump, Donald 5, 63, 71–72, 74,
    81–83, 87, 92–93, 106–107, 120,
    132, 134, 136, 140, 148–150, 151,
    155, 166, 167, 168, 170
Tuchman, Gaye 107, 123n29
Tunstall, Jeremy 141
Turing, Alan 23, 25–26, 36, 101
Turing Machine, the 23, 101
Turner, Ted 163
Twitter 7, 50, 57, 74, 79, 81–82, 89,
    107, 134, 135, 136, 150, 166
Tworek, Heidi J. S. 103, 122n15

Uber 14, 165–166, 168
UK Press Gazette 48, 49
Ulanoff, Lance 111, 116n53
Universal Music Group 28, 29

Vaidhyanathan, Siva 59–60, 66n76,
    69, 89, 97n41
Veblen, Thorstein 17, 35n29
Verge, The 109

Viacom 63
Viewtron 11, 30, 33
Villas-Boas, Antonio 14, 34n14
Vincent, James 109, 124n48
Vos, Tim 86–87, 95, 96n28

Walker, John Brisbane 51
Wall Street Journal, The 61, 146
Wallace, Lauren 65
Walmart 2, 52, 140
Walter, W. Grey 26, 36n60
Walton, Henry 39, 41, 43
Washington Post, The 1, 9, 71, 92,
    128, 137, 140, 141–150, 167
Wason, Peter 59
Watkins, Leo 60, 69n79
Watson, Paul Joseph 131
WEA 29
Web 2.0 14
Weizenbaum, Joseph 25
Welbers, Kasper 87, 96n34
Wertheimer, Linda 118, 125n71
West, Sarah Myers 96
WH Smith 41
White, David Manning 85, 87, 96n27
Wikileaks 92–93
Wikipedia 13
Williams, Kevin 102–103, 122n11
Willson, Michelle 6, 10n12

Wilson, Charles 40, 41, 65n1, 66n11
Winston, Brian 19, 36n41
Witt, Stephen 29, 37n68
Woehlert, Romy 107, 123n33
Woetzel, Jonathan 53–54, 68n58
Woodward, Bob 146, 150
Wordsmith 111–113, 116, 169
Wozniak, Steve 27
Wu, Brianna 78
Wyllie, Christopher 93

Xerox 52

Yahoo! 57, 110, 166
Yang, Jerry 166
Yiannopoulos, Milo 80–81, 95
Yorkshire Post, The 49
Young, Mary Lynn 101, 122n5
YouTube 8, 45, 46, 58, 133,
    134, 143

Zaitchik, Alexander 129, 155n11
Zentner, Alejandro 47, 67n31
Zephoria 91
Zhu, Christina 111–112, 124n66
Zodiak Broadcasting Station
    (ZBS) 152
Zuckerberg, Mark 6, 18, 35, 55, 58,
    59, 60, 68, 69, 87, 90, 97, 134, 135